SANDRA GUSTAFSON'S

GREAT EATS ITALY

FLORENCE • ROME • VENICE

FOURTH EDITION

D1550500

CHRONICLE BOOKS
SAN FRANCISCO

Printed in the United States of America

FOURTH EDITION

ISBN: 0-8118-3209-0
ISSN: 1074-5084

Cover design: Ayako Akazawa
Book design: Words & Deeds
Typesetting: Jack Lanning
Series Editor: Jeff Campbell
Author photograph: Marv Summers

Distributed in Canada by
Raincoast Books
9050 Shaughnessy Street
Vancouver, B.C. V6P 6E5

10 9 8 7 6 5 4 3 2 1

Chronicle Books LLC
85 Second Street
San Francisco, CA 94105

www.chroniclebooks.com
www.greateatsandsleeps.com

*For Sara, Theresa, Diane, Sandy, Samantha,
and Michael, who shared many Great Eats
with me in Italy*

Contents

To the Reader

In Florence you think, in Rome you pray, and in Venice you love. In all three, you eat.

—Italian proverb

Italians tend to think of themselves first as Romans, Venetians, Florentines, and Sicilians, and only secondarily as Italians. But what unites them all is their love of and appreciation for food—whether the simple cooking of Tuscany, the seafood in Venice, the garlic, aromatic herbs, spices, and meats in Rome, or the Parma ham and robust pastas of Bologna. Italians have been trendsetters at the table ever since the Middle Ages. They were the first to use a fork, the first to wash their hands before a meal, and among the first to make a point of preparing food using the freshest ingredients. When it comes to cuisine, few countries in the Western world have given so much to so many. Just think of all the foods you love, and no doubt a majority will be Italian: pasta, pizza, balsamic vinegar, Parmesan cheese, sundried tomatoes, porcini mushrooms, polenta, osso buco, prosciutto, minestrone—the list is endless. When we want satisfaction, comfort, or pure enjoyment, we eat Italian.

To Italians, life is meant to be lived fully, and much of everyday life in Italy revolves around eating. Food is not considered mere sustenance but rather a work of art to be enjoyed and relished at every meal, and meals are meant to be shared with company. In fact, the word *company* is derived from two Italian words: *con,* meaning "with," and *pane,* for "bread"— which means "breaking bread in friendship." But a meal only starts with the bread. From there you move on to the appetizer, a first and second course, vegetables, salad, cheese, fruit, dessert, coffee, and, finally, a digestive, which you will need after a lengthy meal. If you seriously overindulge, a shot of the strong herbal mix Fernet-Branca, available in most bars, will set you straight in no time.

In the last forty years, Italy has gone through a complete economic transformation. It is now the world's fifth-largest industrial power. As a result, prices have skyrocketed, the dollar goes up and down like a yo-yo, and inflation is rampant. *Nothing* is cheap in Italy—certainly not the food. Today it costs almost $2 to buy and send a postcard back to the States, many restaurants charge $30 to $35 for a meal, and you can easily spend too much on a mediocre sandwich and a glass of rough house wine if you don't know where to eat.

Eating well takes planning, and this is where *Great Eats Italy* comes to your rescue: it is your reliable dining guide to the best quality food at the best prices. Longtime readers will note that, for its fourth edition, *Cheap Eats in Italy* has a new name, but this hasn't changed the spirit in which it is written. My commitment in *Great Eats Italy* remains the same: to help you find the best value in all price ranges, so whatever your budget may be, you know you will be getting a good meal—whether it's a romantic Big Splurge or a simple picnic on the piazza. Just as important, you will dine where the natives dine, not where the tour buses stop.

When it comes to research, other guidebooks may send a questionnaire, or have someone stop by a random selection of restaurants. I do not do that. I am personally responsible for every entry in this book, and I visit every address, new or old, for every edition. Updates are frequent. In doing the research for this edition of *Great Eats Italy,* which includes more than two hundred dining selections, I spent months in Italy, plotting maps, walking hundreds of miles in every type of weather, checking on countless addresses, and eating food that ranged from terrible and indifferent to delightful and gourmet. In the write-ups, I describe the atmosphere and decor, and tell you about the history of the restaurant and the family who runs it, even mentioning any children or pets who may greet you when you arrive. I describe the other diners; how the food is prepared, presented, and tastes; and what it all costs. I recommend dishes to give you an idea of what the restaurant does best, and I warn you about any dishes to avoid. Because most menus in Florence, Rome, and Venice reflect the four seasons of the year and very often change on a daily basis, many of the foods I describe may not be served when you visit, but the quality and value will still be firmly in place. One subject I do not cover is that of Italy's many fine wines . . . that would necessitate another book, and many excellent ones have already been written on it. However, I do comment on some of the house wines and tell you if they are drinkable.

In the back of the book is a "Readers' Comments" page for your notes, suggestions, and comments. I hope you agree with my selections, and let me know when you do, but it is just as important to me to know about changes you may find, and any Great Eating discoveries you have made that you would like me to know about for the next edition. Please take a few minutes to drop me a note telling me about your experiences. As the countless readers who have written to me know, your letters are very important to me, and I read and answer every one I receive.

Whether you are traveling to Italy for business or pleasure, I urge you to go with an open mind. When you leave home, don't expect to encounter your way of life, or your favorite comfort foods. Enjoy the moment wherever you are—the people, the sights, the sounds, and even the smells. Sample a wide variety of foods, and roll with the punches, since travel is rarely trouble free. If you can see the humor in a difficult situation, you will come home a more knowledgeable person, with a lifetime of happy memories.

By using this edition of *Great Eats Italy,* I hope you will return with some of the best memories of all: those of delicious meals in wonderful settings, enjoyed all the more because they were affordable. If I have been able to help you do this, I will consider my job well done. I wish you *buona fortuna* and above all . . . *buon appetito!*

Tips for Great Eats in Italy

The President could solve all the country's problems by having a big plate of spaghetti once a week. Congress can supply the meatballs.

—Will Rogers

1. If you want to eat dinner with the tourists, eat early. If you want to eat with the locals, eat late. Most places do not require men to wear a tie, but Italians always dress with casual elegance when they eat out. You will never see a well-dressed Italian man or woman dining out in shorts and athletic shoes . . . except at beach resorts.

2. If you see a headwaiter or chef standing in the doorway, tour buses parked outside, or an empty restaurant during prime time, keep going.

3. When dining out, remember to order appropriately according to the place and the chef's abilities. Do not expect gourmet fare in a snack bar, and do not go to a fancy restaurant and order only a bowl of soup. You do not have to order something from every course, but you should have at least two courses in better restaurants.

4. Italians make a big fuss over children; therefore, taking children to restaurants in Italy is not the problem it can be in France. You can ask for a high chair (*seggiola* or *sediolina*) and for half portions (*mezze portione*).

5. By law, all eating establishments must post a menu outside. *Always* read it before going in. This prevents you from being seated before finding out that you do not like what is being served, or worse, that the prices are too high. Generally, it is best to avoid places that have laminated, printed menus in four or five languages.

6. Pay attention to the daily specials and the house specialties. You can be sure these will be the best the chef has to offer and will usually consist of seasonally fresh foods. If they are not on your menu, look for them on a chalkboard, or ask your server.

7. Try to include a trip to a daily outdoor market. This is not only a colorful look at local life but a window on what your plate may contain that night.

8. If your budget is tight, consider the *menù turistico* (set-price meal). Even though the choices may be boring and limited, it is usually a good buy because it includes at least two courses and often the cover and service charges. Some also include dessert and/or a beverage.

9. To keep the tab lower on an à la carte meal, skip the antipasto course and head straight for the pastas and entrées. Keep in mind that main courses on an à la carte menu are usually not garnished, and orders of vegetables and salads will be extra.

10. Restaurants in Italy must indicate when frozen food is used by adding an asterisk (*) by any such menu items. Most often you will find that if anything is frozen (in Italian, *congelato* or *surgelato*), it will be the fish. Most Italians would never order anything frozen, and neither should you. Make sure what you are ordering is *fresco* (fresh).

11. Don't sit down in a bar! Drink your morning cappuccino and eat your snack or sandwich for lunch while standing. If you sit down in a bar, you risk being charged up to twice as much for the privilege of occupying a chair. If you sit at an outside table, the tab could be even more. The benefit of sitting is that you acquire something akin to "squatter's rights" and can linger at your table for the price of a coffee for hours without being bothered.

12. The cover charge (*coperto*) is *per person*. The service charge (*servizio*) is a percentage of the total bill. The good news is that *the service charge is the tip*. You do not have to pay one euro more unless you feel the service has been out of the ordinary. (For more information on cover and service charges, see page 14).

13. Every restaurant in Italy is required to give you a formal bill, which you are legally required to take with you when you leave. Before leaving, compare the bill with the prices on the menu and add up the figures. Do not hesitate to question anything you do not understand. Mistakes are all too common.

14. If you are twenty-nine years old or younger and plan to visit Venice, invest in a Rolling Venice Card (Carta Giovani). This bargain to end all bargains entitles the holder to discounts at participating restaurants, hotels, shops, and certain museums. For further details, see page 180.

15. If you have enjoyed a place recommended in *Great Eats Italy*, tell the owner or manager where you found out about them. They are always very appreciative.

How to Use Great Eats Italy

Each listing in *Great Eats Italy* includes the following information: the name and address of the establishment, the area of the city in which it is located, the telephone number (plus fax, email, and Internet if available), the days and hours it is open and closed, annual closing dates, whether reservations are necessary, whether and which credit cards are accepted, the average price of a three-course à la carte meal without beverages, the price of the *menù turistico* (set-price meal), the cover and service charges, and whether or not English is spoken. If there is a nonsmoking section, this is noted. Most listings include a map key number in parentheses to the right of the restaurant name; an entry without a number means it is located beyond the parameters of the map. A dollar sign ($) to the right of the name means that it is a Big Splurge.

At the end of the restaurant listings, you will find a glossary of Italian menu and restaurant terms; an index of all restaurants, including indexes by category; and, finally, a "Readers' Comments" page.

Big Splurges

Restaurants in the Big Splurge category are included for those who have more flexible budgets, or for special-occasion dining to celebrate a birthday, anniversary, or any other memorable day. However, as with all the restaurants in this book, they represent the best values in their price range. These restaurants are marked by a dollar sign ($). See the index for a complete list of Big Splurges in Florence, Rome, and Venice.

The Euro

The euro became the official currency of the eleven-nation European Union, of which Italy is a part, on January 1, 2000; euro notes and coins began to be used as legal tender in January 2002. Euros will be used alongside the national currencies until July 2002, at which point, the euro will become the sole legal tender for the European Union. As such, prices in this book are given in euros only, though you may see prices displayed in both national currencies and the euro for a while. Note that euro prices were based on the conversion rate with the lira at presstime, and this will undoubtedly change.

Holidays

Very few restaurants in Italy are open 365 days a year. Most are closed at least one day a week and for an annual vacation of up to one month (those few places with no annual vacation are noted as NAC, for no annual closing). Many close on some or all of the holidays listed below, and those closings depend on the economy at the moment as well as the whims of the owner. You can also count on most places being closed at least a few days between Christmas and New Year's Day. If a holiday falls on a Tuesday or Thursday, many will also take the Monday and/or Friday off. Because of these constantly changing policies, please call ahead to check if your visit falls during these holiday times or in the months of December, January, July, or August.

New Year's Day (*Capo d'Anno*)	January 1
Epiphany (*La Befana*)	varies; early in January
Good Friday	varies; March or April
Easter Sunday (*Pasqua*)	varies; March or April
Easter Monday (*Lunedì Pasqua*)	varies; March or April
Liberation Day (*Venticinque Aprile* or *Festa della liberazione*)	April 25
Labor Day (*Primo Maggio* or *Festa del Lavoro*)	May 1
National Day	June 2
Assumption of the Virgin (*Ferragósto*)	August 15
All Saints' Day (*Tutti Santi*)	November 1
Feast of the Immaculate Conception (*Festa dell'Immacolata*)	December 8
Christmas Day (*Natale*)	December 25
Day after Christmas (*Santo Stefano*)	December 26

Patron Saints' Days:	
Florence: St. John the Baptist's Day	June 24
Rome: St. Peter's Day	June 29
Venice: St. Mark's Day	April 25

Hours and Days Closed

All eating and drinking establishments have a regular *giorno de chiusura*: the one or two days a week they are closed (*chiuso*). That doesn't mean much. Due to holidays, local customs, government red tape, the ever-present threat of *scioperi* (strikes), yearly vacations, restoration and remodeling, the weather, and much more than the non-Italian can ever fathom, the one place you really want to try may be closed. Though *Great Eats Italy* lists each establishment's days and hours of operations, be sure to call ahead to double-check, especially if you do not have a backup choice nearby or your heart is set on a particular place.

Bakeries, fruit and vegetable shops, and other food stores are closed all day Sunday and one afternoon per week. Pastry shops are often open on Sundays until early afternoon, and some supermarkets are staying open for a few hours on Sunday . Food shopping hours are generally 8:30 A.M. to 1 P.M. and 3:30 to 7:30 P.M. Open-air markets are open Monday through Saturday from 8 A.M. to 1 P.M.

Maps

Great Eats Italy has an accompanying map and restaurant key for each city, and in the text, these map key numbers appear in parentheses to the right of the restaurant's name. If a restaurant does not have a number, it is located beyond the boundaries of the map.

Please note that the maps in *Great Eats Italy* are designed to help the reader locate the restaurant listings; they are not meant to replace fully detailed street maps. Italian cities can be very confusing to get around in, so no matter what your length of stay is, I strongly recommend that you buy a locally produced city map. These are generally available at any news kiosk or bookstore. See the introductions to Florence and Venice for more information on negotiating these notoriously convoluted cities.

Smoking

I am happy to report that Italians are smoking less than ever before. Still, there is no Italian campaign saluting the health benefits of a smoke-free environment . . . or any hint of one in the future. During peak hours, especially in bars, smaller restaurants, and trattorias, the haze can get thick. If a restaurant listed in *Great Eats Italy* is one of the places where smoking is prohibited or that has a special nonsmoking section, it is noted. Otherwise . . . *buona fortuna!*

Paying the Bill

Italian restaurant bills can be confusing. With the following information, you will be better able to avoid the pitfalls of overcharging or confusion when *il conto* (the bill) is presented.

In many small places, especially bars, *pasticcerias, tavola caldas,* or *rosticcerias,* cash is king and plastic money is out. Most restaurants, though, take credit cards. Every listing in *Great Eats Italy* states the credit-card policy. The following abbreviations indicate which credit cards are accepted:

American Express	AE
Diners Club	DC
MasterCard	MC
Visa	V

Italian law requires that all establishments give a bill to the customer and that the customer carry the bill out of the restaurant. Who knows if anyone ever checks, but it is a protection for the consumer—you must get a proper bill for your money spent. And don't waste the protection: always add up the bill yourself and question any discrepancies. There are too many mistakes.

Prices

All *Great Eats Italy* listings give the prices for à la carte meals and the *menù turistico* (fixed-price meal) if one is available. All printed menus are required to list whether or not there is a *coperto* (cover charge) and/or a *servizio* (service charge) and the amount. The à la carte prices quoted in this book represent the *average cost of a three-course meal only;* they do not include the cover or service charge if there is one or any beverages (unless otherwise noted). In determining the average price of a meal, the cheapest and the most expensive foods were avoided. Thus, you could spend more, or less, depending on what you decide to eat and drink. In using *Great Eats Italy,* you should expect prices to increase each year based on the margin of labor costs, inflation and most important . . . the owner's view of the economy.

Cover Charge (*Coperto*)

The cover charge is levied per person and is not to be confused with the service charge. In Rome, the cover charge has been theoretically banned, but Roman restaurateurs don't give up easily, so there is now a bread charge, called *pane,* to take its place; in establishments you will see it noted as *pane, pane e coperto,* or still just *coperto.* Supposedly it is not applicable if you do not touch the basket of bread, but theory and fact do not always agree. In Florence and Venice the cover charge is intact and referred to simply as *coperto.* No matter what it is called, or in which city, the cover charge includes the table settings, flowers, and everything else the owner wants to toss into this catch-all charge, *plus* the bread, whether or not you want it or eat it. All menus *must* clearly state the cost of the bread/cover charge, which is listed separately on the bill, and added to the total on which you will pay service. Usually, if you order the *menù turistico,* and always if you eat or drink standing at a bar counter, you will avoid the cover charge, and in most cases the service charge as well. In *Great Eats Italy,* each establishment's cover and service charges are noted.

Service Charge (*Servizio*)

Just as menus must state the cover charge, they must also state the service charge, or lack of it. *Servizio incluso* and *servizio compreso* mean the service charge is included in the price of the meal, and no further tip is necessary (nor will there be another charge added to your bill). *Servizio non-incluso* or *servizio non-compreso* means that the service charge has not been added; it is technically discretionary, but you will be expected to pay an additional 10 to 15 percent of the total bill. "*Servizio* 15%" means that the restaurant will automatically add 15 percent to your bill, and this will appear as a separate charge. All of the listings in *Great Eats Italy* describe how the service charge is handled: either "service included," "service discretionary," "15% service added" (the percentage will vary), or "no service charged."

Please remember that *the service charge is the tip,* and you are not required to leave anything more unless the service has been especially good and you are feeling generous, in which case you can round off the total. For service above and beyond, consider the ultimate tip: informing the person's employer by writing a letter of praise.

Reservations

Every *Great Eats Italy* listing states the reservation policy. If reservations are advised, please make them. It is always better to arrive with reservations than to wish you had. If you feel uncomfortable calling yourself, ask your hotel to do it for you. They may even be able to get you a better table. Only a few places that are very busy do not honor their reservation times. However, you should arrive on time, call if you will be late, and definitely call to cancel if you will be unable to keep your reservation.

Italian telephone numbers are not as crazy as they once were, but the improvement is slight. In Rome, some phone numbers have only five or six digits, while newer numbers have seven digits. The area codes for Florence, Rome, and Venice, including the beginning zero, are part of the number you dial. For example, in Florence you dial 055 plus the restaurant number; in Rome, dial 06 plus the number, and in Venice, 041 and the number. All telephone numbers in this book include the entire number you are required to dial, for example, 055 123 456. If you have difficulties, try calling the operator (dial 12). Operator assistance offers no guarantees, but it is worth a try.

Transportation

It is beyond the scope of *Great Eats Italy* to note all of the public transportation options in the three Italian cities covered in this book. Of the three, only Rome has a metro system, and it consists of two lines, which are designed to take people through or across the city, not around it. Since the system is only marginally useful as a way to travel to the restaurants listed in this guide, metro stops are not mentioned. Rome's buses are a more comprehensive way to get around, though the city is small enough that you can walk comfortably to many places.

Florence and especially Venice are cities where walking is not just the most convenient but the preferred way to travel. Otherwise, Florence has a public bus system, and in Venice one travels on foot or by canal, whether in a vaporetto, an expensive private water taxi, or a very expensive gondola.

General Information about Italian Dining

Everything you see I owe to spaghetti.
—*Sophia Loren*

No man is lonely while eating spaghetti; it requires too much attention.
—*Christopher Morley*

When to Eat

Breakfast (*La Prima Colazione*)

Hotels and pensiones usually serve at least a Continental breakfast (normally served between 7:30 and 10 A.M.) that consists of coffee, tea, or hot chocolate, fresh rolls, butter, and preserves. In the last few years, many hotels have expanded their breakfast into a buffet where guests help themselves to a full range of breakfast foods—from fruit and fruit juice, cereals, and assorted pastries to cheese, cold meats, yogurt and all the coffee, tea, or hot chocolate you can drink. While this may seem like a great idea, it is seldom in your best fiscal interests. Hotels make up to 200 percent on these buffets, but you never see the cost because hotel rates are quoted including breakfast. Savvy, budget-minded Great Eaters should try to get their hotel to deduct this cost—which can be as much as $15 per person—from their bill and eat their breakfast at a bar or *caffè*. Doing so will cost a fraction of what the hotel charges, and the coffee will be better, the pastry fresher, and the local scene far more interesting.

Lunch (*La Colazione*)

Lunch usually starts at noon or 12:30 P.M. and lasts anywhere from thirty minutes (standing up) to three hours (sitting down). Last order is supposed to be the time the restaurant lists as closing, but more often the last order will be taken about thirty minutes *before* closing. Lunch can be anything from a quick sandwich eaten standing at the corner bar to a full-blown four- or five-course meal ending with a strong coffee under the umbrellas on a busy piazza . . . which has to be one of the true pleasures of eating in Bella Italia. Time, cost, calories, location, and hunger are the factors that go into deciding what to do for lunch. Sandwiches are available in a *paninoteca,* a bar selling sandwiches either made to order or ready-made and displayed under napkins in a case. If you are staying in one place for a few days, it is fun to become a "local" by eating your lunch each day in the same bar or small, family-run trattoria. The first day you will be treated with politeness. The second, your waiter will be pleased to see you back, and on the third, you will be treated as a "regular," and your waiter will already know what type of wine you like. Try it . . . you will be surprised. In most trattorias and restaurants, the menus for lunch and dinner are the same, and there is no price break offered at lunch.

Dinner (*La Cena*)

If you want to eat with other foreigners, reserve a table for 7:30 P.M. If you want a more Italian experience, dine at 9 P.M. or later; dinner is usually served until 10:30 P.M. Solo diners, especially women, may be relegated to poor table locations. To avoid this as much as possible, reserve a table for two. Upon arrival, say your dining companion had to cancel at the last minute and tell the waiter how sad this makes you. It is amazing how well this works, and how much the service improves.

Where to Eat

At one time there was a distinct difference between a trattoria and a *ristorante,* based on the type of clientele and the prices charged. Now they are virtually interchangeable. A trattoria is generally a family affair, with Mama or Papa in the kitchen, and children helping out as needed. The decor and the menu are simple and the prices only *slightly* less than in a *ristorante.*

Fast-food *italiano* is a boon to all Great Eaters, and I am not talking McDonalds, where a burger, fries, and shake can cost upward of $14. Besides, who wants a Big Mac in Italy? Bars offer some of the best food, from an early-morning *cornetto,* the Italian croissant (either plain or filled with custard or jam), to *tramezzini,* sandwiches made with sliced white bread, and *cicchetti,* bite-sized hors d'oeuvres served in Venice. Inexpensive meals can also be found in stand-up snack bars that feature a *tavola calda,* which means "hot table." Usually frequented for lunch, these places feature a buffet of hot and cold dishes either to eat there or take out. *Rosticcerie* also offer hot and cold dishes to eat in or take out. At either the *tavola calda* or *rosticceria,* items are priced by the portion. You choose your food, pay the cashier, get a receipt, and give that to the person behind the counter, who will dish up your food. You will also encounter pizzerias (very often open only in the evening, especially in Rome and Florence) and places called *pizza al taglio* or *pizza rustica.* These hole-in-the-wall shops sell slices of ready-made pizza sold by weight. It is fun to try several small pieces. Alcoholic beverages are usually not served, but you can get soft drinks and bottled mineral water. Seating is virtually nonexistent.

Other places for a quick bite or a simple meal include a *latteria,* which sells cheese, yogurt, and other dairy products; a *gelateria,* which serves ice cream; and a *pasticceria,* which sells fresh pastries all morning and in the afternoon. At *il forno* you can buy bread, and at an *alimentari*, which is a combination grocery and deli, you can order a custom-made sandwich on a roll or piece of *pizza bianca.* In a *salumeria,* or *gastronomia,* you can buy cold cuts, cheese, wine, bread, mineral water, and other foods to put together a picnic in the piazza or back in your hotel room. For a glass or two of wine and a light meal or upmarket snack, go to an *enoteca,* or wine bar. *Osterias* were wine bars years ago, but now they are more restaurant than wine bar and feature old-fashioned homestyle cooking.

The Italian Menu

One cannot think well, love well, or sleep well, if one has not dined well.
—*Virginia Woolf*

The most important thing about eating in Italy is not to let the length of the menu frighten you, and to order according to the establishment. If you are in a simple trattoria, you probably will not be expected to order every course, and the overworked waiters won't have much time to go into detail about the dishes they are serving. In restaurants, the pace is not as frantic and waiters should explain the dishes and help you select a wine. Portions tend to be smaller, and thus you will be expected to order more.

Bread is served with all Italian meals and is part of the *coperto.* Butter is not served, but if you ask for it, you will probably get it.

Salad is generally eaten after the main course, even if you are ordering only a pasta or a pizza.

Don't order fish on Sunday, when the markets are closed: the fish will be at least one day old. In Venice, extend this to Monday, since the Rialto fish market is closed then as well.

Most Italian menus follow this order:

antipasti, or appetizer—which can be as simple as a few olives brought to your table or as lavish as a serve-yourself buffet, whereby you can almost make a meal from this course alone.

I primi, or *primo*—the first course, a choice of pasta, risotto, soup, or a light vegetable dish.

I secondi, or *secondo*—second or main course of meat, fish, or game.

contórni—vegetables and salads.

formaggi—cheese.

dolci—dessert.

caffè—espresso *only.*

digestivo—after-dinner liqueur (*grappa, amaro,* or *limoncello*).

Some restaurants and trattorias offer a *menù turistico* at an all-inclusive price. Do not let the name turn you off . . . it is only a fixed-price menu that at the very least includes pasta, a main course, and either a vegetable or a salad. It may also include dessert, beverage, *coperto* (cover charge per person) and *servizio* (service charge), in which case there will be no additional expenses tacked onto your final bill. While this can be the best budget way to go, the quality, quantity, and selection might not be up to the standard of an à la carte meal. You cannot expect the finest beef, soft-shell crabs, or the chef's best dishes. You *can* expect a filling if unsurprising meal.

If you are handed the English menu, it may not list the daily specials. Always ask to see the Italian menu along with the English one, otherwise you may miss out on the best dishes at the best prices. If you are a woman dining with a man in a better restaurant, you may be handed a menu without prices; this chauvinistic practice will probably fade in time, but for now, simply insist on seeing a menu with the prices clearly marked.

For a complete list of menu terms, and for phrases to help you while ordering, please see the Glossary, page 243.

Finally, it cannot be said enough: Double-check your bill before you pay, and ask questions if you think something is incorrect. Mistakes, unfortunately, happen with great regularity.

How to Drink Italian Style

A wine is like a man; it can have flaws and still be pleasing.
—Italian village salami-maker

An Italian bar is much more than a place to drink coffee or alcoholic beverages. Here you can eat breakfast, have a snack, sandwich, or hot lunch, make phone calls, use the toilet, read the newspaper, listen to or watch sporting events, meet your neighbor or lover, and argue over politics. If there is a black-and-white "T" (for tobacco) displayed outside, you can also buy cigarettes, matches, some toiletries, stamps, and bus tickets. No wonder there are more than five thousand such places in central Rome alone. In Rome and Florence, when the bar is busy, you pay for what you want at the *cassa* (cash desk) before you order it at the bar. Then take your receipt and put it on the bar for the barman to see. Remember, standing costs less. If you sit at a table, you will be charged more, but you can stay at your table as long as you like for the price of a cup of coffee or glass of beer.

What kind of coffee should you order? The possibilities can be confusing to many Americans. This is a list of the most popular caffeine-laden drinks.

caffè/caffè espresso	A small cup of very strong coffee, i.e., espresso
caffè Americano	American-style coffee
caffè corretto	Coffee "corrected" with a shot of grappa, cognac, or other spirit
caffè doppio	Double espresso
caffè freddo	Iced coffee
caffè Hag/decaffeniato	Decaffeinated coffee
caffè latte	Hot milk mixed with espresso and served in a glass for breakfast
caffè lungo	More water added, similar to *caffè Americano*
caffè macchiato	Espresso "stained" with a drop of steamed milk—a small version of a cappuccino

caffè moka	Equal mix of espresso, chocolate, hot milk
caffè ristretto	Short, *very* strong espresso
cappuccino	Espresso infused with steamed milk and consumed in the morning but never, ever after lunch or dinner
cappuccino senza schiuma	Cappuccino without the froth
granita di caffè con panne	Iced coffee with whipped cream

Like the French, Italians never drink coffee or tea *with* any meal except breakfast, although coffee (*caffèP*) is often ordered after a meal. Tea is considered a morning or between-meal beverage, or one to be used for medicinal purposes. Only unknowing tourists order a cappuccino in a restaurant after lunch or dinner.

Coffee accounts for almost 80 percent of a bar's earnings, but there are other things to drink, starting with *birra* (beer). Beer is either *alla spina* (on tap) or *alla bottiglia* (in the bottle). If you order it *alla spina,* ask for it as *una birra piccola* (small), *media* (medium), or *grande* (large). Wine is always available by the glass, but unless you are in an *enoteca* (wine bar), chances are it will be of low quality. Every bar has grappa, but be careful; it can be lethal. The most popular *aperitivi* (aperitifs) are Spritz, a traditional Venetian drink (made with white wine, selzer, a twist of lemon rind and Campari soda), Martini *rosso* or *bianco,* and the everpresent *prosecco* (dry sparkling white wine). Finally, there is water, either from the tap, called *acqua naturale,* or bottled, which comes *non gassata* (still or plain) or *gassata* (with gas).

FLORENCE

Their smiles and laughter are due to their habit of thinking pleasurably about the pleasures of life.
—*Peter Nichols,* Italia, Italia, *1973*

Whichever way you turn, you are struck with picturesque beauty and faded splendors.
—*William Hazlitt,* Notes of a Journey
through France and Italy, *1826*

For nearly three centuries, from Giotto's time to Michelangelo's, Florence was the cultural center of Europe, producing countless art treasures and generating ideas that formed the cornerstone of twentieth-century thought. Five centuries after the Renaissance was born here, Florence has become a victim of her own beauty and is in danger of being consumed by traffic, pollution, and crowds from the four corners of the planet. Streets designed to accommodate horse-drawn carriages and pedestrians now cope with cars, trucks, Vespas, and hundreds of smog-inducing tour buses. Despite this, visitors continue to flock to this beautiful city to immerse themselves in the art, the literature, and the soft Tuscan light. The home of Dante and *David,* Machiavelli, the Medicis, and the Guccis, Florence is still the perfect place to fall in love, for the first time or all over again.

The food in Florence is simple and hearty, without rich sauces or elaborate spices. The cuisine reflects the Tuscan emphasis on bread, beans, deep-green extra-virgin olive oil, wild game, free-range poultry, and grilled and roasted meats. Most of Florence's restaurants are not gourmet, but many regional dishes are prepared so well that the food is considered some of the best in Italy. Because of the influx of more than a million visitors a year, the good-value restaurants are known to visitors and natives alike. To avoid eating with your fellow compatriots, plan to eat dinner when the Italians do, around 9 P.M.

In Florence you will probably consume more bread than you will pasta. Most of the bread is baked without salt, which seems odd at first, but once you develop a taste for it, the plain unsalted bread is almost addictive. Stale bread goes into some of the best dishes. *Crostini* (toasted bread spread with pâté) is a delicious antipasto or light snack. *Ribollita,* a hearty vegetable soup with beans and black cabbage, reheated and poured over a thick slice of bread, is a favorite first course. In summer, *panzanella,* a salad of torn bread tossed with tomatoes and onion in red wine and virgin olive oil, is a light and refreshing lunch. Not to be forgotten is *bruschetta,* made with thick slices of bread, toasted on the grill, rubbed with garlic, and sprinkled with olive oil and usually topped with chopped

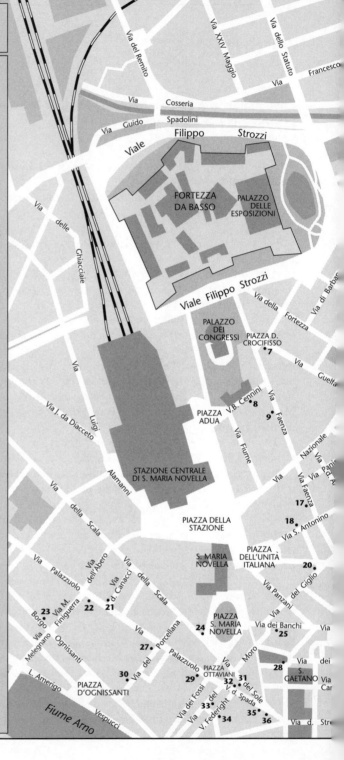

Florence
Map 1

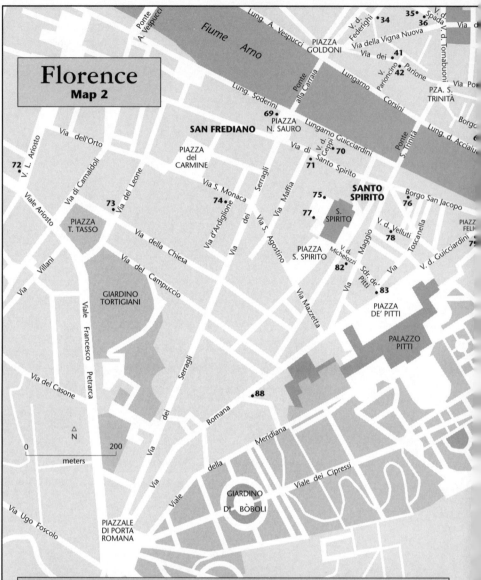

Florence
Map 2

Fiume Arno

Lung. A. Vespucci

Ponte A. Vespucci

PIAZZA GOLDONI

Via della Vigna Nuova

Via dei •41

V. d. Federighi •34

35• •V. d. Spada
36•

V. d. Tornabuoni

Via d

Lung. Soderini

Lungarno

Corsini

V. Parioncino Parione •42

PZA. S. TRINITÀ

Via Po

Ponte alla Carraia

Borgo

Lung. d. Acciaiu

69• PIAZZA N. SAURO

SAN FREDIANO

Lungarno Guicciardini

Via dell'Orto

PIAZZA del CARMINE

Via di V. d. Coppi •70
Santo Spirito •71

Ponte S. Trinità

72• V. L. Ariosto

Viale Ariosto

Via di Camaldoli

Via del Leone

Via S. Monaca

Serragli

Via Maffia

75•

SANTO SPIRITO

Borgo San Jacopo

73• Via del Leone

74•

Via d'Ardiglione

Via dei

Via S. Agostino

77•

S. SPIRITO

76•

V. d. Velluti

PIAZZA FELI

PIAZZA T. TASSO

Via della Chiesa

Via del Campuccio

PIAZZA S. SPIRITO

V. d. Michelozzi

82•

V. Maggio

78•

Toscanella

V. d. Guicciardini 7

Villani

Via

GIARDINO TORTIGIANI

Sdr. de' Pitti •83

PIAZZA DE' PITTI

Viale Francesco Petrarca

Serragli

Via del Casone

dei

Via

Via Mazzetta

PALAZZO PITTI

△ N

0   200

meters

Romana

•88

Meridiana

della

Viale

Viale dei Cipressi

Via

GIARDINO DI BÒBOLI

Via Ugo Foscolo

PIAZZALE DI PORTA ROMANA

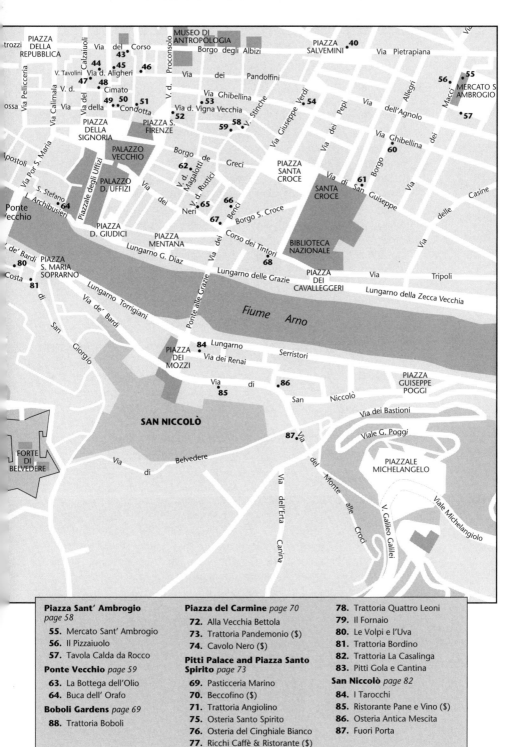

tomatoes. A pasta staple on every menu is pappardelle, wide flat pasta strips served with hearty meat and sauces laced with red wine. The meat courses are a delight to all carnivores, especially the *bistecca alla fiorentina*, a two- to three-inch slab of Chianti beef, salted and coated with olive oil and served juicy rare. Tuscan beans are another favorite dish, especially the white cannellini beans that are served with meat, or plain with extra-virgin olive oil. Olive oil is synonymous with Italy, and in Florence you will find the best to be a murky, dark green, with a robust edge to it. Chianti wine is always a fit accompaniment to any meal, but it can have a very rough taste. For the best Chianti, look for Chianti Classico, with the DOCG guarantee of quality and the *gallo nero,* or black rooster, label on the neck.

Dessert is not the main focus of the meal. It is usually a piece of fresh fruit or a glass of *vin santo,* a sweet wine made from dried grapes. *Cantuccini di Prato* (also called *biscotti di Prato*) are hard almond cookies usually dipped in the wine and a nice finish to any Tuscan meal.

Street Addresses in Florence

In Florence, the street numbers of commercial establishments (stores, restaurants, and businesses) are indicated by a red "r" following the number of the address (i.e., 34r). A blue or black "b" means the address is a private residence. To add to the fun, addresses seldom follow a strict numerical sequence, as we might expect them to. Instead, they are in sequence according to the "r" or the "b" numbers, but they are not necessarily next to one another, which can create confusion for the unknowing visitor.

Cooking Classes

If you love good food and long to be Italian, even for only a day, treat yourself to one of Judy Witts Francini's wonderful Divina Cucina cooking classes. Judy is an enthusiastic, dynamic American with an extensive food background who came to Florence, met and married her Italian husband, and has never looked back. She is a hands-on cook and teacher, and classes are small and kept to a six-student maximum. Judy's programs range from one to five days. The one-day class includes a guided shopping trip to the Mercato Centrale, preparation of the ingredients in her colorful kitchen, and finally, savoring the fruits of your labor. If you have more time, by all means consider her five-day program, which includes a full-day trip to Chianti, three days of cooking classes, plus shopping and walking tours of Florence.

Contact information for Judy Witts Francini: Via Taddea, 31, 50123 Firenze, Italia; Tel & Fax: 055 29 25 78; Email: diva@divinacucina.com; Internet: www.divinacucina.com.

Restaurants *Di Qua d'Arno*

The listings have been organized into two main sections: those on the Uffizi Gallery and Il Duomo side of the Arno, known as *Di Qua d'Arno* (which literally means "this side of the Arno") and those across the Ponte Vecchio on the Pitti Palace side of the Arno, *Di La d'Arno*, or *Oltrarno* (literally, "the other side of the Arno").

Il Duomo, Piazza della Repubblica, and Piazza della Signoria

Florence is a city-museum, whose art treasures are unparalleled anywhere in the world. This city of refinement and elegance gave Italy its national language and was the birthplace of the Renaissance. The city symbol is Il Duomo, the thirteenth-century cathedral crowned by a dome by Brunelleschi and with a distinctive pink, white, and green marble exterior that dominates the Piazza del Duomo and all around it.

Ringed by *caffès* and with countless shops lining the streets leading into the large square, the Piazza della Repubblica is the commercial heart of Florence. In ancient times it was a huge marketplace that was filled with merchants, farmers, and beggars, all doing business successfully.

South of Piazza della Repubblica and Il Duomo, the Piazza della Signoria, although never completed, is considered one of the most beautiful in Italy, and is certainly Florence's civic showplace. The square, once the forum of the Republic and the center of secular life during the rule of the Medici family, is dominated by the magnificent Palazzo Vecchio and a series of magnificent statues, including a copy of Michelangelo's *David* (the original is housed in the Galleria dell'Accademia on Via Ricasoli), an equestrian bronze of Cosimo I by Giambologna, and the *Fountain of Neptune* by Ammanati.

Also here is the Uffizi Gallery, which contains some of the best Renaissance art in the world. To avoid spending hours standing in line with literally hundreds of hapless tourists, you can book a morning or afternoon time in advance. There is a small surcharge, but when you see the line, you will be happy to pay it. The booking number for the Uffizi, as well as other major museums, is 055 294 883. This office is open Mon–Fri 8:30 A.M.–6:30 P.M., Sat 9 A.M.–noon. There are also two Websites: www.weekendafirenze.com and musa.uffizi.firenze.it.

RESTAURANTS

GELATERIAS

GOURMET FOOD AND WINE SHOPS

GROCERY STORES AND SUPERMARKETS

Restaurants

CAFFÈ GILLI (37)
Piazza della Repubblica, 36-39R

Caffè Gilli has been serving coffee, picture-perfect pastries, wonderful chocolates, and light meals in this original Belle Epoque setting since 1910. Go early and have a warm fruit pastry with your first cappuccino of the day. Come back around noon and treat yourself to lunch on the terrace, which will cost more than eating a sandwich at the bar, but it gives you a great vantage point for unparalled people-watching to your heart's content. The whole experience is very Florentine, and by far the best on the piazza.

TELEPHONE
055 213 896

OPEN
Daily: 8 A.M.–midnight, continuous service

CLOSED
Never

RESERVATIONS
Not necessary

CREDIT CARDS
AE, DC, MC, V

À LA CARTE
From 2.58€ (coffee and pastry at the bar) to 12.91€ for light lunch on the terrace

MENÙ TURISTICO
None

COVER & SERVICE CHARGES
None

ENGLISH
Yes, and menu in English

CAFFÈ ITALIANO (49)
Via della Condotta, 56r

The strong coffee will definitely jump-start your day; the house pastries satisfy sweet-tooth yearnings, and the lunches keep you going for the rest of the day. Join the locals at the bar for your morning cappuccino or an espresso laced with bitter chocolate and a buttery *cornetto* pastry. If you are here for lunch, head upstairs for a seat at one of the maroon velvet banquettes that line each side of the narrow room, which features changing art exhibits and a selection of daily papers and periodicals. The seasonal, daily-changing menu is short, offering pasta, huge summer salads, and plates of smoked fish or cheese and salami, topped off with a fresh fruit tart. Locals pack it between 12:30 and 1:30 P.M., so time your lunch visit accordingly.

TELEPHONE
055 289 020

OPEN
Mon–Sat: bar 8 A.M.–8 P.M., lunch 12:30–3 P.M.

CLOSED
Sun; NAC

RESERVATIONS
Not necessary

CREDIT CARDS
None

À LA CARTE
Sandwiches 1.55–2.32€; lunch 4.65–10.85€

MENÙ TURISTICO
None

COVER & SERVICE CHARGES
None

ENGLISH
Usually

CANTINETTA DEI VERRAZZANO (44)
Via dei Tavolini, 18–20r

TELEPHONE & FAX
055 268 590

EMAIL
cantinetta@verrazzano.com

INTERNET
www.verrazzano.com

OPEN
Mon–Sat: 8 A.M.–9 P.M.,
continuous service

CLOSED
Sun; NAC

RESERVATIONS
Not accepted

CREDIT CARDS
AE, DC, MC, V

À LA CARTE
From 3.10–9.10€

MENÙ TURISTICO
None

COVER & SERVICE CHARGES
Both included

ENGLISH
Yes

On one of my early morning walks, I found this elegant *caffè*, which is also a bakery, wine bar, wonderful lunch stop, and elegant teatime rendezvous. Starting at 8 A.M., the bakers send out heaping trays of breakfast goodies along with loaves of brown, white, olive, or wine-flavored breads. I would stop in after walking, order a glass of freshly squeezed orange juice, a *cornetto,* and a double cappuccino to enjoy while glancing through the morning paper. The gleaming glass display cases are filled with a colorful assortment of individual tarts, marvelous cakes sold whole or by the slice, beautiful piles of *biscotti,* and sandwiches made with salmon, cucumber, thinly sliced beef, or ham. By noon, the wood-burning oven along the back is in full force, turning out individual pizzas or focaccia bread split in half while still hot and layered with your choice of fillings. I also loved the assorted open-faced sandwiches garnished with a slice of hard-boiled egg, a sprinkle of chives, and a splash of olive oil. Later in the day, it is a good choice for a glorious Italian pastry treat to eat here or have packaged to go; and any time between noon until 8 P.M., it is a nice place to sip a glass of wine while contemplating your next shopping, sightseeing, or walking destination. The wine bar is part of the Castello da Verrazzano in Chianti, and offers the best vintages, including a Reserva Grand Cru.

DA PENNELLO (46)
Via Dante Alighieri, 4r

TELEPHONE
055 294 848

FAX
055 294 881

OPEN
Tues–Sat: lunch noon–2:30 P.M.,
dinner 7–10 P.M.

CLOSED
Mon, Sun; Aug, Dec 25–Jan 2

RESERVATIONS
Definitely

CREDIT CARDS
AE, DC, MC, V

À LA CARTE
23.24–25.82€, 3 courses;
antipasti only, from 5.16–
8.26€

MENÙ TURISTICO
18.08€, 3 courses, beverage
extra

Da Pennello was founded in the sixteenth century by Mariotto Albertinelli, a painter who preferred cooking and good wines to painting. The *osteria* is in the same building where Dante Alighieri lived, and has been discovered, but never mind. The brightly lit restaurant is deservedly popular with everyone who visits or lives in Florence and is always packed to the walls, so if you arrive without a reservation, especially during prime lunchtime, be prepared to wait up to an hour. It is located on a narrow street about a five-minute stroll from Il Duomo in the direction of the Uffizi Gallery and the Arno River. The kitchen is known for producing an impressive variety of outstanding antipasti, and if you wish, you can make an entire meal out of these wonder-ful appetizers.

The *menù turistico* also offers some Great Eating. There is a choice of *primi piatti* (first courses) of several pastas or the soup of the day. The *secondi piatti* usually lists a roast, veal scaloppine, and an omelette of some sort, along with vegetables or a salad and dessert. The value here is that you can exchange either the first or second courses with a trip to the antipasto table. Wine is extra. If you want *only* to take advantage of the groaning antipasti table, that is a nice option for Great Eaters who want a light meal. If you are going to do this, I suggest going for lunch when it is fresh. Dinnertime antipasti tables are usually recycled from lunch.

I FRATELLINI (48)
Via dei Cimatori, 38r

One of the best ways to cut food costs and have a Great Eat in the bargain is to have lunch at a snack bar. Here you will be joined by savvy Italians who know they can order the blue-plate special or a meaty sandwich and a glass of wine for a mere fraction of a restaurant meal. Further savings are possible if the meal is eaten while standing rather than seated at a table. Only you can decide how far you want to pinch your euros on that score.

This brings me to I Fratellini, a stand-up wine bar and sandwich counter that has been going strong since 1875 and is now run by two friendly, hardworking brothers. You can order your freshly made sandwiches to eat here or to go. They serve twenty to twenty-seven sandwiches, specializing in those piled with *prosciutto crudo* (air-dried, salt-cured ham) and homemade chicken liver pâté spread on thinly sliced bread. To round out the repast, order a glass of their Chianti Classico . . . but be careful. If you ask for the large, it will be served in a tall water tumbler. There are no tables; you are expected to stand. If you can't manage holding both your big sandwich and glass of wine at the same time, look for a spot along the little shelves on each side of the stand. That's where you can place your wineglass between sips.

OSTERIA VINI E VECCHI SAPORI (51)
Via del Magazzini, 3r

Look for the Chianti bottle sitting on a wine barrel and the green plants hanging in front of Emore Cozzani's great little Florentine wine bar, around the corner from Piazza della Signoria. *Little* is the operative word here: there are only six tables inside. This is a hands-on operation for Emore, who works both the bar and the dining tables, proving that the best things do come in small

---

COVER & SERVICE CHARGES
None

ENGLISH
Yes, and menu in English

TELEPHONE
055 239 6096

OPEN
Mon–Sat: 8 A.M.–8 P.M., continuous service; also Sun in Jan, Mar–May, Sept–Oct, Dec

CLOSED
Sun in Feb, June–Aug, Nov; 2 weeks in Aug

RESERVATIONS
Not accepted

CREDIT CARDS
None

À LA CARTE
Sandwiches from 2.32€, wines from 0.52€

MENÙ TURISTICO
None

COVER & SERVICE CHARGES
None

ENGLISH
Very limited

TELEPHONE
055 293 045

OPEN
Tues–Sun: 10 A.M.–11 P.M. (till 3 P.M. Sun), continuous service

CLOSED
Sun night, Mon; NAC

RESERVATIONS
Not necessary

packages. The food and wines celebrate the goodness of Tuscany with *pasta e fagioli* (pasta and white beans), *salsicce e fagioli* (sausage and white beans), penne with mushrooms and peas, tripe, roast pork, *crostini,* and *biscotti* to dip in *vin santo* for a semisweet ending.

TRATTORIA GABRIELLO (50)
Via Condotta, 54r

The three dining areas in Trattoria Gabriello have a country look created by red- or green-and-white table-cloths and sturdy blue-and-white Tuscan pottery. The simple menu of Tuscan classics draws a local lunch crowd, as does the reasonable *menù turistico,* which offers two courses and includes the cover and service charges. Ordering only a pasta and a salad, or one main course, is perfectly acceptable and will definitely keep the prices well within budget.

Start with a crostini topped with *funghi porchini* and melted *scamorza* cheese, then maybe a bowl of rich *ribollita* soup or spaghetti with fresh clams. The beef stew is a popular cold-weather dish, and so is the rich osso buco. Desserts aren't the strong suit here . . . treat yourself to a gelato later instead.

TRIPE STAND (45)
Via Dante Alighieri, 22r

Almost all American visitors to Florence eventually find themselves in the American Express office on Via Dante Alighieri. If you are here between 9 A.M. and 2 P.M., or later from 5 to 7:30 P.M., a portable food cart with a blue-and-white awning will be sitting out front. There will be a line, and the busy man behind the cart won't miss a beat as he serves his hungry customers. What is he selling at this popular pit stop? Tripe. Thirty kilograms per day—which equals sixty-six pounds. That is a lot of tripe!

Wait a minute . . . tripe isn't *that* bad, and here it is really quite good. Obviously it is a big success among local tripe fanciers, who have been stopping by Miro Pinzauti's cart for two decades. Big pieces of tripe are pulled from two steaming pots, sliced thinly onto fresh rolls, dipped into the juice (optional), served with salt, pepper, and green salsa, and rolled in wax paper. Afraid to go whole hog on a sandwich? Then order a small helping of just the tripe, served again on waxed paper and accompanied by toothpicks. If you are cooking in, you can buy fresh tripe from this stand at 0.57€ for 100 grams. What to drink with your repast? Remember, this *is* Italy, so you can purchase a chilled minibottle of wine, a more pedestrian soda, or a beer to complement your meal.

COVER & SERVICE CHARGES
None

ENGLISH
No

Gelaterias

PERCHÈ NÒ! (47)
Via dei Tavolini, 19r (near Via dei Calzaiuoli)

Perchè Nò! opened its doors in 1939 and is recognized today as the oldest *gelateria* in Florence. In addition to its longevity, it has an impressive history. During World War II, it supplied the American troops stationed in Florence with ice cream. When the city's electrical supply was shut off, officers ordered soldiers to reconnect the electrical supply that serviced Perchè Nò! and the surrounding area. After the war, the owners installed the first counter showcase for ice cream, which became a model for all others.

From the beginning, they have been known for their varieties of *semifreddo,* that illegally rich and creamy ice cream that has untold fat grams and tastes like a gift from heaven. Be sure you also sample their white chocolate, rum crunch, hazelnut mousse, or coffee mousse. In summer, the green apple *sorbetto* is a refreshing change of pace. The yogurt ice cream is a big seller, as is the brioche filled with whipped cream. You can have your gelato in a cone or a cup and dipped in a flurry of chocolate pieces and nuts if you've tossed aside all thoughts of dieting.

TELEPHONE
055 239 8969

OPEN
Daily in summer: 10:30 A.M.–midnight; Mon, Wed–Sun in winter: 8 A.M.–8:30 P.M.

CLOSED
Tues in winter; Nov 5–25

CREDIT CARDS
None

PRICES
From 1.81€

ENGLISH
Limited

Piazza della Indipendenza

Piazza della Indipendenza is a large green space near the train station.

RESTAURANTS

GROCERY STORES AND SUPERMARKETS

($) indicates a Big Splurge

Restaurants

IL GIARDINO DI BARBANO (5)
Piazza della Indipendenza, 3/4r

TELEPHONE
055 486 752

OPEN
Mon–Tues, Thur–Sun;
6–11 P.M., until midnight in summer

CLOSED
Wed; 2 weeks Aug (dates vary)

RESERVATIONS
Not necessary

CREDIT CARDS
AE, DC, MC, V

À LA CARTE
Salads from 5.16€, pastas from 5.16€, pizzas from 4.65€, 2 course meal from 15.49€

MENÙ TURISTICO
None

COVER & SERVICE CHARGES
Cover 1.03€, service included

ENGLISH
Yes, and menu in English

Handsome Gian Carlo and his pretty wife, Tosca, have been running this successful restaurant for almost twenty years. Gian told me, "I was born in Florence, my entire family lives here, and I will die here." He has definitely captured the essence of being Florentine. From 6 to 11 P.M. every night but Wednesday, most of the restaurant's 120 seats are filled with a happy crowd that ranges from tourists and tradesmen to fashionable locals. In summer, request a table in either the glassed-in or outdoor garden; in winter, ask for a booth in front. The specialties include *pappardelle al cinghiale* (wide, flat noodles sauced with wild boar meat), fusilli with sausage and porcini mushrooms, and grilled veal chop with potatoes. If those don't speak to you, perhaps one of the thirty other pastas and risottos will. Still not enticed? Then order one of the thirty or more wood-fired pizzas made with *fior di latte* mozzarella and extra-virgin olive oil. There are also large salads, appetizers, and a host of desserts, including the house version of profiteroles, all guaranteed to keep you fully contented for some time.

IL VEGETARIANO (2)
Via delle Ruote, 30r

Exceptional vegetarian food, served in a warm, friendly atmosphere, is dished out cafeteria style to faithful diners, who return with great regularity. Murals of Tuscany, fresh flowers on the tables, and a summer garden create an appealing natural setting.

The menu changes daily and varies with the seasons, and it is executed by a team of Italians and one Irish woman, Brenda, who has been making the desserts for twenty years. Once you enter the restaurant, check the printed blackboard, decide what you want, write it down on the form provided, and take it to the cashier to pay. The dishes for each course are priced the same, allowing you to add up your total easily. After paying, take your menu form to the cafeteria counter to be served. You eat at communal tables in either the smoking or nonsmoking sections. The varied selection of food usually includes soup, rice and pastas, casseroles made from beans and legumes, quiches, soufflés, vegan and macrobiotic choices, salads, and for dessert, anything from pumpkin pie and fruit crumble to vegan cake or brownies.

NOTE: There is no sign outside the restaurant. Look for the round sign with a red telephone receiver hanging above the entrance at Via della Ruote, 30r.

TELEPHONE
055 475 030

OPEN
Tues–Sun: lunch 12:30–2:30 P.M., dinner 7:30–10:30 P.M.

CLOSED
Mon; holidays, Aug

RESERVATIONS
Not accepted

CREDIT CARDS
None

À LA CARTE
12.91–18.08€

MENÙ TURISTICO
None

COVER & SERVICE CHARGES
None

ENGLISH
Yes

TAVERNA DEL BRONZINO ($, 3)
Via delle Ruote, 25r

Eating at the Taverna del Bronzino is always a great pleasure. It is the perfect place for Big Splurge occasion dining, be it a birthday, an anniversary, or a romantic evening with the love of your life. The understated and elegant interior is done in muted colors with flattering lighting. Seating is comfortable and the nicely appointed tables have crisp linens, heavy silver, and fresh flowers. Formal waiters offer gracious and unobtrusive service that is always one step ahead of what you need.

You are bound to be as impressed with the food as with the surroundings. It all starts with a glass of the house aperitif and a plate of tiny appetizers to enjoy while you decide what to order. If you ask, your waiter will make knowledgeable suggestions to help you plan your meal. The imaginative dishes are inspired by the seasonal best of the Italian harvest, and each is cooked to order. The appetizers lean toward fresh prawns, shrimp, and smoked fish. The fresh pastas are blanketed under

TELEPHONE
055 495 220

FAX
055 462 076

OPEN
Mon–Sat: lunch 12:30–2 P.M., dinner 7:30–10 P.M.

CLOSED
Sun; last 3 weeks of Aug

RESERVATIONS
Essential

CREDIT CARDS
AE, DC, MC, V

À LA CARTE
41.23–51.65€

MENÙ TURISTICO
None

COVER & SERVICE CHARGES
Cover 3.10€, service included

ENGLISH
Yes

robust sauces of seafood, *funghi porcini,* or black truffles; the creamy risottos are filled with delicate artichokes or perhaps morelles lightly seasoned with fresh mint. The meat, poultry, and fresh fish are perfectly cooked, gently perfumed with wines and herbs, and attractively served. Even a plate of springtime asparagus is beautifully executed. Sublime desserts and a distinguished wine list round out a meal you will favorably recall long after you have forgotten many others.

TRATTORIA DA TITO (1)
Via San Gallo, 112r

TELEPHONE
055 472 475
OPEN
Mon–Sat: lunch noon–3 P.M.,
dinner 7–10:30 P.M.
CLOSED
Sun; Aug
RESERVATIONS
Advised
CREDIT CARDS
MC, V
À LA CARTE
20.66–25.82€
MENÙ TURISTICO
15.49€, 3 courses, vegetables,
and beverage; cover and service
included
COVER & SERVICE CHARGES
Cover 1.03€, 10% service
added
ENGLISH
Yes, and menu in English, but
not the daily specials

Tito remains one of my Florentine favorites because it is so typically Tuscan—complete with yellowing walls lined with photos and paintings of dubious value, quick and friendly service by family members (it has been family owned since 1913), and reasonable prices for food of uncompromising quality. It is also out of the tourist mainstream, thus attracting a very local crowd who consider this their neighborhood command post. At lunchtime you will need a shoehorn to get in. Great Eaters will like the all-inclusive, three-course *menù turistico,* which is a virtual steal, considering the choices. Otherwise, you could loosen the money belt a notch or two and order from the *piatti del giorno* (daily specials). Carbohydrate fans will have a field day with the long list of authentic pastas and rice dishes. Especially good choices include the *ribollita;* tortelloni with spinach, ricotta cheese, and asparagus; or any of the seasonal pastas, which could include fresh *funghi porcini,* wild boar, or artichokes. Carnivores can choose from a range of top-quality meats, and fish eaters will like the grilled salmon or baked sole. In the event that you have room for dessert, indulge in the *dolce della casa* (special house dessert of the day) or an assortment of Tuscan cheeses and another glass of wine.

TRATTORIA SAN ZANOBI (4)
Via San Zanobi, 33A/r

TELEPHONE
055 475 286
FAX
055 496 520
OPEN
Mon–Sat: lunch noon–2:30 P.M.,
dinner 7–10:30 P.M.
CLOSED
Sun; 1 week in Aug

It's a simple trattoria, with red-tile floors, original brick archways, wood-framed windows, and a Liberty-style bar brought from the north of Italy. Each room takes its design cue from a famous Florentine landmark: Il Duomo, the Palazzo Vecchio, and the Palazzo da Vanzati. The printed à la carte menu covers the bases, but, as usual, prime plates are those the chef recommends that day. These are neatly written on a small sheet of paper fastened to the inside of the menu, and they represent uncomplicated interpretations of *ribollita, pasta e fagioli,* risotto, tagliatelle with duck, roast lamb with potatoes, grilled salmon, and roast beef with arugula salad. Desserts offer several ice cream choices, fresh fruit, and of course *cantuccini di prato con vin santo* (almond cookies dipped in sweet wine).

The Pasta Lunch Break, available Monday to Friday, offers fast-food value for those seeking a quick meal without sacrificing quality. The Pasta Lunch Break offers one-plate meals; choose from fifteen different toppings on the pasta of your choice, as well as two salads, eggplant Parmesan, or a big bowl of vegetable soup.

RESERVATIONS
Advised for dinner

CREDIT CARDS
AE, DC, MC, V

À LA CARTE
15.49–20.66€

MENÙ TURISTICO
None; one-dish Pasta Lunch Breaks are 4.13–6.20€

COVER & SERVICE CHARGES
Cover 2.07€, service included

ENGLISH
Yes, and menu in English

Piazza Goldoni and Via de' Tornabuoni

The Piazza Goldoni serves as a crossroads joining the Ponte alle Carraia with Via del Fossi leading to the Piazza Santa Maria Novella, the train station, and Lungaro Amerigo Vespucci and Lungaro Corsini following the Arno.

Completing a rough triangle with these streets northeast of the piazza is Via de' Tornabuoni, which leads from Piazza Santa Trinità up to Piazza Antinori. Florence is justly famous for its wealth of shopping opportunities, and none are more elegant or expensive than those along Via de' Tornabuoni.

RESTAURANTS

Cantinetta Antinori ($)	38
Coco Lezzone ($)	38
Il Latini ($)	39
I' Parione ($)	40
La Martinicca	40
Trattoria Garga ($)	41
Trattoria Marione	41

PASTRY SHOPS AND BAKERIES

Forno Top	42

GOURMET FOOD AND WINE SHOPS

Antica Bottigliera del Centro	86

($) indicates a Big Splurge

Restaurants

CANTINETTA ANTINORI ($, 28)
Piazza Antinori, 3r

TELEPHONE
055 292 234

FAX
055 235 987

OPEN
Mon–Fri: lunch 12:30–
3:30 P.M., dinner 7–11:30 P.M.

CLOSED
Sat–Sun; Aug 4–28,
Dec 24–Jan 8

RESERVATIONS
Essential for a table; not
accepted at the bar

CREDIT CARDS
AE, DC, MC, V

À LA CARTE
36.15€ (3 courses); appetizers
and cheeses from 7.75€,
beverage extra

MENÙ TURISTICO
None

COVER & SERVICE CHARGES
Cover 2.58€, 10% service
added

ENGLISH
Yes, and menu in English

Many years ago, owners of large estates around Florence kept small cellars in their palaces and sold products from little windows on the street. Following this long-standing tradition, the Antinori family has established the Cantinetta in their fifteenth-century Renaissance Palazzo Antinori in the heart of Florence. Without question, this is a showplace for the vintages of the oldest and most distinguished wine producer in Tuscany, and knowledgeable visitors and beautifully clad Florentines have made this one of the most popular wine bars in the city. Full meals can run into the Big Splurge category and frankly are not worth the price. I think the best way to enjoy the Cantinetta Antinori is to sit at the bar (saving both the cover and service charges) and order an appetizer or plate of assorted cheeses along with a glass or two of their excellent wines.

COCO LEZZONE ($, 42)
Via Parioncino, 26r

TELEPHONE
055 287 178

OPEN
Mon–Sat: lunch noon–2:30 P.M.,
dinner 7–10:30 P.M.

CLOSED
Sun; holidays, July–Aug
(5 weeks), Dec 22–Jan 7

RESERVATIONS
Not accepted for tables, but
must call ahead to order
Florentine steak

There is no sign outside, but that does not mean that this beloved spot has not been found by everyone from Florentine workers and blue bloods to Prince Charles and Luciano Pavarotti. The inside has barely changed since it opened a century ago. It still has plain white-tile walls and elbow-to-elbow seating along narrow tables. The hearty, traditional cooking is prepared with high-quality, fresh ingredients. The only nod to modern times is the note printed on the menu, *il trillo dei telefoni cellulari disturba la cottura della ribollita*—"the ringing of your cellular telephone disturbs the cooking of the *ribollita.*"

There is a weekly menu, but not all of the dishes are available every day. Listen to what the waiter says about the daily specials, and remember that you can always depend on osso buco on Monday, beef stew on Tuesday, veal scaloppine or *involtini* (stewed rolls of meat) on Wednesday and Saturday, tripe for your Thursday main course, and *baccalà* on Friday. Diners are expected to order full meals, to eat them with zeal, and to drink plenty of wine in the process. That is very easy to do, especially if you start out with a light *primo piatto* (first plate) of *pappa al pomodoro,* their famous *ribollita,* or the seasonally available *farfalle con piselli* or *tartufo* (pasta with peas or truffles). For the *secondo piatto,* go with the daily special, or if you have been working up the courage to try tripe, here is your chance. Served in a tomato sauce with freshly ground Parmesan cheese, it is perfectly tender and delicious. Beef eaters can dig into one of the Florentine steaks, cooked rare and literally overflowing the plate. But, be forewarned, even though you cannot make a table reservation, you must call ahead to reserve your steak. The desserts are all made here and reflect the season and mood of the chef, but don't expect an after-dinner coffee, because it is not served.

CREDIT CARDS
None. The restaurant states: "We accept any foreign currency, eurochecques and traveler's checks, but we don't accept any credit cards."

À LA CARTE
25.82–30€

MENÙ TURISTICO
None

COVER & SERVICE CHARGES
Cover 2.07€, 10% service added

ENGLISH
Yes

IL LATINI ($, 34)
Via dei Palchetti, 6r

Narciso Latini opened Il Latini in the early 1900s as a *fiachetteria,* or wine shop. In the fifties, his nephew took over, expanded, and began to serve sandwiches and hot food prepared by his wife, first in her own kitchen at home and later in the restaurant. For most of us, the popular trattoria became synonymous with good food, good wine, and good cheer. It was everything one expected and hoped for, from the interior crowded with hanging hams and trestle tables to the big servings of typical Tuscan dishes accompanied by plenty of their own bottles of wine and extra-virgin olive oil.

Unfortunately, things have changed drastically since the last edition of this book, and not for the better. Il Latini is now overrated, overpriced, and impossibly crowded with *only* tourists (the Florentines have long since sworn off it). Service has become rude, the food mediocre and unappetizingly presented. It is extremely disappointing when an old standby fails to live up to its longheld reputation, but I feel I must warn readers that Il Latini is no longer a recommended choice. Hopefully it will improve in the future.

TELEPHONE
055 210 916

OPEN
Tues–Sun: lunch 12:30–2:30 P.M., dinner 7:30–10:30 P.M.

CLOSED
Mon; Aug (dates vary)

RESERVATIONS
Advised

CREDIT CARDS
AE, DC, MC, V

À LA CARTE
28.41–33.57€

MENÙ TURISTICO
None

COVER & SERVICE CHARGES
None

ENGLISH
Yes

I' PARIONE ($, 41)
Via del Parione, 74/76r

TELEPHONE & FAX
055 214 005

OPEN
Mon, Wed–Sun: lunch 12:30–
2:30 P.M., dinner 7:30–
10:30 P.M.

CLOSED
Tues; Aug (dates vary)

RESERVATIONS
Essential for dinner, advised for
lunch

CREDIT CARDS
AE, MC, V

À LA CARTE
25.82–28.41€

MENÙ TURISTICO
None

COVER & SERVICE CHARGES
Cover 2.07€, service charge
included

ENGLISH
Enough

The crowd is a buzzy mix of attractive locals and savvy visitors; the atmosphere is slightly chaotic when things get going; and the food is deliciously inventive, but not fussy. The entrance from the street opens directly onto the kitchen, with two distinct dining areas on each side. To the left is a small space, set with country tables and chairs, brightly colored Tuscan-style painted pottery, and linen napkins. On the right is a slightly larger room completely enveloped in massive paintings in the style of Picasso, Diego Rivera, or some say, Michaelangelo . . . you decide. The same furniture and table settings prevail.

While the paintings may be the source of some differing speculation, all will agree that the food is consistently good and fairly priced. Start with a plate of seasonal vegetables, lightly grilled and dusted with shavings of fresh Parmesan, an arugula salad laced with slices of raw baby artichokes, or marinated fresh salmon with a sprinkling of fresh chives. The asparagus risotto is soul-food at its best, and so is the gnocchi with pesto and tomato sauce. The fresh fish selection depends on the chef's trip to the market, and it might include lightly grilled fat shrimp or a moist swordfish in a Mediterranean tomato sauce. If you like lamb, here is the place to order quickly cooked little rib chops or roast lamb sliced from the bone. A side order of rosemary seasoned potatoes and fresh spinach drizzled with olive oil can easily be shared. Not so the chocolate torte with rich dark chocolate sauce. I thought I was too full to even think of finishing it . . . but it was just the right ending to a very nice meal in Florence.

LA MARTINICCA (31)
Via del Sole, 27r

TELEPHONE
055 218 928

OPEN
Mon–Sat: lunch noon–2:30 P.M.,
dinner 7:30–10:30 P.M.

CLOSED
Sun; NAC

RESERVATIONS
Preferred

CREDIT CARDS
MC, V

A meal at La Martinicca is pleasant and unhurried, with hearty Tuscan food and wine to match. The interior is typical trattoria style with assorted artwork in three small rooms set with pink linens. Arrive early and you will be surrounded by other foreigners or neighborhood guests with children in tow. Go around nine, when both the service and noise level is better. The all à la carte seasonal menu covers the important bases, including a tempting list of homemade pastas. The cheese-dressed gnocchi is a rich choice, and so is the *tagliatelle genovese,* loaded with fresh basil, garlic, and Parmesan cheese. As always, pay attention to the daily specials, watching for grilled baby lamb chops, roast chicken, veal scaloppine with asparagus, or a satisfying osso bucco with spinach. A dessert cart is wheeled around at the appropriate time, and their version of *torta della nonna* is good, but they really don't have a handle on crème brûlée. The best bet is the *cantucci con vin santo*—almond cookies dipped into sweet wine.

À LA CARTE
25.82–30.99€

MENU TURISTICO
None

COVER & SERVICE CHARGES
None

ENGLISH
Yes, and menu in English

TRATTORIA GARGA ($, 33)
Via del Moro, 48r

Trattoria Garga is one of the most sought after dining destinations in Florence, and rightfully so. Once you get used to the wild, brightly colored interior, which my dining companion dubbed "tastefully hideous," and settle in for an evening of good wine and food, you, too, will be making plans for your next visit. I have one, no, make that two words to say about the food . . . absolutely wonderful. On several visits, every dish ordered displayed high quality, not only in the ingredients, but in their execution and presentation.

Portions are generous, so my advice is to share an antipasto and pasta to save room for a main course and dessert. Start with the *insalata del Garga,* a colorful mix of baby greens, avocados, fresh tomatoes and maybe a handful of fresh anchovies in olive oil marinade. The risotto with fresh asparagus is delicious, and so is the tagliatelle tossed with the season's best vegetables, or rich *funghi porcini.* For a main course, consider the thick, moist piece of swordfish with a Sicilian tomato sauce or veal scaloppine with lemon, avocado, or chantal mushrooms as unbeatable choices. The vanilla ice cream with fresh strawberries is a cool finish, but chocoholics will not want to miss the illegally rich chocolate tart.

TELEPHONE
055 239 8898

OPEN
Tues–Sun: lunch 12:30–2:30 P.M., dinner 7:30–10:30 P.M.

CLOSED
Mon; NAC

RESERVATIONS
Essential, at least a day in advance

CREDIT CARDS
AE, MC, V

À LA CARTE
53.20–61.97€

MENÙ TURISTICO
None

COVER & SERVICE CHARGES
Cover 1.55€, 12% service added

ENGLISH
Yes

TRATTORIA MARIONE (35)
Via della Spada, 27r

Trattoria Marione is a crowded, happy place where Sergio and his extended family prove their Italian pedigree with their versions of *cucina casalinga* (homestyle cooking). The typical decor consists of rows of wine bottles, assorted paintings, and rush-seated chairs positioned around tightly packed tables. Especially appealing for some is their *menù turistico,* which includes two courses, fruit for dessert, wine or water, and the cover

TELEPHONE & FAX
055 214 756

OPEN
Mon–Sat: lunch noon–3 P.M., dinner 7–10 P.M.

CLOSED
Sun; holidays, Aug

RESERVATIONS
Not necessary

CREDIT CARDS
AE, DC, MC, V
À LA CARTE
15.49–20.66€
MENÙ TURISTICO
12.91€, 2 courses, plus fruit
and wine or water; cover and
service included
COVER & SERVICE CHARGES
Cover 0.77€, 10% service
added
ENGLISH
Yes

and service charges. While this *prezzo fisso* (fixed-price menu) has several choices for first and second courses, it offers few surprises. Upping the ante a bit and going à la carte is not fraught with budget peril, and it allows for a more interesting dining experience, including their *ribollita*. The name means "reboiled," and this dense vegetable soup is thickened with bread and left a day before reheating and eating; Trattoria Marione's won an award as one of the best in Florence from the Academy of Italian Cooking. There is also gnocchi with salmon, pappardelle with wild boar sauce, fresh grilled fish, roast lamb or veal served with creamy potatoes, and a moist roast chicken. Dessert? Not here, thank you, unless you want fruit or *biscottini con vin santo*.

Pastry Shops and Bakeries

FORNO TOP (36)
Via della Spada, 23r

TELEPHONE
055 219 854
OPEN
Mon–Tues, Thur–Sat:
7:30 A.M.–1 P.M., 5 P.M.–
7:30 P.M.; Wed: 7:30 A.M.–1 P.M.
CLOSED
Sun; NAC
CREDIT CARDS
None
PRICES
From 0.52€ for a roll to 4.13€
for a strawberry tart; sandwiches
are around 1.29€
ENGLISH
Very limited, depends on server

Mmmm . . . I can still smell the wonderful breads and pastries from this popular bakery and pastry shop that was just down the street from my apartment—and a source of endless temptations. If you go by in the morning, you'd think they couldn't possibly sell everything on display: breads, cookies, cakes, tarts, pizzas, and more. However, if you arrive in the late afternoon, all that may be left are crumbs. So come as early as possible, grab a number, and try to make your deliciously difficult decisions by the time they call you to the counter. Forno Top has several locations throughout Florence.

Piazza Santa Croce

Santa Croce Church, founded by Franciscans in 1228, is considered the richest medieval church in Florence. It is also the pantheon of Italy's great men: Michelangelo, Machiavelli, Galileo, Rossini, and Foscolo are buried here. Inside are frescoes by Giotto. To the right of the church stands Brunelleschi's beautiful Pazzi Chapel. The Piazza Santa Croce is anchored by the church and ringed with lovely medieval *palazzo*s and scores of tourist hawker stalls. In back of the piazza is one of the most interesting working areas of Florence and the bustling Sant' Ambrogio Market (see page 89).

RESTAURANTS

GELATERIAS

GROCERY STORES AND SUPERMARKETS

($) indicates a Big Splurge

Restaurants

ACQUA AL 2 (53)
Via della Vigna Vecchia, 40r (at Via dell'Acqua)

Everyone loves Acqua al 2, one of the most firmly established and well-known casual restaurants in Florence. It consists of three rooms with stone walls, arched brick ceilings, wooden banquettes, hard wooden chairs and benches, and tables set with fresh flowers, candles, and paper place mats. The animated diners come from all walks of life and every corner of the globe to enjoy the hearty food. The menu doesn't leave much to chance, with twenty-six pastas (many of which are vegetarian), chicken prepared five ways, a few omelettes, as well as several variations of veal and beef. You can just order one course, go whole hog and have the works, or land somewhere in between and share. The house specialties offer some particular treats that lend themselves to sharing. Start with the *assaggio di primi,* your choice of any five

TELEPHONE
055 284 170

INTERNET
www.acquaal2.it

OPEN
Daily: 7:30 P.M.–1 A.M., continuous service

CLOSED
NAC

RESERVATIONS
Advised

CREDIT CARDS
AE, DC, MC, V

À LA CARTE
15.49–25.82€

MENÙ TURISTICO
None

pastas; follow that with the *assaggio di insalate,* which gives you several salad selections; and then the *assaggio di formaggi* or *assaggio di dolci,* which offer an assortment of cheeses or desserts of the day. The house wine is good and priced to flow . . . which it does in large quantities.

NOTE: The restaurant has a second location in the Gaslamp quarter of San Diego, California, at 322 Fifth Avenue, 92101; Tel: 619-230-0382.

ENOTECA BALDOVINO (61)
Via San Guiseppe, 18r

TELEPHONE
055 234 7220

OPEN
Daily; in winter noon–4 P.M.,
6 P.M.–1 A.M.; in summer noon–
1 A.M., continuous service

CLOSED
Christmas

RESERVATIONS
Recommended, and essential
for terrace tables

CREDIT CARDS
AE, DC, MC, V

À LA CARTE
5.16–12.91€

MENÙ TURISTICO
None

COVER & SERVICE CHARGES
1.55€ cover charge, 10%
service suggested

ENGLISH
Yes

Enoteca Baldovino, run by the same owners as Trattoria Baldovino nearby (see page 51), is an informal place, serving lighter dishes geared to go well with the weekly featured wines (twenty of which are available by the glass) and other drinks poured here from morning until night. In the summer, the action expands to coveted seats on the terrace. If I am going for lunch, I like to have the *gran piatto misto,* an assortment of four of the daily specials, perhaps a spinach and pecorino torte, a chicken salad spiked with stilton cheese, a spicy chicken curry served over rice and potato, and tuna salad tossed with fresh green beans. I also love the endless varieties of *crostini* and *carpacci* made with everything from wild boar to smoked salmon, eggplant, and zucchini. Salads, cheeses, and foie gras served on toast round out the menu. Enoteca Baldovino also has a section of Italian wines, Tuscan extra-virgin olive oil, and balsamic vinegar that can be shipped tax free anywhere in the world.

FIASCHETTERIA AL PANINO (67)
Via dei Neri, 2r

TELEPHONE
055 216 887

OPEN
Mon–Sat; bar 10 A.M.–9:30 P.M.;
lunch 12:30–3 P.M., or until the
food is gone

CLOSED
Sun; 1 week in Aug (dates vary)

RESERVATIONS
Not accepted

CREDIT CARDS
None

À LA CARTE
Sandwiches from 2.58€, two
courses for 5.16–7.75€

Smart Italians eat their lunches in snack bars that serve a hot noon meal. One of the best of these around the Santa Croce Church is the Fiaschetteria al Panino. You won't be able to miss its corner location . . . just look for the hungry crowd standing outside patiently waiting for their food reward. This is a fast-paced place where dallying over long conversations is not part of the lunchtime game plan, when everyone eats quickly at the bar or sits on a stool at the marble counters circling the windows. At other times things slow down, and you may see the same cast of neighbors sitting at the same tables playing cards, nursing a glass of wine, or engaged in the same people-watching you are.

COVER & SERVICE CHARGES
Cover 1.03€, 10% service
added

ENGLISH
Yes

The food is guaranteed to do wonders for your well-being. Following the Italian tradition of preparing a special dish each day, the chef has *pappa al pomodoro* on Monday and *zuppa di faro* on Tuesday. Wednesday he makes tagliatelle, and on Thursday, cannelloni stuffed with spinach and ricotta cheese. Friday is always fish, and the pasta has a clam sauce. Every day you can count on lasagna, an assortment of *frittatas*, and warm foccacia, split and filled with meat or cheese. For dessert, abandon all diet worries and try the chocolate mousse torte, a rich pie that will haunt the dreams of chocoholics for years to come. The other desserts are a lemon and honey torte that is good but not fabulous and fried doughnut holes that are absolutely forgettable, heavy lumps that sit like wet laundry in the pit of your stomach. Espresso is served, but no other coffee drinks.

MENÙ TURISTICO
None

COVER & SERVICE CHARGES
No cover, service included

ENGLISH
None

I' CCHÈ C'È C'È (62)
Via d. Magalotti, 11r

In Italian the name means "what you find, you find," which in this case always means excellent Tuscan fare and service. Owner and chef Gino Noci is a native Florentine with lots of experience in the restaurant business, including time spent in a French restaurant in London and being invited to do guest-chef, demonstration cooking in the States. He emphasizes that his establishment is a casual, family-run place where everyone is welcomed in the same friendly way. For lunch, the long wooden tables are set with paper place mats and napkins. At night, linen replaces the paper. Ringing the room are shelves of wine bottles and paintings of varying quality.

Budget-watching Great Eaters will want to pay close attention to the *menù turistico,* which includes a first and second course and either a salad or frozen fried potatoes. When deciding what to order, always ask your waiter what Gino is cooking that day, and do your best to order these dishes. Also take a look at the grilled fresh fish. Everything is kept simple, using only the best olive oils and fresh ingredients. The house wine, poured from large barrels, is drinkable.

TELEPHONE
055 216 589

FAX
055 290 485

OPEN
Tues–Sun: lunch 12:30–2:30 P.M., dinner 7:30–10:30 P.M.

CLOSED
Mon; Aug 17–Sept 10

RESERVATIONS
Essential; not accepted for *menù turistico* for lunch

CREDIT CARDS
AE, DC, MC, V

À LA CARTE
23.24–28.41€

MENÙ TURISTICO
12.91€, 2 courses; cover and service included, beverage extra

COVER & SERVICE CHARGES
Cover 1.03€, service not included

ENGLISH
Yes

IL BARROCCIO (52)
Via della Vigna Vecchia, 31r

For Sunday lunch, Il Barroccio is a full house with a mix of Italian families, area regulars, and tourists visiting the Santa Croce Church. The closely spaced tables are set with white and red linen cloths, polished silver,

TELEPHONE
055 211 503

OPEN
Mon–Tues, Thur–Sun: lunch 12:15–2:30 P.M., dinner 7:15–10:30 P.M.

china, and fresh flowers. Tuscan watercolors crowd almost every inch of space on the smoke-yellowed walls.

The menu has all the Tuscan standbys, plus a selection of seasonal and daily specials. All the pastas, sauces, and desserts are made here and are free of preservatives and additives. You can actually taste the potatoes in the gnocchi, with its fresh basil and tomato sauce. The *ravioli alle noci* (ravioli with nuts in a cream sauce) is a very interesting first course. Main courses to rely on include the *carpaccio Parmigiano e rucola*—thin slices of raw beef served with fresh Parmesan and bitter greens. Veal is fixed several ways, and there are always grilled meats and vegetables. The desserts consist of *panna cotta,* a pudding, tiramisù, *biscotti con vin santo,* sorbet, and fresh fruit. A nice alternative is the plate of assorted Italian cheeses paired with a glass of wine.

NOTE: If you are the host for a small group, the restaurant can provide a set menu with wines if notified in advance.

LA BARAONDA ($, 60)
Via Ghibellina, 67r

La baraonda means "hubbub," an apt description of this trattoria at noon, when the prices are lower than at night and every seat is occupied. It is owned by Duccio Magni and his wife, Elena, who is responsible for the kitchen. Florentine regulars flock here for the wholesome yet imaginative food prepared with only seasonally grown produce. The three-room interior consists of pure white tiles halfway up the walls, beamed ceilings, a bar with a few antique prints of boxing matches. Villeroy and Bosch china graces the white linen-clad tables.

The well-priced lunches keep everyone coming back for more, especially between October and May, when favorite dishes are featured several days of the week. Wednesday it will be pigeon; Thursday, rabbit; Friday, codfish; and Saturday, a delicious roast leg of pork. During the hot months, the menu offers lighter fare, including meat salads and fresh goat cheese. And every day for the past twelve years they have served veal meatloaf covered in fresh tomato sauce, which always sells out, and vegetable soufflés, which are actually more like a quiche than an airy soufflé. Another favorite is La Francesina, a beef stew made with onions that are cooked until melted and caramelized.

CLOSED
Wed; NAC

RESERVATIONS
Advised for weekends

CREDIT CARDS
AE, DC, MC, V

À LA CARTE
20.66–25.82€

MENÙ TURISTICO
None

COVER & SERVICE CHARGES
Cover 1.03€ 10% service added

ENGLISH
Yes

TELEPHONE & FAX
055 234 1171

OPEN
Mon: dinner 7:30–10:30 P.M.;
Tues–Sat: lunch 12:30–
2:30 P.M., dinner 7:30–
10:30 P.M.

CLOSED
Mon lunch, Sun; Aug

RESERVATIONS
Essential for dinner, and
strongly advised for lunch

CREDIT CARDS
AE, DC, MC, V

À LA CARTE
Lunch: 20.66–23.24€, includes
water, wine, and coffee; dinner:
36.15–38.73€, includes house
wine, other beverages extra

MENÙ TURISTICO
None

COVER & SERVICE CHARGES
Lunch: cover 1.55€; dinner:
cover 2.58€; 10% service added
for both lunch and dinner

ENGLISH
Yes, and French

At dinnertime, there is no printed menu, and each course has only one price. The meal begins with complimentary appetizers served with a basket of homemade bread and a crock of black olive pâté. I like the risotto baked with greens and the penne tossed with lots of garlic and broccoli as sturdy first courses. If I don't have one of the daily specials or the veal meatloaf, then I might order the braised beef in a lemon sauce or the fresh fish. All main courses are garnished, saving the extra expense of a side order of vegetables or a salad. An apple torte, similar to a thin pancake piled high with lightly cooked apples, and a chocolate cake made with candied orange peel are special house desserts. A glass of Italian grappa or Nocino (a walnut liqueur) finalizes the excellent meal.

OSTERIA DEI BENCI (66)
Via de' Benci, 13r

The three rooms with arched brick ceilings are informal. Colorful pottery adds zip to the bare wooden tables covered in paper place mats and matching napkins. In warm weather, the action moves to the sidewalk terrace. House wine and water are served in glass tumblers, but if you upgrade your wine, they will pour it into a proper wine glass. The monthly changing menu at this popular Santa Croce osteria keeps the young, hip food cognoscenti always interested and coming back for more. The kitchen owes its success to an imaginative use of fresh ingredients and its ability to offer more than the obvious Tuscan staples. Admittedly, the full menu takes some study, not only to decide, but to decipher. However, if you stick to the one-page monthly offering, you not only will have an easier time ordering but a better meal in the bargain. In late winter, you might start with fresh anchovy crostini or a bracing tagliolini in a rich pork sausage sauce made with balsamic vinegar and topped with Parmesan cheese. A lighter alternative is the spaghetti laced with fresh artichokes and plenty of fresh garlic. Only Sumo wrestlers could finish the Florentine beefsteak, which literally falls off the platter onto the table. The roast beef *di filetto di Chianina,* served with a creamy potato purée, is a more manageable choice, especially if accompanied by an array of seasonal vegetables drizzled with thick Tuscan olive oil. For dessert, try an assortment of pecorino cheeses and another glass of bracing red wine, or the heavenly cheese cake.

TELEPHONE
055 234 4923

OPEN
Daily: lunch 12:30–2:30 P.M., dinner 7:45–10:45 P.M.

CLOSED
Major holidays, but call to check

RESERVATIONS
Essential, and on weekends a day in advance

CREDIT CARDS
AE, DC, MC, V

À LA CARTE
18.08–28.41€

MENÙ TURISTICO
None

COVER & SERVICE CHARGES
Cover 1.29€, 10% service added

ENGLISH
Limited

PALLOTTINO (58)
Via Isola delle Stinche, 1r

TELEPHONE
055 289 573

OPEN
Tues–Sun: lunch 12:45–
2:30 P.M., dinner 7:30–
10:15 P.M.

CLOSED
Mon; 15 days in Aug (dates
vary)

RESERVATIONS
Accepted for dinner only

CREDIT CARDS
AE, DC, MC, V

À LA CARTE
Dinner only, 18.08–23.75€

MENÙ TURISTICO
Lunch only, 7.23€, 2 courses
and dessert or coffee; cover and
service included, wine extra;
5.16€, one-plate meal, cover
and service included, beverages
extra

COVER & SERVICE CHARGES
For dinner: cover 1.55€, 10%
service added

ENGLISH
Enough, and à la carte menu in
English

Ask the natives living around Santa Croce Church where they eat, and the unanimous reply is: "Pallottino! Where else?" I have had the opportunity of trying it several times, and I certainly share the enthusiasm, especially for the *menù turistico,* served *only* at lunch Tuesday to Saturday, but never on holidays. This is a Great Eat to behold. To keep the regulars interested and coming back in droves, the menu, two courses plus dessert or coffee, changes daily and offers several choices for each course. Whole-wheat bread comes with the meal, but veggies and wine do not. The house wine is cheap and drinkable.

What about dinner? The *menù turistico* is replaced by seasonal à la carte choices, which provide enough variety of the usual Tuscan favorites to keep everyone well fed and happy. Naturally, the offerings are a little more sophisticated, but the prices are still reasonable enough not to crash the budget. There is a two-course minimum order at night.

RISTORANTE DEL FAGIOLI (68)
Corso dei Tintori, 47r

TELEPHONE
055 244 285

OPEN
Mon–Fri: lunch 12:30–
2:30 P.M., dinner 7:30–
10:30 P.M.

CLOSED
Sat–Sun; 1 week at Christmas
and Easter, Aug

RESERVATIONS
Recommended

CREDIT CARDS
None

À LA CARTE
20.66–25.82€

MENÙ TURISTICO
None

COVER & SERVICE CHARGES
Cover 1.55€, no service charge

ENGLISH
Yes

During one research trip to Florence, I stayed in a beautiful penthouse apartment facing the Piazza Santa Croce. My neighbors were a delightful couple who were celebrating retirement by spending six months in Florence and another six months in a villa in Tuscany. What a way to start retirement! As part of their immersion into Italian life in Florence, they ate out at least once a day and would often report their findings to me. One of their standbys was this family-owned and -run trattoria right around the corner from our flats.

The restaurant has been here since 1966, and I can assure you not one thing has changed in its two rooms, nor has the Tuscan food prepared by Luigi, the father, and leisurely served by his two sons, Antonio and Simone. While contemplating what to have, ask for the *pinzimonio misto di stagione,* a plate or bowl of raw seasonal vegetables to dip into olive oil, a light and refreshing way to start your meal. The portions are more than generous, especially the *ribollita,* brought to you in a big bowl so you can help yourself to as much as you want. It would be easy to make a meal on this rich, twice-cooked bean and bread soup highlighted with vegetables, garlic, oil, and herbs, but save room for the comforting dishes that follow, such as osso buco, *baccalà* with tomato, and spicy sausages. Forget the steaks; they are tough and tasteless. The owners make all of their own desserts, but frankly, I never had room for more than a few *biscotti* dipped in *vin santo*.

RISTORANTE FRANCESCANO ($, 61)
Largo Bargellini, 16r

Ristorante Francescano has had a varied past. Before World War II, it was a *canova di vina*, an early type of wine bar where wine was only dispensed by the glass. Later it became a restaurant where anyone who was someone, or thought they were, made an appearance. Scattered around the rooms are pictures of these stars who ate here in its heyday. Today it is run by the same delightful Scottish couple who own Trattoria Baldovino (see page 51).

The back room decorated with old sewing machines and radios is especially romantic and cozy when the candles are lighted at night. A glass case by the entrance, filled with salamis, wild boar sausage, Chianti hams, and trimmed with ropes of garlic and peppers tells you the food is going to be rich and robust. The country-style Tuscan food focuses on all the sausages and cured meats you see in the entry display case, along with seasonal vegetables marinated in olive oil and herbs, barley soup, penne tossed with meatballs and peppers, spaghetti in a mutton ragù, and pumpkin-flavored potato gnocchi in a sausage sauce. And these are just the beginning courses. From the chargrill come pork chops, more sausages, and prime beef steaks. Slow-cooked stews, duck served on a bed of baby onions, and braised pork answer all your carnivore yearnings. Battered and fried foods are not forgotten; especially notable are the mixed plate of chicken and rabbit, the lamb with artichoke hearts, and the mixed plate of deep-fried vegetables. It is almost impossible to contemplate dessert after this enormous meal, but there are some who can polish off the pear cheesecake with caramel sauce, the fresh fruit tart, or the double Swiss chocolate cake with whipped cream. The wine list is huge, with an emphasis on Tuscan varieties.

TELEPHONE
055 241 605

OPEN
Mon, Wed–Sun: lunch noon–2:45 P.M., dinner 7–11 P.M.

CLOSED
Tues; NAC

RESERVATIONS
Essential

CREDIT CARDS
MC, V

À LA CARTE
28.41–33.57€

MENÙ TURISTICO
None

COVER & SERVICE CHARGES
Cover 1.55€, 10% service added

ENGLISH
Yes, and English menu

RISTORANTE LA GIOSTRA ($, 39)
Borgo Pinti, 10r

TELEPHONE
055 241 341
FAX
055 226 8781
EMAIL
lagiastrarest@iol.it
OPEN
Daily: lunch 12:30–2:30 P.M.,
dinner 7 P.M.–midnight
CLOSED
Never
RESERVATIONS
Essential
CREDIT CARDS
AE, DC, MC, V
À LA CARTE
25.82–30.99€
MENÙ TURISTICO
None
COVER & SERVICE CHARGES
Cover 1.55€, service not
included
ENGLISH
Yes

The motto on the business card says, "In Food We Trust, and in Love." Judging from the restaurant's popularity, it is obvious Florentines have come to trust the food and fall in love with La Giostra.

You will recognize Dimitri, the Russian owner of this very "in" place, when he comes out of the kitchen in full chef's garb and goes from table to table greeting his guests. He is a dignified and well-educated man, with doctorates in both chemistry and biology. Always a lover of fine food and cooking, he was told for years by his friends, "You are such a good cook—why don't you open your own restaurant?" Several years ago he came out of retirement and opened La Giostra with the help of his twin sons and his daughter. The restaurant was an instant hit, and it remains fully booked for both lunch and dinner seven days a week. The name means "carousel," and there is a picture of one to the right of the entry.

Lunchtime does not seem to be a drawn-out affair, though dinner can be. If you go when the restaurant opens, chances are the service will be more attentive. As the evening progresses, the waiters are stretched beyond their limits, resulting in long delays between courses. Almost the minute you are seated, you are served a flute of champagne and a plate of assorted *crostini,* toast with various toppings. This helps with the long lag until the waiter comes back to take your order, and again until the appearance of the first course. Be patient—the menu is small but choice. All of the *primi piatti* (first courses) are good, especially the ricotta-filled crepe, the pappardelle with artichokes and ham, and the tagliatelle with a flavorful sauce of *funghi porcini.* One of the most popular main courses is the *spinata,* finely sliced beef flavored with sage, bay leaves, rosemary, salt and pepper and baked only two minutes in the oven and brought to your table on a sizzling hot plate. Another favorite is the *scamorza,* slices of ham covered with cheese that has been browned and bubbled under the broiler just before it arrives at your table. For dessert, forget the *torta di mele,* a dreary apple tart, and opt instead for a cool lemon sorbet or the wickedly fattening tiramisù. The wine list is not cheap, but vintages are happily served by the glass, thus enabling you to sample more than one without ruining the budget completely.

SALUMERIA/GASTRONOMIA VERDI (54)
Via Guiseppe Verdi, 36r

Glorious picnics, terrific takeout, and Great Eater–friendly lunches all begin at Pino's Salumeria/Gastronomia Verdi, a few short blocks from Piazza Santa Croce. Walking by, you can smell the good things awaiting you inside, where the artistically presented food is as delightful to the palate as to the eye. Pino gets up with the chickens to be at the market when it opens to find the best ingredients, which are skillfully prepared into wonderful dishes by Antonella, a sweet French cook who grew up in Monte Carlo. With these two virtuosos in my neighborhood, I would never have to go near the kitchen to cook again! They work long hours every day, including Sunday, dishing out a fabulous selection of pastas, sweet and savory crepes, tortes, salads galore, and a host of sandwiches made with the best cold meats and cheeses—or any other ingredient you can think of to put between two slices of freshly baked bread. Tuscan and Venetian wines are available to complement your repast.

Everything can be packaged to go, or consumed in the small side room dedicated to what Pino calls "speed lunches." You must ask for these meals, which are put together from the deli counter and consist of a first and second course with vegetable garnish and a half bottle of mineral water for less than a hamburger, shake, and fries would cost you in a State-side fast-food joint.

TELEPHONE
055 244 517

OPEN
Mon–Sat: 8 A.M.–3 P.M., 5–8 P.M.

CLOSED
Sun; NAC

RESERVATIONS
Not necessary

CREDIT CARDS
MC, V

À LA CARTE
Sandwiches from 2.07€, all other food sold by weight

MENÙ TURISTICO
Lunch: 6.20€, 2 courses plus vegetable and mineral water

COVER & SERVICE CHARGES
None

ENGLISH
Yes, and French

TRATTORIA BALDOVINO (61)
Via San Giuseppe, 22r

Follow the *bel mondo* to Baldovino, one of the best, and definitely most popular, trattorias in Florence. Opened a few years ago on a shoestring by a delightful Scottish duo, David and Catherine Gardner, it hit the ground running and became a favorite among Florentines and visitors alike. Success allowed them to expand up the street, and there you will find Enoteca Baldovino, their wine bar and outdoor terrace (see page 44). A little further down is their more upscale Ristorante Francescano (see page 49), and across the Arno is their latest venture, Beccofino (see page 74).

Trattoria Baldovina has several rooms, each painted in wild color combinations of orange and purple, or just plain green. Once you are inside the front door, wend your way through the first room and the exhibition kitchen to the more desirable back rooms, which have less waiter and patron traffic. The inventive menu puts

TELEPHONE
055 241 773

FAX
055 246 6684

EMAIL
baldovino.beccofino@inwind.it

OPEN
Nov–March, Tues–Sun; April–Oct, daily; lunch noon–2:30 P.M., dinner 7–11 P.M.

CLOSED
Mon in Nov–March; last week of Nov and first week of Dec

RESERVATIONS
Recommended for lunch, essential for dinner

CREDIT CARDS
AE, DC, MC, V

À LA CARTE
Pizza from 5.15€, 3-course meal 20.66–25.82€

MENÙ TURISTICO
None

COVER & SERVICE CHARGES
Cover 1.55€, 10% service
suggested

ENGLISH
Yes, and menu in English

an imaginative twist on the bounty of the Tuscan region. Appetizers to whet your appetite include grilled vegetables marinated in olive oil and served with a hunk of fresh mozzarella. A plate of smoked fish gets star billing, as do several types of rosemary-flavored focaccia seasoned with olive oil and topped with either chopped tomatoes, garlic, and basil; Parmesan and oregano; or smoked salmon, arugula, and Parmesan. Six meal-in-one salads start with the Baldovino, featuring chicken breast, grapes, walnuts, and celery, and finish with a raw vegetable combination dusted with shavings of pecorino cheese. Soups, pastas, and wood-fired pizzas, calzoni, main courses of ovenbaked rabbit seasoned with marjoram, chargrilled chicken shiskebab, or roast lamb with juniper berries all prove winners in the eyes of the trendsetters who fill the restaurant on a daily basis. The tempting homemade desserts—guaranteed to keep you on the treadmill an extra twenty minutes per day for the next week—include apple pie with pinenuts and raisins topped with warm custard, double chocolate torte served with vanilla ice cream, and cheesecake with strawberry salsa.

NOTE: There is a no-smoking dining room.

Gelaterias

GELATERIA DEI NERI (65)
Via dei Neri, 20–22r

TELEPHONE
055 210 034

OPEN
Mon–Tues, Thur–Sun: 1 P.M.–
midnight

CLOSED
Wed; NAC

CREDIT CARDS
None

PRICES
Cups or cones 1.55–5.16€;
cakes from 10.33€

ENGLISH
Limited

How do you know the gelato here is made from fresh ingredients? One look through the streetside window into the kitchen presided over by Mauricio, the hardworking owner, tells it all. This ice cream maestro works six days a week from 1 P.M. until midnight churning out some of the best gelato I have ever tasted. If you are lactose intolerant, not to worry; he has developed a sugarless, vegetarian soya ice cream that belies all notions that anything healthy can't possibly taste good. His chocolate mousse *semifreddo* is alone worth a trip to his shop, as is the lemon cream yogurt ice cream. Not content to rest on his laurels, Mauricio also makes ice cream cakes to order. Clearly he has orders, and lots of them, because I have never passed his shop without admiring his masterpieces displayed in the front window, waiting to be picked up.

VIVOLI (59)
Via Isola delle Stinche, 7r

Since 1930, the largest and creamiest selections of ice cream have been scooped out at Vivoli, located across the street from one of Florence's English-language movie houses. It is most active in the evening, when young Florentines strut their stuff, and on Sundays, when it becomes a family affair. These are the times you will be able to witness the Italian phenomenon of the *passeggiata,* the see-and-be-seen stroll all Italians love.

Baskets of fresh berries, cases of bananas, and crates of oranges go into the thousand-plus quarts of ice cream made and consumed here *each day.* For my gelato euro, the absolute best flavor, and one of their specialties, is the orange-chocolate cream, a cloudlike mixture of chocolate, cream orange liqueur, and pieces of fresh orange. Any of the *semifreddo* choices are fabulous, provided you can stand the fat-gram blowout from the whipped cream–based ice cream. Dieters need not feel left out: the fruit flavors are fat free, with the exception of the banana. The gelato is served only in cups, and you pay for the size of the cup, not the number of flavors you want in it. Avoid the strange rice cream flavor, a bland-tasting vanilla with hard pieces of almost raw rice sprinkled throughout. Also available are drinks at the full bar and homemade morning pastries and sandwiches.

TELEPHONE
055 292 334

FAX
055 230 2621

OPEN
Tues–Sun: 7 A.M.–1 A.M.

CLOSED
Mon; Jan, last 2 weeks in Aug

CREDIT CARDS
None

PRICES
Gelato from 2.07–8.78€

ENGLISH
Depends on server

Piazza Santa Maria Novella

The Gothic Renaissance church of Santa Maria Novella was the Florentine seat of the Dominicans. The piazza outside, one of the largest in the city, is frequented by backpackers coming and going from the train stations and assorted other foreigners just hanging out.

RESTAURANTS

Armando ($)	54
Da Giorgio	54
Il Contadino	55
Ristorante Buca Mario ($)	55
Sostanza ($)	56
Trattoria 13 Gobbi ($)	56

GELATERIAS

L'Angolo del Gelato	57

($) indicates a Big Splurge

Restaurants

ARMANDO ($, 23)
Borgo Ognissanti, 140r

TELEPHONE & FAX
055 216 219

EMAIL
trattoria.armando@iol.it

OPEN
Mon: dinner 7:30–10:30 P.M.;
Tues–Sat: lunch 12:30–3 P.M.,
dinner 7:30–10:30 P.M.

CLOSED
Mon lunch, Sun; major
holidays, Aug (dates vary)

RESERVATIONS
Advised, especially for dinner

CREDIT CARDS
AE, MC, V

À LA CARTE
28.41–36.15€

MENÙ TURISTICO
None

COVER & SERVICE CHARGES
Cover 2.07€, service included

ENGLISH
Yes

Armando, on my short list of best-value restaurants in Florence, offers cooking that is not only pleasing but nourishing. Handed down from father to son, and now mother to daughter, this typically Tuscan trattoria is as authentic as the cuisine, with friendly service provided by family and long-term staff in an ever-crowded and cheerful atmosphere. As the evening wears on, it can get loud, but that is part of the fun of eating here. Keep in mind that Italians dine late; in fact, at 9:30 P.M. they are still milling about waiting for a table to clear.

The Oscar for the best pasta dish goes to their *ravioli al burro e salvia,* homemade ravioli stuffed with ricotta cheese and sage and lightly covered in a buttery sauce. Throw cholesterol and fat counting to the wind just once and treat yourself to this. Another hands-down favorite in the pasta category goes to the *spaghetti alla carriettiera,* pasta topped with a spicy sauce made from garlic, fresh basil, tomato, and red pepper. This dish will wake up your taste buds in a hurry. Even if you have spent a lifetime turning up your nose at liver, please consider it here and try the *fegato alla salvia,* calves' liver broiled just to the tender pink stage. In the dessert department, keep in mind their homemade offerings, especially the decadently rich bitter chocolate cake.

DA GIORGIO (21)
Via Palazzuolo, 100r

TELEPHONE
055 284 302

OPEN
Mon–Sat: lunch noon–3 P.M.,
dinner 6–10 P.M.

CLOSED
Sun; Aug

RESERVATIONS
Not accepted

CREDIT CARDS
AE, DC, MC, V

À LA CARTE
None

If the line is too long down the street at Il Contadino (see below), walk up to Da Giorgio, another cheap eat with a set-price-only menu. If I had to choose between the two, I would give the edge to Da Giorgio. In spite of the shared tables with plastic-covered linen, there are cloth napkins, green plants, a few pictures scattered on the walls, and a larger selection of dishes.

Of course, there is no printed menu; you must depend on the waiter to tell you what is available that day. For starters, there might be macaroni with a spicy sauce; *pasta al pesto;* risotto with peas, tomatoes, and meat; or *fettuccine al freddo.* On Thursday, there is always gnocchi, and fresh fish on Friday. Your second course of meat, chicken, or fish is garnished with vegetables, salad, or potatoes. Wine or mineral water is included, but coffee is extra. The only dessert option is a piece of fresh fruit, which costs extra and is not worth it.

MENÙ TURISTICO
Lunch, 8.78€, dinner, 9.30€; both include 2 courses, vegetables, beverage, cover, and service; coffee and fresh fruit are extra

COVER & SERVICE CHARGES
Both included

ENGLISH
Yes

IL CONTADINO (22)
Via Palazzuolo, 69/71r

You will probably have to wait in line with the Italians at lunch and the tourists at dinner if you want one of the cheapest eats in Florence. Il Contadino is across the street from the area's other bargain eat, Da Giorgio (see above), and they both serve just about the same food and appeal to the same type of thrifty eater.

Except for a few old photos of Florence, interior decor is almost nonexistent in the two white-tiled rooms, which are filled instead with eager eaters, sleeves rolled up and ties loosened. The food is unimaginative but filling, and there is plenty of it. House wine or mineral water is included. For both courses, there are usually at least five selections, such as ravioli, minestrone, lasagna, *pasta e fagioli,* pork, beef, chicken, and frozen fish on Wednesday and Friday. The main courses are garnished with either a salad, vegetable, fries, or beans. Coffee and fresh fruit cost extra.

TELEPHONE
055 238 2673

OPEN
Mon–Sat: lunch noon–2:30 P.M., dinner 6–9:30 P.M.

CLOSED
Sun; 3 weeks in Aug (dates vary)

RESERVATIONS
Not accepted

CREDIT CARDS
None

À LA CARTE
None

MENÙ TURISTICO
Lunch, 8.78€, dinner, 9.30€; both include 2 courses, beverage, cover, and service; coffee and fruit are extra

COVER & SERVICE CHARGES
Both included

ENGLISH
Yes

RISTORANTE BUCA MARIO ($, 29)
Piazza Ottaviani, 16r

To best appreciate a meal at Buca Mario, avoid the front dining area, which serves as a passageway, and request a table in one of the other rooms in this large, meandering restaurant. Slightly on the formal side, with career waiters in black pants and burgundy bow ties, it is hardly in the fast track of hot Florentine dining spots. However, it has courteous and correct service, and above all, consistently good food. In the spring, I like to start with a salad of designer greens mixed with tender, raw, baby artichoke slices and shavings of Parmesan cheese, splashed with fresh lemon and extra virgin olive oil. Another favorite is fragrant melon served with prosciutto, or creamy *mozzarella de bufala* sandwiched between bright red tomatoes and accented with fresh sprigs of basil. For the *primi piatti,* look for *taglierini* with

TELEPHONE
055 214 179

FAX
055 264 7336

OPEN
Mon–Tues, Thur–Sun: lunch noon–3:30 P.M., dinner 7:30–10:30 P.M.

CLOSED
Wed, Aug (dates vary)

RESERVATIONS
Advised

CREDIT CARDS
AE, DC, MV, V

MENÙ TURISTICO
None

À LA CARTE
28.41–33.57€

smoked salmon, pappardelle with wild boar, or a classic *ribollita*. If you are ordering a *secondo piatto* of either meat or fish, perhaps go easy on the pastas, and head straight for their roast lamb flavored with rosemary and garlic or one of the veal scallopini renditions. Most fried foods are on everyone's no-no list, but here they are worth a special indulgence, especially if you order the chicken, zucchini, artichoke, and *melanzane* mix or the fried calamari and shrimp served with a soothing tartar sauce. Desserts? Frankly, they are uninspired. Order a grappa instead.

SOSTANZA ($, 27)
Via del Porcellana, 25r

TELEPHONE
055 212 691
OPEN
Mon–Fri: lunch noon–2:10 P.M., dinner seatings 7:30 P.M. and 9 P.M.
CLOSED
Sat–Sun; last 2 weeks of Dec, all Aug
RESERVATIONS
Essential
CREDIT CARDS
None
À LA CARTE
23.24–28.41€
MENÙ TURISTICO
None
COVER & SERVICE CHARGES
Cover 2.07€, 10% service added
ENGLISH
Enough

Sostanza is one of the city's oldest and best-loved trattorias, frequented by the great, the near-great, and just plain folks. Forty places are crammed into a long room that despite its pristine plainness becomes hectic as the meal progresses and the diners crowd in together. The waiters wear jackets, but formality ends there. The wine is served in tumblers, bread is handed to you, and plates are passed. Lots of hugging, kissing, and waving goes on among the regulars. Reservations are essential for the two nightly dinner seatings.

The handwritten menu is easy to read, and states at the top, *si serve solo pranzo completo.* That generally translates as, Don't come here if you are only going to order a pasta and a salad. Dishes to remember are the *tortino di carciofi* (artichoke omelette) and the *bistecca alla Fiorentino*—a six-hundred-gram T-bone steak geared for lumberjacks but ordered, and finished, by wafer-thin models—and the *bollito di manzo con salsa verde:* boiled beef with a green sauce of chopped parsley, capers, anchovies, dill pickles, bread, garllic, onion, vinegar, and olive oil. The only dessert made here, a meringue cake, is a must—you will think you don't have room but will end up enjoying every bite.

TRATTORIA 13 GOBBI ($, 30)
Via del Porcellana, 9r

TELEPHONE
055 284 015, 055 213 204
OPEN
Mon–Sat: lunch 12:30–2:30 P.M., dinner 7:30–10:30 P.M.
CLOSED
Sun; NAC

"Artistically rustic" are the words that come to mind when asked to describe the interior of this popular trattoria not far from either Piazza Goldoni and Piazza Santa Maria Novella. Bare wooden tables are covered with linen place mats and painted Tuscan pottery. The back room overlooks the summer patio and some apartments next door, where you can often see the occupants' laundry lazily flapping in the breeze. The menu is encased in a picture frame, and offers a good, but not overwhelming, selection of seasonally local dishes; the excellent house wine is served in big pitchers. On Friday the focus is on fresh fish. On other days, I like to start with the *antipasti della casa,* an assortment of *crostini* topped with various cured meats and pâtés, or share one of their huge salads, especially the pear and pecorino or raw zucchini tossed with gorgonzola and pine nuts. Next I order a vegetable risotto, a bubbling eggplant *parmigiana,* or a pasta tossed with garlic, peppers, bacon, and olive oil. The roast lamb is wonderfully tender, and so is the liver flavored with sage. I can't say this about any of the veal dishes, all of which suffered from overcooking and oversaucing. The *dolci* (desserts) are worth the guilt trip, especially the chocolate pear tart and the cheesecake. Some of the waiters have an attitude problem, and they actively discourage leisurely lingering on crowded weekends when the tables are turned at least twice . . . meaning they will (hopefully) get more tips.

RESERVATIONS
Advised for lunch, essential for dinner
CREDIT CARDS
AE, MC, V
À LA CARTE
28.41–30.99€
MENÙ TURISTICO
None
COVER AND SERVICE CHARGE
Cover 1.03€, 10% service charge
ENGLISH
Yes

Gelaterias

L'ANGOLO DEL GELATO (24)
Via della Scala, 2r

Italians are addicted to gelato, and nowhere is this more evident than in Florence, where *gelaterias* seem to be a dime a dozen. For the best ice cream near Santa Maria Novella, drop by L'Angolo del Gelato, a corner store owned by a friendly man named Fabrizio and his mother, Grazia. Everything they serve is made here from fresh ingredients and seasonal fruits. It is all sold by the size of the cup, and you can have as many flavors as you want in whatever cup size you select. The most popular flavors are chocolate and, in summer, lemon. In winter, look for creamy *semifreddo* flavors and the *fiesta,* an almost illegally rich chocolate ice cream laced with Grand Marnier. In summer, indulge to your waistline's content with their fat-free fruit *sorbettos* or fruit-based yogurt ice cream. The servings are generous. Those in the know always ask for their gelato with some *panna montata* on top . . . or freshly whipped cream.

TELEPHONE
055 210 526
OPEN
Summer: daily 10 A.M.–1 A.M.; winter: Tues–Sun 11 A.M.–midnight
CLOSED
Mon in winter; NAC
CREDIT CARDS
None
PRICES
Gelato from 1.03–5.16€
ENGLISH
Yes

Piazza Sant' Ambrogio

This is an interesting working-class neighborhood and has the most local of Florence markets. The best time to experience all the fauna and flora is on a Saturday morning.

RESTAURANTS

Il Pizzaiuolo	58
Tavola Calda da Rocco	58

INDOOR/OUTDOOR MARKETS

Mercato Sant' Ambrogio	89

Restaurants

IL PIZZAIUOLO (56)
Via dei Macci, 113r

TELEPHONE
055 241 171
OPEN
Mon–Sat: lunch 12:30–3:30 P.M., dinner 7:30 P.M.–midnight
CLOSED
Sun; 4 days at Easter and Christmas, Aug
RESERVATIONS
Required for dinner
CREDIT CARDS
None
À LA CARTE
Pizza 4.65–9.30€, pasta from 6.20–11.3€
MENÙ TURISTICO
None
COVER & SERVICE CHARGES
None
ENGLISH
Sometimes

Pizza pundits debate who has the best pizza in town, but all of them would agree on one thing: if you like Neapolitan pizza, this place has the best in Florence. It is a casual spot, across the square from the busy market at Piazza Sant' Ambrogio. You can arrive for lunch without a reservation, but forget it if you arrive without one at dinner. In the evening, reservations are taken for 8, 9, 10, or 11 P.M., and without your name on the book for one of these times, you will not get in. The twenty-five or so pizzas range from a simple *Napoli*—with tomatoes, mozzarella, anchovies, capers, and oregano—to the *pizza bomba ripena,* which has the usual tomato and mozzarella, plus *prosciutto cotto* (cooked prosciutto), ricotta, mushrooms, and salami. If you don't see the combination you want, they will create it for you. Also on board are a half dozen pastas, but bypass these for another meal. If you are eating here, you eat pizza and perhaps share a salad.

TAVOLA CALDA DA ROCCO (57)
Mercato di Sant' Ambrogio

TELEPHONE
Not available
OPEN
Mon–Sat: lunch noon–2 P.M.

You know everything is fresh . . . the Rocco family shops at the market daily for the food they prepare in their open kitchen in the center hall of this wonderful Florentine dining landmark. The hot dishes are ready by noon, and are served to seriously hungry market workers and regulars who lap it up while perched on stools closely placed at formica tables. The menu, which changes daily and is written on a board, always includes robust soups and stews, hearty pastas, and in winter, baked pears in red wine for dessert. Even if you ordered every course, you would have trouble spending $12, and that would include a generous plastic cup filled with the rough-and-ready house *vino*. After your meal, saunter across the aisle to the Bar-Jolly Caffè–La Caffetteria del Vecchio Mercato and have one of the cheapest espressos in town.

CLOSED
Sun; Aug

RESERVATIONS
Not accepted

CREDIT CARDS
None

À LA CARTE
First courses 2.58€, main courses 3.62€, vegetables 2.07€, dessert 1.03–2.07€

MENÙ TURISTICA
None

COVER & SERVICE CHARGES
Cover 0.52€, service charge included

ENGLISH
Enough

Ponte Vecchio

The famous Ponte Vecchio dates from 1345. It is lined with small shops displaying an awe-inspiring collection of gold and magnificent jewels, and it is thronged with tourists on their way to and from the Pitti Palace, window shopping, and posing for countless photos.

Restaurants

BUCA DELL' ORAFO (64)
Volta dei Girolami, 28r
Hidden under an archway near the Ponte Vecchio is the tiny Buca dell' Orafo, a favorite for years with Florentines and visitors for its good value and authentic cuisine. The two owners are on tap every day to run the kitchen and serve their guests. Everyone seems to know one another, particularly at lunch, when lots of laughing and talking goes on between the tables. If you go for lunch or after 9 P.M., you will likely share your dining experience with Italians. If you go for an early dinner,

TELEPHONE
055 213 619

OPEN
Tues–Sat: lunch 12:30–2:30 P.M., dinner 7:30–10:30 P.M.

CLOSED
Mon, Sun; Aug

RESERVATIONS
Essential as far in advance as possible

CREDIT CARDS
None

À LA CARTE
23.24–30.99€

MENÙ TURISTICO
None

COVER & SERVICE CHARGES
Cover 2.07€, service included

ENGLISH
Yes

you will hear mostly English spoken and probably run into your cousin's neighbor from Detroit.

The regulars know to come on the specific days their favorite dishes are served. Friday it is always fresh codfish. Thursday, Friday, and Saturday *ribollita* headlines the openers. And every day you can count on finding a special, such as *stracotto e fagioli,* braised beef with beans in a sauce with garlic, onions, and sage. A spring favorite is the *tortino di carciofi,* an artichoke omelette that will change your mind about what can be done with an artichoke. The dessert to melt your heart and your willpower is the house special *dolce,* a sponge cake with cream layers and meringue and almonds on top. It will be one of the best desserts you have on your entire trip.

San Lorenzo Central Market

The Piazza Mercato Centrale, which celebrates the glories of Tuscan food, is a nineteenth-century cast-iron landmark housing one of the largest and most interesting markets in Europe. It is a must-see in Florence for all food lovers. Crowding the surrounding streets are countless stalls with sellers hawking more than enough goods to fill up an extra suitcase. For even the least committed Great Chic shopper, it is definitely worth a look, though the stalls sell basically the same things: polyester scarf copies of the real Guccis or Fendis, leather bags, belts, jackets, boxes, T-shirts, Florentine paper goods, souvenirs, and accessories. Despite what the setting suggests, bargains are rare because the competition is so intense that the prices are almost fixed, so look around and buy from the vendor who treats you the best.

RESTAURANTS

Restaurants

ANTICHI CANCELLI (17)
Via Faenza, 73r

At Antichi Cancelli, which means "the old gate," it does not take newcomers long to blend in and quickly catch the mood of the place. With its hanging peppers and garlic braids, potted plants, brick ceiling, and tiny paper-covered marble-topped tables, it looks like the quintessential movie set for an Italian film. The difference, of course, is that the food and jovial ambience are real, and so is its popularity. Do not even *think* of arriving without reservations, and even then you can count on having to wedge yourself into the crowd and wait for a table.

It is important that you come prepared to eat. Management, especially Romeo and Enzo, takes a dim view of dieters or anyone else not ordering at least a pasta, main course, and dessert. The daily menu is based on what is best at the market during each season and is handwritten on a scrap of paper stapled to the regular menu. The dishes of Tuscany are well prepared, and everything from the antipasti and pasta to the sauces and desserts is made here. The filling portions promise that no one will be thinking about the next meal for a long time.

NOTE: Especially appealing to many Great Eaters are the hours. Dinner is available at the unheard-of hour of 6 P.M., and on Saturday and Sunday, the restaurant serves continuously from noon until 10:45 P.M.

TELEPHONE
055 218 927

OPEN
Tues–Fri, lunch noon–2:45 P.M., dinner 6–10:45 P.M.; Sat–Sun noon–10:45 P.M., continuous service

CLOSED
Mon; NAC

RESERVATIONS
Absolutely essential

CREDIT CARDS
AE, DC, MC, V

À LA CARTE
18.08–20.66€

MENÙ TURISTICO
12.91€, 3 courses; beverages, cover, and service included

COVER & SERVICE CHARGES
Cover 1.29€, 10% service added

ENGLISH
Yes, and *menù turistico* in English

CAFAGGI (11)
Via Guelfa, 35r

One of the best ways to discover good places to eat is to ask the natives where they go. The top contender on Via Guelfa, between Piazza della Indipendenza and Piazza San Marco off Via Cavour, is Cafaggi. This plain-Jane restaurant has been in the Cafaggi family for decades and consists of two rather large cream-colored rooms. The second room off the kitchen is slightly more appealing owing to a few plants scattered about. Smart Great

TELEPHONE
055 294 989

OPEN
Mon–Sat: lunch noon–2:30 P.M., dinner 7–10:30 P.M.

CLOSED
Sun; 1 week in Jan and 4 weeks between July and Aug (dates vary)

RESERVATIONS
Advised, especially weekends
and holidays

CREDIT CARDS
AE, MC, V

À LA CARTE
25.82–30.99€

MENÙ TURISTICO
15.49€, 2 courses; cover and
service included, beverage extra

COVER & SERVICE CHARGES
Cover 2.58€, service included

ENGLISH
Yes, and menu in English

Eaters will join the well-dressed businesspeople at lunch and the attractive neighborhood crowd in the evening, all of whom come prepared to dine well, not to lounge in magnificent surroundings. After you have had your first glass of wine and have tasted the fine food, you will quickly forget about the dull atmosphere. Some Great Eaters will want to stay with the set-priced menu, which includes a first and second course. However, with a bit of careful ordering, à la carte will not be prohibitively expensive.

The real boss in the kitchen is Sra. Cafaggi, who oversees it all, including her son Leonardo, who is the chef and prides himself on turning out carefully prepared dishes using the freshest seasonal ingredients. In fact, the front window has a vivid display of the types of fresh fish, meat, and produce you can expect to see on your plate. They are wizards with fresh fish and veal, especially the veal served in a buttery asparagus sauce, and they always prepare a special vegetarian main dish. The desserts are all made here; try the brownie with a scoop of the famous Vivoli ice cream. The house wine is adequate, so there is no need to splurge on anything else. The service is friendly yet professional and to the point.

CASA DEL VINO (16)
Via dell' Ariento, 16r

TELEPHONE
055 215 609

INTERNET
casadellvino.it

OPEN
Mon–Fri: 9 A.M.–2 P.M., 4:30–
8 P.M.; Sat: 9 A.M.–2 P.M.

CLOSED
Sat afternoon, Sun; Aug

RESERVATIONS
Not accepted

CREDIT CARDS
AE, DC, MC, V

À LA CARTE
4.13–5.16€, sandwich and
glass of wine

MENÙ TURISTICO
None

COVER & SERVICE CHARGES
None

ENGLISH
Enough

Wine has been flowing at the Casa del Vino for more than 150 years. Since 1960, this Florentine institution has been run by the third generation of the founding family. Located behind the Mercato Centrale de San Lorenzo, the wood-paneled and mirrored wine bar pours Italian wines and sells sandwiches made to order to a devoted following.

Table seating is nonexistent: you will eat your sandwich and drink your wine standing at the bar, or if you get lucky, perched on one of the three bar stools.

i' TOSCANO (10)
Via Guelfa, 70r

The chef at i' Toscano displays his varied skills with dishes of fresh, flavorful food attractively presented in two rather formal rooms—formal by Florence standards, that is. A collection of black-and-white pictures of Florence adds the only point of interest in the brightly lit, stark white surroundings. The properly set tables are spaced wide enough to prevent your being a part of your neighbor's conversation, and the friendly waiters make an effort to explain any dish you are not sure about.

The food is just creative and imaginative enough to lift it out of the ordinary. The three-course *menù turistico,* an excellent value, changes every two weeks and offers three or four choices for the first two courses and fresh fruit or cheese for dessert. For not too much more, you can order à la carte and have a more interesting meal. Depending on the season, you might start with a plate of cold slices of wild boar, deer, and other game meats, or something typically Florentine, toasted bread topped with black cabbage, garlic, and olive oil. The spinach ravioli with herbs and fresh tomato is a satisfying first course, as is the gnocchi with truffle cream sauce. For the main dish, if you are here on a Friday, by all means order the *baccalà*—stockfish served with a fresh tomato sauce. On other days, it is a toss-up between the veal scaloppine with herbs and the savory beef stew. For your vegetable, the *gobbi alla fiorentina* (*gobbi* is a thistlelike plant with leaves and stalks that are eaten like celery), served here lightly braised in a butter sauce, is an interesting choice you seldom see. Saving room for dessert takes some willpower, but at least share a slice of the lemon cake or order an assortment of local cheeses served with apple jam.

TELEPHONE
055 215 475

FAX
055 296 843

OPEN
Mon, Wed–Sun: lunch noon–2:30 P.M., dinner 7:30–10:30 P.M.

CLOSED
Tues; 1st week of Aug

RESERVATIONS
Advised for dinner

CREDIT CARDS
AE, DC, MC, V

À LA CARTE
23.24–28.41€

MENÙ TURISTICO
15.49€, 3 courses; mineral water, cover and service included

COVER & SERVICE CHARGES
Cover1.55€, service included

ENGLISH
Yes, and menu in English

NERBONE (15)
Stand #292, Piazza del Mercato Centrale (next to the San Lorenzo Church)

The Mercato di San Lorenzo, Florence's huge indoor market, is the main source of food for a region that takes food very seriously, and it is without peer for its wide variety and enormous selection. Be sure you allow yourself enough time to appreciate the displays of food, which provide a quick study course in the art and ingredients of Italian cooking. While here you will see several Italian-style fast-food stalls, but the most famous, and unquestionably the best, is Nerbone, Stand #292, where

TELEPHONE
055 219 949

OPEN
Mon–Sat: 7 A.M.–2 P.M., continuous service

CLOSED
Sun; Aug (dates vary)

RESERVATIONS
Not accepted

CREDIT CARDS
None

À LA CARTE
From 2.32€

MENÙ TURISTICO
None

COVER & SERVICE CHARGES
None

ENGLISH
None

hot meat sandwiches have been the major drawing card since 1872.

Nerbone, which is under the same ownership as Alla Vecchia Bettola (see page 71), appeals to those with hearty appetites who don't mind a noisy, no-frills setting. The menu lists bowls of beans, mashed potatoes, tripe, and pastas. Never mind any of these. The standard order here is a sandwich of boiled beef (*bollito*), sliced onto a crusty roll and then dipped into the meat juices (*bagnato*). After you are handed your food, take it to the tables across the aisle, or stand at the bar with a beer or a glass of *vino rosso* and enjoy!

PALLE D'ORO (18)
Via Sant' Antonino 43/45r

TELEPHONE
055 288 383

FAX
055 35 48 11

OPEN
Mon–Sat: lunch noon–2:30 P.M., dinner 6:30–9:45 P.M.

CLOSED
Sun; Aug

RESERVATIONS
Not necessary

CREDIT CARDS
AE, DC, MC, V

À LA CARTE
Lunch, 15.49€, sandwiches from 2.07€; dinner, 20.66€

MENÙ TURISTICO
Lunch, 10.33€, dinner, 12.91€; both include 3 courses, mineral water, cover and service; other beverages extra

COVER & SERVICE CHARGES
Cover 1.03€, service included

ENGLISH
Yes, and menu in English

Sooner or later, all cost-conscious eaters in Florence learn about Palle d'Oro, which sits on a crowded shopping street leading to the big Mercato Centrale. For more than a hundred years this fourth-generation family-run jewel has provided dependable and good fast food *alla italiano*. It is so crowded at noon you probably won't be able to see the walls, which means you will miss the interesting black-and-white family photos showing Lorenzo, the great-grandfather (whose nickname was Palle d'Oro), bringing the country wine to Florence piled high on a horse-drawn two-wheeled cart.

At lunchtime, you will be joining Florentines ordering freshly crafted sandwiches up front or quick and easy hot dishes in the back. In the evening, take a seat and order a brimming bowl of soup or pasta, a fragrantly roasted chicken with a green salad, or a piece of grilled fish seasoned with fresh lemon and a splash of olive oil and a carafe of the house red.

RISTORANTE DE' MEDICI (20)
Via del Giglio, 49–51r

TELEPHONE
055 218 778

FAX
055 29 52 92

OPEN
Daily: noon–1 A.M., continuous service

CLOSED
Christmas

If you order a pasta, a wood-fired pizza, or one of the succulent grilled meats—and avoid the tiny, overpriced salads—you will do just fine at this large, rather formal restaurant only fifty meters from the Medici Chapel and the Basilica of San Lorenzo. I think it is an all-purpose place to remember for several reasons.

First, it is open from noon until 1 A.M., and you can go in anytime for a full meal or a light snack, great advantages if you have children. Second, the wide selection of pastas and pizzas are offered at prices that won't send you and your budget into orbit. The grilled meats are all of the finest quality, and the house specialty is *bistecca alla fiorentina,* sold by the gram. Watch out . . . this can make your bill soar. Chianti wines are featured, as are several beers that pair well with a pizza.

RESERVATIONS
Not necessary

CREDIT CARDS
MC, V

À LA CARTE
20.66€; pizza from 4.13€

MENÙ TURISTICO
None

COVER & SERVICE CHARGES
Cover 1.55€, 10% service added

ENGLISH
Yes

TRATTORIA GOZZI (19)
Piazza San Lorenzo, 8r

There are many places to eat around the Mercato Centrale de San Lorenzo, some very good and others appallingly bad. One of the most authentic and tourist free is this trattoria, a true worker's hangout where you can enjoy hearty Tuscan food (for lunch only) with burly market men and women. The only menu is posted outside. When you are seated, the waiter will tell you what's cooking. You are expected to order a full meal—just a salad and a glass of wine is *out.* You can count on chunky minestrone and bean soups, roasted meats, sturdy boiled brisket, and always fresh fish on Friday. Follow the lead of fellow diners and order a bottle of the house Chianti while enjoying the friendly service and a lunch that will leave some money in your pocket.

TELEPHONE
055 281 941

OPEN
Mon–Sat: lunch noon–3:30 P.M.

CLOSED
Sun; major holidays, Aug

RESERVATIONS
Not necessary

CREDIT CARDS
DC, MC, V

À LA CARTE
15.49–18.08€

MENÙ TURISTICO
None

COVER & SERVICE CHARGES
Cover 1.03€, no service charge

ENGLISH
Yes

TRATTORIA MARIO (12)
Via Rosina, 2r

Mario's boasts many avid, loud, and local regulars, all of whom seem to be on a first-name basis. Consequently, there is a great deal of good cheer and camaraderie, with everyone swapping tall tales and telling jokes. They all know to arrive early and order a glass or two of the house red while waiting for the lunch service to begin. Late-comers will have to wait, or worse yet, they won't get their favorite dish, since the kitchen often runs out early.

The daily menu is posted on a board by the open kitchen. Friday is *fish only* day, and on Thursday gnocchi is the dish to order. On any day smart choices include the vegetable soup, pasta with meat or tomato sauce, or a slab of roast veal or beef garnished with their own fresh fries cooked in olive oil. You don't need to save room for

TELEPHONE
055 218 550

OPEN
Mon–Sat: bar 7 A.M.–5 P.M., lunch noon–3:15 P.M.

CLOSED
Sun; Aug (dates vary)

RESERVATIONS
Not accepted

CREDIT CARDS
None

À LA CARTE
10.33–12.91€

MENÙ TURISTICO
None

dessert because all they serve is fresh fruit or a glass of sweet wine with wonderful, hard, almond-flavored *biscotti.* No coffee is served either, but there are dozens of bars around the market that make fun places to merge in and stand for an after-lunch espresso in order to recharge your batteries for more afternoon market browsing.

TRATTORIA ZÀZÀ (13)
Piazza del Mercato Centrale, 26r, at the corner of Via Rosina

Every visitor to Florence eventually hears of Trattoria Zàzà, a long-standing market trattoria that offers a winning mix of atmosphere and hearty Tuscan food. Wooden picnic tables with long benches and hard stools line both the upstairs and downstairs dining rooms. The walls are papered with framed newspaper clippings of famous trotting horses and film posters of vintage movie legends, including Ingrid Bergman and Humphrey Bogart in the famous *Casablanca* farewell scene. Overhead are three rows of shelves stacked high with the Chianti you will be drinking with your meal.

The wide-ranging menu offers a multitude of choices for every course. To start, order the trio of their best soups, which includes a bowl of *ribollita, pomodoro fresca* (fresh tomato), and *passato di fagioli con faro* (bean soup). The roast chicken or veal scaloppine are good entrées. Lighter eaters will appreciate their *insalate giganti*—six salads that are meals in themselves. These seem to appeal to just about everyone. The de rigueur dessert is Zàzà's own *torta di mele alla Zàzà,* an upside-down apple tart similar to the French *tarte Tatin.* Please note that service can be irritatingly slow.

TELEPHONE
055 215 411

FAX
055 210 756

OPEN
Mon–Sat: Winter lunch noon–3 P.M., dinner 7–11 P.M.; summer noon–11 P.M., continuous service

CLOSED
Sun; major holidays

RESERVATIONS
Advised

CREDIT CARDS
AE, DC, MC, V

À LA CARTE
18.08–23.24€

MENÙ TURISTICO
12.91€, 2 courses; cover and service included, beverage extra

COVER & SERVICE CHARGES
Cover 1.03€, service included, but tips appreciated

ENGLISH
Yes, and menu in English

COVER & SERVICE CHARGES
Cover 0.52€, service included

ENGLISH
Yes

Train Station

All long-distance trains arrive at the Santa Maria Novella railway terminal that joins Piazza di Santa Maria Novella and the great church of the same name. The station is a comfortable ten- or fifteen-minute walk from the center. Almost all buses in and out of Florence stop nearby, as do taxis and pickpockets, who work the area on a twenty-four-hour basis. Attached to the station are a series of shops and, in one corner, a handy mini-supermarket with so much stock that two people cannot get down the aisles at the same time.

Restaurants

TRATTORIA ENZO E PIERO (9)
Via Faenza, 105r

Enzo and Piero's trattoria is very simple, with rough stuccoed walls and lots of well-fed habitués sitting at the yellow linen–clad tables. On each table is a bottle of Chianti wine vinegar and another of good olive oil so you can dress your own salad or, as the Italians do, sprinkle olive oil on just about everything but dessert.

Both Enzo and Piero are on hand each day to ensure that all runs well. They greet their guests at the table, suggest what is best to order, and check back periodically to see that everyone has everything needed for a fine meal. They also keep an eagle eye on the kitchen, where their high standards ensure absolutely fresh ingredients prepared with care. Whenever you come, be sure to ask for the daily specials, which sometimes are not given with the regular menu. If you are here on a Friday, try the *baccalà alla livornese,* salt cod cooked in a nippy red sauce with liberal doses of garlic; on Wednesday, order the osso buco cooked in a tomato sauce. Other flavorful options are the *tortellini alla cardinale* (with cream, tomatoes, and ham), one of the better *pasta al pomodoro* in Florence, and the stuffed and baked breast of turkey and ham. For dessert you want the *panna cotta,* a cooked custard surrounded by fresh strawberries and chocolate. The *menù turistico* is a Great Eat buy if ever there was one, even though it does not include a beverage. For a little more, you can add a quarter or half carafe and still walk away for under 22€ per person.

TELEPHONE & FAX
055 214 901

OPEN
Mon–Sat: lunch noon–3 P.M., dinner 7–10 P.M.

CLOSED
Sun; 10 days at Christmas, 3 weeks in Aug (dates vary)

RESERVATIONS
Advised for dinner

CREDIT CARDS
AE, DC, MC, V

À LA CARTE
20.66€

MENÙ TURISTICO
12.39€, 3 courses; cover and service included, beverage extra

COVER & SERVICE CHARGES
Cover 1.55€, service included

ENGLISH
Yes

TRATTORIA GUELFA (7)
Via Guelfa, 103r

The Trattoria Guelfa is a hands-down favorite, with regulars filling it every day for lunch and dinner. Reservations are crucial, but even with them, be prepared to wait up to half an hour, especially on weekends. Service can be slow, but when you consider that only two waiters,

TELEPHONE & FAX
055 213 306

OPEN
Mon–Tues, Thur–Sun: lunch noon–2:30 P.M., dinner 7–10:30 P.M.

CLOSED
Wed; NAC

RESERVATIONS
Essential

CREDIT CARDS
AE, MC, V

À LA CARTE
18.08–23.24€

MENÙ TURISTICO
9.30€, 3 courses; beverage,
cover, and service included

COVER & SERVICE CHARGES
Cover 1.55€, service included

ENGLISH
Yes

including hardworking Claudio, the owner, are on duty to serve the congenial crowd, it is amazing anyone gets anything, let alone having it always arrive piping hot.

The key to success here is the wonderful back-to-basics Italian homecooking. If you stay with the chef's specialties, or the daily offerings scribbled on a two-by-two inch piece of white paper, you cannot go wrong. Depending on the day and time of year, expect to find fat green and white tortellini filled with ham and mush-rooms, pappardelle with wild boar sauce or *cappellacci,* three big pasta tubes stuffed with cheese and spinach and served in a white mushroom cream sauce. Other standouts include roast pork, grilled veal chops served with rosemary-roasted potatoes, and a delightful *pinzimonio di verdure crude* (a selection of seasonal raw vegetables served with oil for dipping). All the desserts remind me of home, especially the *panna cotta con cioccolato,* a cold pudding with hot chocolate poured over it, and the rich chestnut pudding, *budino di castagne.*

TRATTORIA I DUE G (8)
Via Cennini, 12/14r

TELEPHONE
055 218 623

OPEN
Mon–Sat: lunch 12:30–
2:30 P.M., dinner 7:30–
10:30 P.M.

CLOSED
Sun; holidays, Aug

RESERVATIONS
Advised

CREDIT CARDS
AE, DC, MC, V

À LA CARTE
20.66–25.82€

MENÙ TURISTICO
None

COVER & SERVICE CHARGES
Cover 1.29€, 10% service
added

ENGLISH
Yes

A big basket of fresh focaccia bread and the house wine will keep you occupied while you wait for your first course at this typical Florentine trattoria. When the jolly, red-faced waiter brought my carafe of wine, I said, "Oh, that's too much wine!" "Nonsense," he replied. "Water makes your stomach rusty. Wine keeps it clean!" I am sure he followed his own drinking advice, and ate rich food to ensure he never felt a hunger pang. Besides plenty of good wine, you can expect wonderful risottos, plump ricotta-filled ravioli, stuffed rabbit, cooked-to-order roast chicken (a thirty-minute wait), beautiful seasonal vegetables, and flavorful summer strawberries drizzled with raspberry vinegar and a dusting of sugar. To say that visitors have not found this place would be dead wrong. All the hotels along Via Fiume and Via Faenza recommend I Due G, but this has not inflated the trattoria's sense of self; it still takes pride in serving good food and plenty of wine at sensible prices.

Restaurants *Di La d'Arno,* or *Oltrarno*

Di La d'Arno, or *Oltrarno,* means "the other side of the Arno." Crossing the Ponte Vecchio from the central part of the city, visitors usually walk and shop along Via Guicciardini until they reach the enormous Pitti Palace, the Medici family showcase that is now an art gallery with works by Titian, Tintoretto, Rubens, and Raphael. Shops and restaurants around the palace are naturally geared toward the tourist trade, but if you get a few blocks away from this, you will find fascinating enclaves of artisans, art galleries, and beautiful antique shops. Restaurants on the Piazza Santo Spirito are some of the most popular in the city, and on the second Sunday of every month, crowds browse through a flea market that spills from the piazza in front of the church onto the neighboring side streets. Also on the *Oltrarno* are the hilly Boboli Gardens, Forte Belvedere, San Miniato al Monte (a thousand-year-old church with an unparalleled view of the city), and the Piazzale Michaelangelo, built in 1869 by Guiseppe Poggi, also with a magnificent view over Florence.

Boboli Gardens

Behind the Pitti Palace are eleven rolling acres of gardens known as the Giardinia di Boboli, which was the playground of the Medicis when they lived here. Laid out by the great landscape architect Triboli, the gardens are popular today for quiet walks and include a long expanse of cypress trees, lovely plantings, statuary, fountains, and L'Isolotto, a miniature island in the middle of a lake.

TRATTORIA BOBOLI (88)
Via Romana, 45r

Do you remember your mother, or a sympathetic friend, ever telling you, "Keep your eyes and ears open, and never give up. You never know what good thing is awaiting you around the next corner"? Well, I can tell you, it's true. Such was the case for me one rainy day in Florence near the Boboli Gardens. I had just reinspected a hotel nearby that unfortunately had to be dropped

TELEPHONE & FAX
055 233 6401

EMAIL
trattoriaboboli@mail.com

INTERNET
www.paginegialle.it/bobolitratt

OPEN
Mon–Tues, Thur–Sun: lunch
noon–3 P.M., dinner 7:30–
10 P.M.

CLOSED
Wed; Aug

RESERVATIONS
Preferred

CREDIT CARDS
AE, DC, MC, V

À LA CARTE
23.24–28.41€

MENÙ TURISTICO
13.94€, 2 courses, beverage
included; *menù desgustazione,*
23.24€, 3 courses, bottle of
Chianti and coffee included;
student menu (Oct–Mar),
9.30€, one main course plus
potatoes, beverage extra; for all,
cover and service included

COVER & SERVICE CHARGES
Cover 1.55€, no service charge

ENGLISH
Yes

from *Great Sleeps Italy* because management had become complacent, favoring deferred maintenance to conscientious upkeep. I was tired and hungry when I noticed this friendly-looking trattoria across the street. Any port in a storm, I thought, as I hung up my dripping raincoat and settled into a cozy corner table. The room itself was typical: crowded with wine bottles, with posters, paintings, and plates on the walls, a few plants here and there, and a ceiling fan.

Since I did not qualify for the bargain student menu, the *menù turistico* looked worthy of consideration. It offered plenty of food and was a good value, with either a soup or choice of three pastas to start, followed by fried chicken, veal scaloppine with tomatoes and peas, pork with potatoes, or liver, and accompanied by wine or water. I decided to splurge a little and ordered the *menù degustazione,* which included a bottle of excellent Chianti wine. I started with *crepes à la Florentine,* a duet of crepes filled with spinach and ricotta and covered with a cream sauce and cheese gratinée. Next I had a grilled steak topped with arugula and a side of potatoes. My dessert was a plate of *biscotti* for dipping into a glass of *vin santo,* followed by coffee. I was graciously served by Gilberto and his wife, who have been taking care of their loyal patrons for almost three decades. While I hadn't stumbled upon an undiscovered gem of destination dining, Trattoria Boboli is much more than a mere port in a storm. If you are near the Boboli Gardens, it is the perfect place for a nice, simple meal.

Piazza del Carmine

Santa Maria del Carmine is a Baroque building with restored frescoes by Masaccio and Masolino; viewing times are limited to a mere quarter of an hour.

RESTAURANTS

($) indicates a Big Splurge

Restaurants

ALLA VECCHIA BETTOLA (72)
Viale Ludovico Ariosto, 32–34r

Tuscany's simplest foods tend to be its most successful, and nowhere is this more evident than at Alla Vecchia Bettola, a picturesque trattoria specializing in the region's native cuisine.

The handwritten but legible menu changes almost daily. A bottle of house wine is on the table for you to pour into green glasses, and you pay only for as much as you drink. Seating is at marble-topped row tables on benches along the wall or on four-legged, backless stools. Despite the rather rustic decor, the atmosphere is upscale and so are the diners, arriving when the doors open and standing in line as the night goes on. As you can see, management does not stress creature comforts. It definitely does, however, stress good food offered at fair prices.

If it is available, start with the *pecorino con baccellie,* a basket of raw, unshelled fava beans (similar to limas) and two slabs of smoky pecorino cheese. You shell the beans and pop them into your mouth with a piece of the cheese and a chunk of country bread. It is different and good, not heavy as one might expect. Move on to *topini al pomodoro,* a light gnocchi bathed in tomato sauce, or *risotto alle zucchine,* followed by a second course of roast veal or rabbit served with crisply fried artichokes. The salads are disappointing, especially the tired spinach version, drenched in too much oil. The desserts, on the other hand, won't let you down. Try the house apple cake or the plate of assorted *biscotti,* consisting of macaroons and almond cookies for you to dip into a glass of sweet *vin santo.*

NOTE: Alla Vecchia Bettola is under the same ownership as Nerbone (see page 63).

TELEPHONE
055 224 158

FAX
055 226 7360

OPEN
Tues–Sat: lunch noon–2:30 P.M., dinner 7:30–10:30 P.M.

CLOSED
Sun–Mon; Aug, Dec 23–Jan 2

RESERVATIONS
Essential

CREDIT CARDS
None

À LA CARTE
2.82–30.99€

MENÙ TURISTICO
None

COVER AND SERVICE CHARGES
Cover 1.55€, service included

ENGLISH
Yes

CAVOLO NERO ($, 74)
Via dell'Ardiglione, 22r

Book in advance, dress up, and treat yourself to a memorable meal at Cavolo Nero. Everything about this upscale pick is right, from the sleek white slipcovered chairs and soft orange sorbet–colored walls (hung with photos of every type of cabbage imaginable) to the jasmine-scented romantic candlelit patio in back. The restaurant owes its success to an imaginative use of fresh

TELEPHONE
055 294 744

OPEN
Mon–Sat: lunch 12:30–2 P.M., dinner 8–11 P.M.

CLOSED
Sun; 2 weeks in Aug (dates vary)

RESERVATIONS
Essential for dinner

CREDIT CARDS
AE, MC, V
À LA CARTE
33.57–38.73€
MENÙ TURISTICO
None
COVER & SERVICE CHARGES
None
ENGLISH
Yes, and menu in English

ingredients highlighting a monthly menu of updated Tuscan classics. In early spring you might start with a creamy goat cheese served with an interesting olive oil and honey sauce, or toasted bread spread with burrata cheese and smoked salmon. Next, try the airy pillows of eggplant ravioli with zucchini and sweet tomatoes or the spaghetti with dried tuna roe. Wonderful main courses include pigeon filled with rich foie grass, roasted sea bass with a fragrant, light ginger sauce, and baked rabbit with wild fennel and mushrooms. Desserts are to die for, especially the pear tart Tatin and the heavenly chocolate cake. The fine food—coupled with fair wine prices and excellent service in a very pleasing atmosphere—adds up to a Great Eat in Florence.

TRATTORIA PANDEMONIO ($, 73)
Via del Leone, 50r

TELEPHONE
055 224 002
OPEN
Mon–Sat: dinner 7:30–10:30 P.M.
CLOSED
Sun; NAC
RESERVATIONS
Abslolutely essential
CREDIT CARDS
AE, MC, V
À LA CARTE
33.57–41.32€
MENÙ TURISTICO
None
COVER & SERVICE CHARGES
Cover 3.10€, 10% service added
ENGLISH
Yes

Whatever your evening dining mood, be it festive, romantic, or just plain starved, Pandemonio always fills the bill, from the first sip of champagne to the complimentary grappa or frosty *limoncello* finale. In-between aperitif and digestif, you will sample creative Tuscan cuisine good enough to pack the attractive, flower-filled dining rooms night after night. The fresh anchovies on a bed of carmelized onions or the tuna served with fat white beans and chopped onions are good beginnings. If you are considering a pasta course, look for scampi risotto, *pappa al pomodoro,* or the rich tortellini with gorgonzola and arugula. Grilled meat and fish dominate the *secondi piatti,* with all-star portions of grilled veal chops, succulent chicken, and mouthwatering scampi. If the fried artichokes make a menu appearance, don't miss these tender morsels. Neither should you overlook the fresh fruit tarts or sweet wild strawberries, if you are lucky enough to be here during the few weeks in the spring when they are in season.

Pitti Palace and Piazza Santo Spirito

The Palazzo Pitti, a fifteenth-century palace designed by Brunelleschi as a residence for Luca Pitti, and later occupied by the powerful Medicis, is across the Arno on Florence's "Left Bank." Only a ten-minute stroll from the Ponte Vecchio, the fortress palace holds one of Europe's greatest art collections, scattered through several museums. The most famous is the Galleria del Palatina, with paintings hung four or five feet high on damask-covered walls. In addition to the galleries, there is the Museo del Costume and the Appartamenti Reali, royal apartments.

The Augustinian church of Santo Spirito was designed by Brunelleschi in 1444. Its austere exterior houses numerous works of art, including a *Madonna and Child* by Filippo Lippi. The piazza has a small morning farmer's market during the week, and on the second Sunday of the month a flea market is mixed in with the organic produce and hippie kitsch.

RESTAURANTS

PASTRY SHOPS AND BAKERIES

($) indicates a Big Splurge

Restaurants

BECCOFINO ($, 70)
Piazza degli Scarlatti, 1r, off Lungarno Guicciardini

TELEPHONE
055 290 076 (for both restaurant and wine bar)
OPEN
Tues–Sun in winter; daily in summer: lunch 12:30–2:30 P.M., dinner 7–11:30 P.M. (wine bar till midnight)
CLOSED
Mon in winter (call about Mon hours in summer); NAC
RESERVATIONS
Essential
CREDIT CARDS
AE, DC, MC, V
À LA CARTE
Restaurant 33.57–38.73€; wine bar 6.20–18.08€, beverage extra
MENU TÙRISTICO
None
COVER & SERVICE CHARGES
Restaurant, cover 2.07€; wine bar, cover 1.03€; at both, service discretionary
ENGLISH
Yes, and menu in English

Beccofino puts the T in trendy as Florence's hottest new restaurant and wine bar. The sufficiently hip clientele makes it as much of a people-watching place as a watering hole and dining destination. In warm weather, the action takes place on the covered terrace overlooking the banks of the Arno River. Inside, the exhibition kitchen and the big, open, loud dining room with wrapped banquette seating around bare wooden tables— everyone tended by buffed, bronzed, and buzz-cut staff dressed in black and speaking Italian-accented English— could be anywhere in Manhattan or Los Angeles and not raise an eyebrow. But in traditional Florence it is causing a stir and has become the talk of the town. With the winning combination of the restaurant and wine know-how of David Gardner (see Trattoria Baldovino, page 51) and the exceptional cooking skills of chef Francesco Berardinelli, it is no wonder that reservations for dinner tables are required days in advance.

Beccofino means good taste and good palate, and you will definitely satisfy both with whatever is on your oversized plate. The menu changes monthly, but if you are here in early spring, I can assure you the poached egg on a bed of braised onions with white truffles will be an antipasto you will never forget. So is the deceptively simple pecorino cheese *crostini* with herbed peppers or the steamed mussels with asparagus served in a spicy parsley broth. The basil pesto risotto with tempura vegetables is fabulous, and so are the tiny clouds of *gnocchetti* bathed in a pecorina fondue and dusted with cracked pepper and fresh thyme. If there are two of you who love lamb, the pink, herbed leg of lamb is required eating. Otherwise, consider the roasted guinea hen with black olives or any fresh fish offering. Don't overlook the nearly perfect desserts, especially the cappuccino-laced crème brûlée or the light lemon mousse with fresh mint. The wine list is exceptional, with vintages priced for everyone.

If a full meal stretched out over the entire afternoon or evening seems too much, then book a table for lunch or dinner in the wine bar, which serves lighter meals featuring salads, cold meat and cheese plates, daily soups, and main courses in addition to irresistible desserts, such as pears in red wine with a cinnamon *zabaione* sauce or prune and armagnac parfait. Featured wines are listed on a blackboard, and more than forty wines are poured by the glass, enabling guests to sample several types before deciding on a favorite.

LE VOLPI E L'UVA (80)
Piazza de' Rossi, 1r

Everything is small at Le Volpi e l'Uva except the quality, which is tremendous. The six friendly owners strive to give good wine at civilized prices, and judging from the smart-looking, upmarket group of devotees, they have succeeded brilliantly. French, German and a smattering of other wines are available, but the specialty here are wines from small producers throughout Italy, with the emphasis on the north. More than forty varieties are sold by the glass, and many more by the bottle. A glass of prosecco will run around 2.07€, and a vintage brunello from 5.16€. The only food served are small sandwiches and platters of cheese and cold meat. The regulars know to stand at the marble bar because if you sit at one of the tables—either inside or on the tiny terrace sandwiched in between parked cars and vespas—you will add 25 percent to your bill.

TELEPHONE
055 239 8132

OPEN
Mon–Sat: 11 A.M.–8 P.M., continuous service

CLOSED
Sun; NAC

RESERVATIONS
Not accepted

CREDIT CARDS
AE, MC, V

À LA CARTE
Wine from 2.07€ a glass, sandwiches from 1.55€, meat and cheese plates from 4.39€

MENÙ TURISTICO
None

COVER & SERVICE CHARGES
None

ENGLISH
Usually

OSTERIA DEL CINGHIALE BIANCO (76)
Borgo Sant' Jacopo, 43r

Massimo Masselli represents the third generation of this well-known Florentine family of restaurateurs. Their popular establishment, set in a fourteenth-century tower, specializes in wild boar, a delicacy best made into sausage, salami, or ham and served as an antipasto or stewed with red wine and vegetables and served with polenta as a main course.

There is a bargain Great Eating *menù turistico,* served only for lunch. Choices for this two-course meal include a large salad, but no wild boar. Headlining the Tuscan dishes on both this and the à la carte menus are *pappa al pomodoro* (a filling bread soup made with tomatoes, garlic, and olive oil) and *ribollita* (a hearty, long-simmered soup made with beans, vegetables, and bread). These age-old recipes date back to the times when peasants did not have much to eat and had to make do with what few ingredients they could find. Homemade pappardelle with hare is a lusty winter dish, as is tripe with tomato sauce. Another choice with admittedly more appeal for

TELEPHONE
055 215 706

OPEN
Mon–Tues, Thur–Sun: lunch noon–2:30 P.M., dinner 7–10:30 P.M.

CLOSED
Wed; 3 weeks in July (dates vary)

RESERVATIONS
Essential

CREDIT CARDS
None

À LA CARTE
20.66–28.41€

MENÙ TURISTICO
Lunch only: 10.33€, 2 courses, glass of wine or mineral water, and cover and service included

COVER & SERVICE CHARGES
Cover 1.03€, service included

ENGLISH
Yes, and menu in English

many is the *strozzapreti al burro,* boiled spinach pasta dumplings filled with cheese and drizzled with butter. Delicately crafted desserts include a *crema di mascarpone* served with cookies and a tiramisù made with ricotta cheese that turns out to be light and less sweet than the regular, heavier versions.

Please keep in mind that reservations are essential for lunch and dinner, and that the romantic mezzanine table must be booked several days in advance.

OSTERIA SANTO SPIRITO (75)
Piazza Santo Spirito, 16r

TELEPHONE
055 238 2383

OPEN
Daily: lunch 12:45–2:30 P.M., dinner 7:45–11:30 P.M.

CLOSED
Never

RESERVATIONS
Advised, especially for dinner and Sun lunch

CREDIT CARDS
AE, MC, V

À LA CARTE
23.24–28.41€

MENÙ TURISTICO
None

COVER & SERVICE CHARGES
Cover 1.55€, service discretionary

ENGLISH
Yes, and menu in English

Osteria Santo Spirito is a neighborhood magnet for an eclectic group that ranges from twenty-somethings on the arms of definitely older men to artists, intellectuals, preppies, and families out for their weekly Sunday lunch get-together. On a warm day or evening, the terrace tables are the natural places to be. Otherwise, tables are in two vibrantly painted rooms: one on the ground level and sharing space with the bar and antipasti offerings, and the other up steep stairs, where pillow-backed banquettes make for slightly more comfortable seating. The waitstaff is young and worked beyond capacity, especially at night when one out-of-breath girl runs up and down the stairs, trying valiantly to serve all the completely full tables on the second level. Crayons are provided, theoretically for children, because the menu covers are children's drawings. But I think the crayons are for any budding artist to use to while away the time between courses and glasses of good wine.

Is the food worth the wait? Yes . . . and who knows, by now maybe there are two waitpersons to handle the upstairs diners. What can you expect? Enormous, artistic presentations of food with an emphasis on beautiful salads and vegetables, which could be successfully split, but unfortunately half portions are not served. In addition to a seasonal menu, there is a page of daily specials. In the late spring, look for plates of razor-thin slices of fresh artichokes or fennel on a bed of arugula, topped with fresh Parmesan shavings and dense Tuscan extra-virgin olive oil, or a baked half avocado filled with feta cheese, olives, and tomatoes. Pastas include *rigatoni Santo Spirito* with tomatoes and smoked ricotta cheese; a simple spaghetti with garlic, oil, and chili peppers; or *taglierini* with basil pesto. Meat eaters can feast on pork filet garnished with apples, sliced duck with balsamic vinaigrette, or smoked tuna with a lemon vinaigrette. For a sweet ending, chocolate lovers will be happy with the chocolate cake with a strawberry salsa, or the cheesecake drizzled with dark chocolate sauce. Otherwise, there is always *biscotti con vin santo*, fruit tart, or a dish of gelato.

PITTI GOLA E CANTINA (83)
Piazza Pitti, 16r

The Pitti Gola e Cantina wine bar occupies a primo location directly across from the Pitti Palace. Open Tuesday through Sunday, it offers Tuscan wines, light lunches, and bar snacks from 11 A.M. until 9 P.M. It is a small spot, the sort of place where it is easy to stop in after a day traipsing through the Boboli Gardens or admiring the museums of the Pitti Palace. Also, it is handy to remember if you have missed the regular lunch hour and want something light to tide you over until dinner. When this happens, I like to order the mixed vegetable plate dressed with Tuscan extra-virgin olive oil, or if it is a hot day, the *mozzarella di bufala* layered with red, ripe tomatoes. The house specialty is *tonno del Chianti*, pork marinated in white wine and bay leaf until it becomes almost flaky. All the wines, olive oils, and vinegars you see here can be shipped worldwide. Remember, when shipping, you will pay the shipping costs, but not the VAT.

Pitti Gola e Cantina is owned by a dynamic wife-and-husband team, Sabina and Giancarlo, who also own two wonderful hotels in Florence, the Hotel Torre Guelfa and the Palazzo Castiglioni (see *Great Sleeps Italy*).

TELEPHONE & FAX
055 212 704

EMAIL
pigola@tin.it

OPEN
Tues–Sun: 11 A.M.–9 P.M., continuous service

CLOSED
Mon; NAC

RESERVATIONS
Not necessary

CREDIT CARDS
AE, MC, V (over 15.49€)

À LA CARTE
4.66–10.33€, wine from 4.13€ a glass

MENÙ TURISTICO
None

COVER & SERVICE CHARGES
None

ENGLISH
Yes

RICCHI CAFFÈ & RISTORANTE ($, 77)
Piazza Santo Spirito, 8–9r

What a pleasant Great Eat destination the Ricchi Caffè & Ristorante continues to be. I dashed into the *caffè* one day several years ago to avoid being drenched by a sudden rainstorm. I had planned to have a quick sandwich and regroup for the rest of the afternoon, but when I saw the lunch plates being served to the eager patrons, I quickly changed my order.

Every time I have visited the Ricchi Caffè since, I have found the food to be simple yet delicious. When you go in winter, sit in the room next to the stand-up bar and settle into a soft, tufted banquette seat before a tiny marble-topped café table. Covering the walls here and in

TELEPHONE
055 215 864

OPEN
Mon–Sat: caffè 7 A.M.–9 P.M. (till 1 A.M. in summer), lunch noon–3 P.M., happy hour 6–9 P.M.; ristorante dinner 7:30–11 P.M.

CLOSED
Sun; last 2 weeks in Aug

RESERVATIONS
Not accepted in caffè, essential in ristorante

CREDIT CARDS
AE, MC, V

À LA CARTE
Caffè: 5.16–10.33€; ristorante
28.41–36.15€

MENÙ TURISTICO
None

COVER & SERVICE CHARGES
Caffè, cover 1.55€; ristorante,
cover 2.58€; at both, service
included

ENGLISH
Yes

the bar is a fascinating display of framed photographs of the Santo Spirito Church. On warm days, enjoy your lunch outside on the terrace with its commanding view of the church.

The power behind the success of the kitchen is Alfonsina, the wife of the owner, who usually positions himself behind the cash register. Her menu selections are limited, but they change every day—with the exception of the roast beef and creamy mashed potatoes and the big one-plate salads, which are served in the summer. On my last visit, in addition to these two staples, she had pasta tossed with either leeks and shrimp or carrot, ricotta, and arugula; moussaka; and *milanese di polo con verdura fritta*—a battered and fried filet of chicken with deep-fried vegetables. It sounds heavy and greasy but is light as a feather. This is *not* the place to skip dessert. Treat yourself and indulge in one of Alfonsina's almost illegally rich pastries, a tiramisù made with wild fruits, a slice of chocolate or apple cake, or a serving of their homemade ice cream. As with most "insider" Great Eats, the best dishes go quickly, so plan to arrive early for lunch. If you are in the neighborhood between 6 and 9 P.M., drop by for "happy hour," where the nibbles at the bar are included in the price of the drinks.

Not content to rest on their laurels with just the *caffè,* the couple has opened a small but very select fish restaurant next door. Because the fish is fresh daily, the choices are seldom the same for any length of time, and are limited to four choices for each course. The *antipasto misto del giorno* for two is a perfect beginning, providing samples of whatever is best that day. After sharing this, you probably will only have room for one more course, their signature pasta with assorted seafood, *taglierini* with baby lobster, or a simple grilled scampi, sea bream (*orata*) or turbot (*rombo*). Save room for desserts, and hope they are serving *sfogliata de mele con crema calda*—flaky layers of pastry with apples and cream. If not, remember all the ice cream is made here.

NOTE: Ricchi Caffè is open for lunch on the second Sunday of every month (except August), when there is a flea market on Piazza Santo Spirito.

TRATTORIA ANGIOLINO (71)
Via Santo Spirito, 36r

Angiolino certainly gets an A for authenticity, with an interior filled with hanging copper pots, garlic braids, bunches of dried herbs, and a pot-bellied stove in the center of it all. You enter along a big marble bar along the first room, and sit at red-and-white linen-clad tables lining the wall. The food matches the setting: strictly Tuscan in scope and presentation. The menu is a textbook for the region's favorites of *ribollita, pappa al pomodoro,* tripe, grilled steaks, and a handful of chef's specialties. It is a good place to remember for a leisurely lunch or dinner anytime you are on this side of the Arno prowling around Piazza Santo Spirito, checking out the outrageously priced antiques along Via Maggio, or walking in the Boboli Gardens.

TELEPHONE
055 239 8976
OPEN
Tues–Sun: lunch 12:30–2:30 P.M., dinner 7:30–10:30 P.M.
CLOSED
Mon; NAC
RESERVATIONS
Preferred
CREDIT CARDS
AE, DC, MC, V
À LA CARTE
23.24–28.41€
MENÙ TURISTICO
None
COVER & SERVICE CHARGES
1.55€ cover, 10% service added
ENGLISH
Yes

TRATTORIA BORDINO (81)
Via Stracciatella, 9r

At Bordino you will sit at closely spaced tables in two rooms outfitted with an amazing collection of flea market finds that range from horns, cowbells, farm implements, and fencing masks to a map of Scottish clans, ears of dried corn, gourd rattles, and black-and-white sketches of a beguiling dog with long silky ears. There's just no accounting for taste . . . even in a Florentine trattoria that serves decent food at decent prices. While it is in the general tourist area that leads across the Ponte Vecchio to the Pitti Palace, it is just far enough off the well-trodden path to escape the madding crowds and attract a local audience. As always, the smart diners are zeroing in on the daily specials, and perhaps upgrading the house red to a better Chianti Classico. You can also order a pasta and a salad and incur the wrath of the waiter. If you do this, remember the risotto with gorgonzola is better than the heavy tortellini with *funghi porchini.* Service is honest and genuine, but there is a lag between courses. Never mind, have another glass of wine and remember no one is in a hurry to go someplace else.

TELEPHONE
055 213 048
OPEN
Mon–Sat: lunch noon–2:30 P.M., dinner 7:30–11 P.M.
CLOSED
Sun
RESERVATIONS
Recommended for dinner
CREDIT CARDS
MC, V
À LA CARTE
18.08–23.24€
MENÙ TURISTICO
None
COVER & SERVICE CHARGES
Cover 1.03€, 10% service added
ENGLISH
Yes

TRATTORIA LA CASALINGA (82)
Via dei Michelozzi, 9r

If you are a collector or just an admirer of fine furniture and antiques, be sure to walk down Via Maggio and browse the many beautiful shops and boutiques selling one-of-a-kind items with prices to match. Try to time

TELEPHONE
055 218 624
OPEN
Mon–Sat: lunch noon–2:30 P.M., dinner 7–9:30 P.M.

your visit to include a meal at this typical Florentine trattoria, which is extremely popular with everyone from students, families, and toothless pensioners to Japanese tourists and ladies-who-lunch.

The two rooms with knotty pine wainscoting and high ceilings have closely spaced white linen–covered tables. It is run by the Bartarelli family: the father is the cook and mother gives him a hand, while out in front an uncle and a sister named Andrea handle the service, which is bright and friendly. The basic menu of pastas, grills, roasts, and vegetables remains the same. The daily specials are handwritten, and, as usual, these are the dishes to pay attention to. Because the tables are turned at least twice during each meal, service is quick, so you can count on being in and out in an hour or so—a real accomplishment in Italy.

TRATTORIA QUATTRO LEONI (78)
Piazza della Passera, Via dei Vellutini, 1r

Florentines hope you won't discover one of their favorite places between the Pitti Palace and Santo Spirito Church. Arriving without a reservation is a big mistake: the place is filled from the minute it opens with dining hopefuls standing in the bar waiting for a miracle. Despite the crunch, the chef and staff pay attention to details that matter, and no one ever makes you feel rushed.

A wider than usual selection of antipasti adds variety to the proceedings. On cold days, you could start with the *crostini misti* (mixed toasts), grilled vegetables, or *mozzarella di bufala* with either tiny tomatoes or prosciutto. In summer, try the *tegamino di zucchine,* with smoked, dried beef, creamy white cheese, zucchini, and tartufo oil, or *cuore di carciofo,* a tempting dish made with smoked meat, small artichokes, gorgonzola cheese, tartufo oil, and pine nuts sprinkled on top. The pasta list is short, offering *pappa al pomodoro,* gnocchi, risotto, and *taglierini* with porcini mushrooms. The fried chicken and rabbit is a typical Florentine main course bet, as is the liver with fresh sage or the tender veal cutlets. For garnishes, you could order deep-fried vegetables, sautéed greens, fat white beans topped with extra-virgin olive oil, or a pedestrian *insalata mista* (mixed salad). Desserts allow you three choices: *biscotti* with *vin santo,* the house sweet of the day, or fresh fruit.

Pastry Shops and Bakeries

IL FORNAIO (79)
Via Guicciardini, 3r

For a sandwich on the run or a pastry to go, you cannot beat Il Fornaio, a chain of bakeries with several locations in Florence. They open early in the morning, selling trays of hot *cornetti* (croissants), brioche, and other treats and temptations. The lunch lines for sandwiches and slices of pizza are legion, proving that when you offer good food at decent prices the world will beat a path to your door. All of the food is to go, and the service is frenetic during the crazy lunch scene. If, however, you go a little before noon, or wait until after 1:30 P.M., when admittedly the selection will be diminished, you will at least be able to place your order without a long wait.

Other popular locations are at the corner of Via Sant'Antonino and Via Faenza near the Mercato Centrale and on Via della Spade, just off Via de' Tornabuoni. These locations have more limited hours and are often closed in the afternoons and on Sunday.

TELEPHONE
055 219 854

OPEN
Daily: 7:30 A.M.–7:30 P.M., continuous service

CLOSED
Never

CREDIT CARDS
None

PRICES
From 1.55€

ENGLISH
Depends on server

PASTICCERIA MARINO (69)
Piazza Nazario Sauro, 19r

For some of the best croissants (called *cornetti* or brioche) in Florence, the name to remember is Pasticceria Marino, a bar and pastry shop on the Piazza N. Sauro at the end of the Ponte alla Carraia. Dozens of other pastries are also made here, but the best are these buttery croissants that come out of the oven all morning long.

The croissants are available plain or filled with chocolate or vanilla custard (called *crema*) or with marmalade. If they are temporarily out when you arrive, be patient—another batch is undoubtedly baking in the back. Order a cappuccino to consume with your treat, and stand with the crowd around the bar or sit at one of the little tables stools placed along one wall.

TELEPHONE
055 212 657

OPEN
Tues–Sun: 6:30 A.M.–8 P.M

CLOSED
Mon; Aug (dates vary)

CREDIT CARDS
None

PRICES
Pastries from 1.03€

ENGLISH
Depends on server

San Niccolò

The Piazzale Michelangelo and the magnificent Romanesque church of San Miniato al Monte provide sweeping views of Florence that you will never forget. The winding road leads you through the old city gates to Via di San Niccolò and the church of the same name with its fifteenth-century frescoes.

RESTAURANTS

($) indicates a Big Splurge

Restaurants

FUORI PORTA (87)
Via del Monte alle Croci, 10r

TELEPHONE
055 234 2483

FAX
055 234 1408

EMAIL
inof@fuoriporta.it

INTERNET
www.fuoriporta.it

OPEN
Mon–Sat: lunch 12:30–3:30 P.M., dinner 7–12:30 A.M.

CLOSED
Sun (except in Dec); Aug 7–20 (dates can vary)

RESERVATIONS
Suggested on weekends

CREDIT CARDS
AE, MC, V

À LA CARTE
10.30–12.91€, wine extra

MENÙ TURISTICO
None

COVER & SERVICE CHARGES
Cover 0.52€, service discretionary

ENGLISH
Yes

Fuori Porta romances patrons with attentive service, good food, and a fabulous selection of wines from around the world, with the emphasis on 650 vintages from Tuscany. Located just beyond the city walls, off Via di San Niccolò and Via San Miniato and below Piazzale Michelangelo, this wine bar, run by knowledgeable wine connoisseur Andrea Conti, is considered one of the best in Florence. While it is known for its fine wines, which are shipped worldwide from their wine shop next door, you need not experience fiscal trauma to enjoy an evening spent sampling some of the thirty-five weekly and monthly featured superior wines (which sell from 2.07€ to 7.75€ a glass).

Patrons also come for the kitchen's simple take on regional foods, which pair well with any of the six-hundred-plus wines available at any one time. Lunch and dinner both feature a daily menu of assorted pastas, fresh fish at night, carpaccio, sandwiches, and cheese and meat plates, plus every *crostino* and *bruschetta* you can possibly imagine. If you are a serious wine buff, visit their Website or email them for a list of wines that can be shipped to your doorstep.

I TAROCCHI (84)
Via dei Renai, 12–14r

Wood-fired pizzas served in laid-back surroundings with bench seating and bare tables tells you this is a young place. The throng at night tells you it is also popular and obviously well priced. While probably not worth a long hike from your hotel, it is a worthy neighborhood choice if you are in the mood for a really good pizza. Pastas also share the menu, and they are also good, especially the *tagliatelle alla certosina,* loaded with shrimp, fresh tomatoes, and arugula, a bitter green that gives it a bite. However, the main event is pizza. If you are looking for something light, try the *stracchinella,* made with two soft cheeses, mozzarella and stracchino, which is a delicate soft cheese from Lombardy, or the house specialty, a thick crust affair called *bella napoli* and loaded with *mozzarella di bufala* and fresh tomatoes. For a pizza with a punch, there is the *capricciosa,* loaded with tomato, mozzarella, prosciutto, mushrooms, pepperoni, olives, and wurstels (German sausage). Nothing light about that! Don't discount desserts, especially the cheesecake, which is made by the owner's mother according to a recipe sent to her by a friend in America.

TELEPHONE & FAX
055 234 3912

OPEN
Tues–Sun: lunch 12:30–2:30 P.M., dinner 7 P.M.–1 A.M.

CLOSED
Mon; NAC

RESERVATIONS
Recommended for dinner on weekends

CREDIT CARDS
MC, V

À LA CARTE
Pizza from 5.16€, 2-course pasta meals from 9.03€

MENÙ TURISTICO
None

COVER & SERVICE CHARGES
Cover 1.03€, service discretionary

ENGLISH
Yes

OSTERIA ANTICA MESCITA (86)
Via di San Niccolò, 60r

Bench seating along exposed stone walls in what was once the crypt of the San Niccolò Church sets the rough-hewn tone of this pleasant osteria in a quiet, non-tourist-plagued section of the *Oltrarno.* For lunch you will be served by members of the Prosperi family; at dinner, other waiters help out. Curious carnivores will be happy with wild boar sausage, a plate of smoked meats, rabbit, or roast pork. Others will be content with vegetable couscous, salad, a plate of assorted local cheeses or fresh fish, which appears on Friday. For dessert there is no contest. Everyone orders the chocolate torte, a thin wedge of shortbread crust topped with dark chocolate. The house wines are adequate, the prices fair, and the service friendly, which adds up to a nice meal just far enough from the hub of tourist Florence to keep it local and appreciated.

TELEPHONE
055 234 2836

OPEN
Mon–Sat: lunch noon–3 P.M., dinner 7:30 P.M.–midnight

CLOSED
Sun; Aug

RESERVATIONS
Advised

CREDIT CARDS
None

À LA CARTE
15.49–18.08€

MENÙ TURISTICO
None

COVER & SERVICE CHARGES
Cover 0.52€, no service charge

ENGLISH
Yes

RISTORANTE PANE E VINO ($, 85)
Via San Niccolò, 70 a/r

TELEPHONE & FAX
055 247 6956

EMAIL
paneevino@yahoo.it

OPEN
Mon–Sat, dinner 7:30 P.M.–
midnight

CLOSED
Sun; NAC

RESERVATIONS
Essential

CREDIT CARDS
AE, DC, MC, V

À LA CARTE
28.41–33.57€

MENÙ TURISTICO
Menù degustazione, 25.88€,
4 courses, beverage extra; must
be ordered by entire table

COVER & SERVICE CHARGES
Cover 1.55€, service charge
included

ENGLISH
Limited, but menu in English

Dining at Pane e Vino puts you in stylish surroundings where you will enjoy dishes that creatively straddle the line between contemporary Italian and international. Book a table in the second room, which is brighter and more comfortable than the spare front room outfitted in black furnishings. When ordering, consider the *menù degustazione*, which must be ordered by everyone at the table. It is a good buy, considering it includes an appetizer, two small first courses, a garnished main course and dessert for less than the sum of these dishes if ordered individually. For example, you might start with a light asparagus souffle with gorgonzola sauce or a pecorino flan with broad bean sauce. Both are rich but served in just the right portions. The buckwheat tagliatelle with rabbit or the fresh pea soup are both winning first courses. So is the fat yellow pumpkin dumpling drizzled with melted butter and sage. Not so the potato ravioli overpowered by a heavy meat and dried mushroom sauce. Follow this with tender medallions of veal dotted with chicken liver mousse or a gamey roast guinea fowl. Vegetarian alternatives include lightly fried, mozzarella-stuffed zucchini flowers or a soft eggplant pudding with a mozzarella cheese and tomato sauce. Desserts are different, and don't always work. One that does is the hazelnut custard with white chocolate sauce. The doughy pear and walnut clafoutis and the caramel mousse inexplicably doused in licorice sauce definitely don't make the grade.

Another thing that doesn't make the grade here is the attire of the waitstaff. Our table was served by a waiter with a two-day beard wearing a wrinkled T-shirt flapping over a pair of rumpled jeans. The waitress in a skimpy tank top that exposed her variety of body tattoos wasn't any more appealing. Maybe these two would be acceptably dressed in some dive for night crawlers only, but in an attractive restaurant with high-quality food and prices to match, they are decidedly out of place.

Food Shopping in Florence

Probably one of the favorite Great Eats you will have in Florence is the one you prepare yourself. It may be an ambitious three-course meal cooked in your apartment kitchen or a snack purchased from the market and eaten on the run or on a bench in a pretty piazza. Whether or not you are buying, strolling through an Italian outdoor market or cruising the aisles of a supermarket gives you a window into the everyday Italian way of life. In Florence, here are the places where I like to shop for food and wine.

Gourmet Food and Wine Shops

ANTICA BOTTIGLIERA DEL CENTRO (25)
Via dei Banchi, 55–57r (Piazza Goldini)

TELEPHONE
055 215 686

FAX
055 293 149

OPEN
Mon 3–7 P.M., Tues–Sat
9 A.M.–1 P.M., 3–7 P.M.

CLOSED
Sun; Sat afternoon in July &
Aug; 1 week in mid-Aug
(dates vary)

CREDIT CARDS
DC, MC, V

The friendly shop, with a knowledgeable staff, sells Italian wines (including a selection of Chianti Classico), pastas, extra-virgin olive oils, the best balsamic vinegar from Modena, *limoncello* from Sorrento, and a big choice of grappas.

I SAPORI DEL CHIANTI (26)
Via dei Servi, 10r (Il Duomo)

TELEPHONE & FAX
055 238 2071

EMAIL
info@isaporidelchianti.it

INTERNET
www.isaporidelchianti.it

OPEN
Tues–Sat 9:30 A.M.–7:30 P.M.,
Mon, Sun 10 A.M.–7:30 P.M.

CLOSED
Holidays

CREDIT CARDS
AE, DC, MC, V

This store has beautiful displays of the food and drink from Chianti, and anything you want can be delivered to your hotel or sent to any address worldwide.

LA BOTTEGA DELL'OLIO (63)
Piazza del Limbo, 2r (Ponte Vecchio)

TELEPHONE & FAX
055 267 0468

INTERNET
www.labottegadellolio.it

OPEN
Mon–Sat 10 A.M.–7 P.M.

CLOSED
Sun

CREDIT CARDS
DC, MC, V

The shop is located on a tiny square, next to SS Apostoli Church, one of the oldest in Florence and the place where the Easter Day parade starts. A visit to La Bottega dell'Olio is a very pleasant education in the joys of olive oil consumption. Almost everything in the pretty shop has something to do with olives or olive oil, and owner Andrea will patiently explain the virtues of his large stock of extra-virgin olive oils, or let you browse to your heart's content. I like the olive-motif kitchen linens, his olive oil-based skin care products and soaps, olive wood cooking and serving implements, and the wonderful array of flavored vinegars, including carob, honey, fig, and, of course, raspberry. Best of all you can taste before you buy. While you are here, please be sure to admire Andrea's beautiful photographs and stop to say hello to the store mascot, a friendly dog named Mozart.

LA GALLERIA DEL CHIANTI (43)
Via del Corso, 41r (Il Duomo)

As the name implies, this store offers food and wines from Tuscany, including a good selection of flavored oils, eighty-year-old balsamic vinegar (193.67€ per bottle) and bags of *cantuccini* for dipping in *vin santo*. Shipping is available.

TELEPHONE & FAX
055 291 440

EMAIL
info@lagalleriadelchianti.com

INTERNET
www.lagalleriadelchianti.com

OPEN
Mon–Sat 9:30 A.M.–7:30 P.M.;
in summer, also Sun 2–7:30 P.M.

CLOSED
Sun in winter

CREDIT CARDS
AE, DC, MC, V

Grocery Stores and Supermarkets

BOTTEGA DELLA FRUTTA (32)
Via della Spada, 58r (Piazza Goldini)

The Bottega della Frutta is sheer heaven if you appreciate fine fruits and vegetables. It is run by a friendly, outgoing husband and wife, Francesco and Elizabetta, who offer the bounty of Tuscany, and of the world, in their tiny shop piled high with the freshest, highest quality produce you are likely ever to see *anywhere*. After two visits, you will feel like a regular. More important, you will be treated as one. On top of this, their prices are very fair, and Elizabetta speaks wonderful English.

TELEPHONE
055 23 98 590

OPEN
Mon–Tues, Thur–Sat 8 A.M.–
7:30 P.M., Wed 8 A.M.–1:30 P.M.

CLOSED
Sun

CREDIT CARDS
MC, V

PEGNA (38)
Via dello Studio, 8r (Il Duomo)

Skip the mops and cat food in front and head for the back of this snazzy grocery store, which sells everything you could possibly want, except produce.

TELEPHONE
055 282 701

OPEN
Mon–Tues, Thur–Sat 9 A.M.–
1 P.M., 3:30–7:30 P.M., Wed
9 A.M.–1 P.M.

CLOSED
Sun

CREDIT CARDS
AE, MC, V

STANDA (40)
Via Pietrapiana, 42/44 (Piazza Santa Croce)

This is the Safeway of Italy, with food, bakery, deli, meat, and liquor sections. It is centrally located, not far from Piazza Santa Croce and across the street from a big post office.

TELEPHONE
Unavailable

OPEN
Daily: 8:30 A.M.–9 P.M.

CLOSED
Never

CREDIT CARDS
AE, MC, V

SUGAR BLUES HEALTH FOOD STORE (6)
Via Ventisette Aprile, 46/48 (Piazza della Indipendenza)

TELEPHONE
055 483 666
OPEN
Mon–Tues, Thur–Sat 9 A.M.–1:30 P.M., 4–7:30 P.M.; Wed 9 A.M.–1:30 P.M.
CLOSED
Sun
CREDIT CARDS
MC, V

This is the only large health food store in town, but compared to those in the States, it's not much to get excited about. The store carries vitamins, packaged foods, a small selection of deli items, cereals, juices, teas, honey, yogurt, and cosmetics. The produce leaves something to be desired unless you happen to be there when it arrives. Otherwise, it sits out and after a day or two goes limp.

There is a second store at Via dei Serraglia, 57, near Piazza Santo Spirito.

Indoor/Outdoor Markets

MERCATO DELLA CASCINE
Cascine Park (past Lungarno Amerigo Vespucci at western edge of Florence)

OPEN
Tues 7 A.M.–1 P.M.

If you can eat it, wear it, water it, feed it, or dust it, chances are it is for sale at the Mercato della Cascine. This weekly outdoor market on Viale Lincoln along the Arno River includes an outdoor food market and endless clothing and houseware stalls pitching everything from aprons to underwear. It is very local, since most tourists don't venture out this far. Go early for the best selection. Watch your wallets and purses, and take your own shopping bags. The English spoken here is very limited. If you don't feel like walking, hop on bus number 1, 9, or 12. Most stalls don't get really going until 8 A.M.

MERCATO CENTRALE DE SAN LORENZO (14)
Piazza del Mercato Centrale

OPEN
Indoor food market: Mon–Sat 7 A.M.–1 P.M.; outdoor stalls: in winter, Tues–Sat 9 A.M.–6 P.M.; in summer, daily 9 A.M.–9 P.M.

The San Lorenzo Central Market is a *must* for every visitor to Florence. Inside, stalls on two levels sell every sort of meat, fish, cheese, fruit, and vegetable imaginable. Outside are hundreds of stalls with hawkers selling a variety of fake Gucci scarves and bags, plus T-shirts for everyone on your list, Florentine paper products, questionable leather goods, and more. No one has a monopoly on any item . . . it's just dozens of sellers all selling the same things at the same prices. Consequently, there's not much bargaining, so pick the seller with the best attitude. Very touristy, but fun and worth at least an hour or so.

MERCATO SANT' AMBROGIO (55)
Piazza Sant' Ambrogio at Piazza Ghiberti

This is a lively indoor/outdoor neighborhood market selling to the locals. If you patronize a stall three or four times, you will be treated just like one of the natives. Here you will find all the same meats, fish, dairy products, fruits, and vegetables found at the Mercato Centrale, but at slightly better prices. Tavola Calda da Rocco (see page 58) is a great place for lunch. The dry-goods stalls outside have some worthwhile buys in cotton underwear and socks. Best day to go: Saturday.

OPEN
Mon–Sat 7 A.M.–1 P.M.

CLOSED
Sun

ROME

Every road does not lead to Rome, but every road in Rome leads to eternity.
— *Arthur Symons,* Cities, *1903*

There are thirty-four McDonald's in Rome, it's true, but there are four hundred Italian restaurants in New York City.
— *U.S. Ambassador Thomas Foglietta, in an interview with Turin daily,* La Stampa

In the eternal city of Rome, antiquity and history are taken for granted as part of everyday life. This city, teeming with humanity and choked with traffic jams and crazy drivers, happily thrives amid some of Western civilization's greatest monuments, piazzas, and landmarks.

Romans originated the first developed cuisine in the Western world and remain famous to this day for their passion for eating. While Rome cannot claim to be the gastronomic capital of Italy, it is the city where food is most pleasurably consumed. The cooking is rich in flavors and aromas, but there is nothing fancy about it. In fact, some may think it almost primitive because many of the famous dishes, such as *coda alla vaccinara* (oxtail stew with vegetables), *trippa alla romana* (tripe cooked with meat sauce, mint, and pecorino cheese), and *cervella fritta* (fried calves' brains), are based on the head, the tail, and the innards. The Jewish community in Rome favors deep-frying and has raised this cooking method to a delicate art form. Consider *carciofi alla giudia* (artichokes flattened and fried until brown and crisp) and zucchini blossoms stuffed with ricotta cheese and anchovies and quickly deep-fried. Other vegetables have a starring role, especially green leafy vegetables cooked in water and served *all'agro,* with lemon juice and olive oil. *Puntarella,* an interesting light green leafy vegetable, is served as a salad with an unforgettable dressing made from pounded garlic and anchovies.

In Rome there are literally thousands of dining choices, from the elegant citadels of fine cuisine to the rapidly vanishing little family-owned and -run trattorias. As in every major world capital, fast-food chains have made their invasion. The good news is that serious chefs are sticking with regional standbys and the basic *cucina* everyone wishes Mama still had the time and desire to prepare. Roman restaurants of all types are noted for serving the same specialties on the same days of the week. Tuesday and Friday, look for fresh fish. On Thursday, it is gnocchi, and on Saturday, tripe. For a traditional Sunday lunch with the extended family, plan on rich lasagna. Pizza is the light meal of choice in the evening. Mouthwatering displays of vegetables, meat, and seafood antipasti are laid out with the precision of a fine jeweler. Favorite pastas are *penne all'amatriciana* (pasta with tomatoes, onions, bacon, and hot pepper), *spaghetti alla carbonara* (pasta with bacon, onion, eggs, cheese, and wine), and *con aglio, olio,* and *prezzemolo,* spaghetti with olive oil, garlic, and parsley. Popular entrées are *saltimbocca* (which means "hop into the mouth" and consists of thin slices of prosciutto and veal sautéed in butter and wine), *abbacchio* (milk-fed baby lamb roasted, or the chops grilled to perfection over an open fire), and *baccalà* (dried salt cod, usually dipped in butter and fried in olive oil).

Desserts are kept simple: usually a piece of fruit or a dish of fresh fruit. If something more is desired, there is the ever-present *dolce* darling of the decade, tiramisù (which means "pick me up"), a rich mix of coffee, cake, chocolate, and mascarpone cheese liberally laced with liqueur. Finally, no trip to the Eternal City could be complete without a liberal sampling of gelato, the favorite Roman between-meal treat. Cones and cups are sold by the size, not the number of scoops, so it is easy to sample two or three flavors at a time—and always with *panna* (whipped cream) on top.

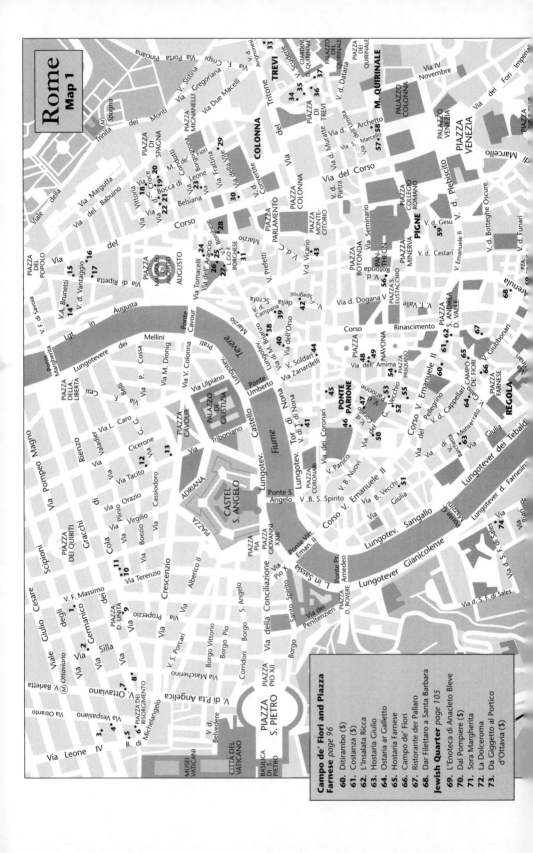

Rome
Map 1

TREVI 33

COLONNA

M. QUIRINALE

PIAZZA VENEZIA

PIGNE

PONTE PARIONE

REGOLA

PIAZZA DEL POPOLO

MAUSOLEO DI AUGUSTO

PIAZZA DI SPAGNA

PALAZZO DI GIUSTIZIA

PIAZZA CAVOUR

CASTEL S. ANGELO

CITTÀ DEL VATICANO

BASILICA DI S. PIETRO

PIAZZA S. PIETRO

MUSEI VATICANI

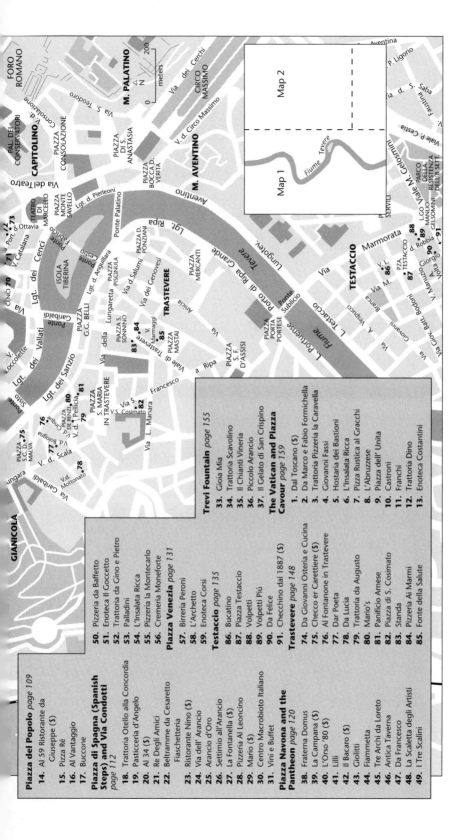

Piazza del Popolo page 109
14. Al 59 Ristorante da Giuseppe ($)
15. Pizza Ré
16. Al Vantaggio
17. Buccone

Piazza di Spagna (Spanish Steps) and Via Condotti page 112
18. Trattoria Otello alla Concordia
19. Pasticceria d'Angelo
20. Al 34 ($)
21. Re Degli Amici
22. Beltramme da Cesaretto Fiaschetteria
23. Ristorante Nino ($)
24. Via dell' Arancio
25. Arancio d'Oro
26. Settimio all'Arancio
27. La Fontanella ($)
28. Pizzeria Al Leoncino
29. Mario ($)
30. Centro Macrobioto Italiano
31. Vini e Buffet

Piazza Navona and the Pantheon page 120
38. Fraterna Domus
39. La Campana ($)
40. L'Orso '80 ($)
41. Lilli
42. Il Bacaro ($)
43. Giolitti
44. Fiammetta
45. Tre Archi da Loreto
46. Antica Taverna
47. Da Francesco
48. La Scaletta degli Artisti
49. I Tre Scalini

50. Pizzeria da Baffetto
51. Enoteca Il Goccetto
52. Trattoria da Gino e Pietro
53. Palladini
54. L'Insalata Ricca
55. Pizzeria la Montecarlo
56. Cremeria Monteforte

Piazza Venezia page 131
57. Birreria Peroni
58. L'Archetto
59. Enoteca Corsi

Testaccio page 135
86. Bucatino
87. Piazza Testaccio
88. Volpetti
89. Volpetti Più
90. Da Felice
91. Checchino dal 1887 ($)

Trastevere page 148
74. Da Giovanni Osteria e Cucina
75. Checco er Carettiere ($)
76. Al Fontanone in Trastevere
77. Dar Poeta
78. Da Lucia
79. Trattoria da Augusto
80. Mario's
81. Panificio Arnese
82. Piazza di S. Cosimato
83. Standa
84. Pizzeria Ai Marmi
85. Fonte della Salute

Trevi Fountain page 155
33. Gioia Mia
34. Trattoria Scavolino
35. Il Chianti Vineria
36. Piccolo Arancio
37. Il Gelato di San Crispino

The Vatican and Piazza Cavour page 159
1. Dal Toscano ($)
2. Da Marco e Fabio Formichella
3. Trattoria Pizzeria la Caravella
4. Giovanni Fassi
5. Hostaria dei Bastioni
6. L'Insalata Ricca
7. Pizza Rustica al Gracchi
8. L'Abruzzese
9. Piazza dell' Unita
10. Castroni
11. Franchi
12. Trattoria Dino
13. Enoteca Costantini

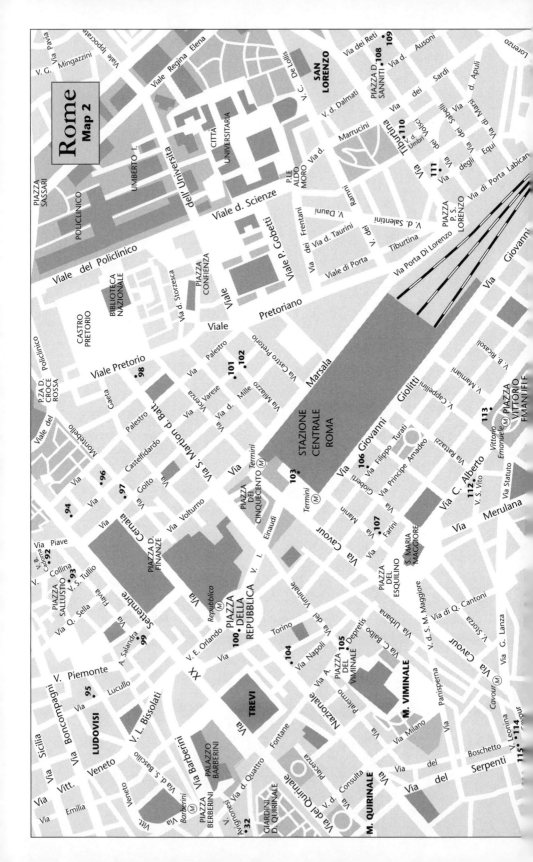

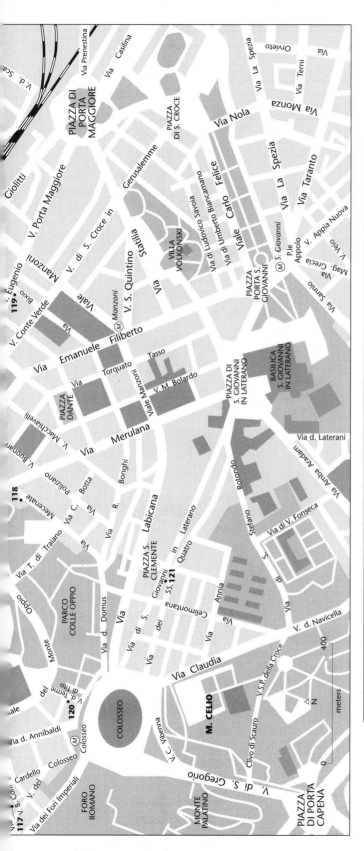

Restaurants in Rome by Area

Campo de' Fiori and Piazza Farnese

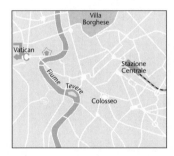

The name Campo de' Fiori means "field of flowers." The original flower market has moved to the outskirts of Rome (see page 169), and now there are only a few flower stalls open during the morning market, which is one of the most colorful in Rome. Around the market is a maze of cobblestone alleys, fading *palazzos,* crumbling churches, bubbling fountains, and restaurants and bars of all types. Not far from Campo de' Fiori is the serenely elegant Piazza Farnese, with its Michelangelo-designed Palazzo Farnese, now the French Embassy.

RESTAURANTS

INDOOR/OUTDOOR MARKETS

($) indicates a Big Splurge

Restaurants

COSTANZA ($, 61)
Piazza del Paradiso, 63/65

TELEPHONE
06 686 1717, 6880 1002

FAX
06 686 5167

OPEN
Mon–Sat: lunch 1–3 P.M., dinner 8–11:30 P.M.

CLOSED
Sun; Aug

Costanza is almost buried in a hidden corner of this tiny piazza a minute or two away from Campo de' Fiori. The rather anonymous exterior masks the warmth of this multiroom *hostaria,* which sits on part of the ruins of the Theater de Pompeo, sections of which are displayed behind glass. The attractive interior is a mix of stuccoed walls, low ceilings, and long beams with the expected roundup of wine bottles, paintings, candles at night, and other bric-a-brac. This dark, cozy atmosphere makes it the perfect place for a romantic meal with a special person.

The wide-ranging menu holds few disappointments, but is admittedly for diners with more flexible budgets. On the pasta front, the *pasta e fagioli Costanza* is delicious—it's a carbohydrate festival of white beans and pasta in a broth with onions, bacon, and tomato sprinkled with grated cheese. Also delicious are any of the risottos, the seasonal ravioli with artichokes, crepes with spinach and cheese, or the *tagliolini* with salmon and radicchio. From here, you move on to a number of main-course dishes, ranging from steak tartare, grilled or roasted veal, pork, baby kid, and beef, as well as fresh fish and vegetable side dishes. The ever-present *dolce,* tiramisù, is featured and is especially rich, as are most of the other homemade desserts. I love the *torta di mirtilli* (blueberry tart) or, for a lighter choice, the zabaglione mousse.

DAR FILETTARO A SANTA BARBARA (68)
Largo dei Librari, 88

All the fast-food fish fanciers in this section of Rome flock to Dar Filettaro. When you arrive, you need only remember one thing about this bargain Great Eat hidden on a tiny side street off Via dei Giubbonari: *filleto di baccalà,* or deep-fried codfish, the house specialty. Their version is batter dipped and quickly deep-fried, leaving the inside moist and the outside crisp. Add a glass of wine and maybe a salad and you should be ready for the next round of sightseeing.

DITIRAMBO ($, 60)
Piazza dell Cancelleria, 74/75

Ditirambo, named after an ancient Greek god of wine and food, is a casual place with beams and planked floors, wines displayed on tiered shelves and servers wearing green aprons that match the green-and-white tablecloths. The quality and freshness of the seasonal products form the base for the food, which is an innovative take on traditional Italian recipes. All bread, pasta,

RESERVATIONS
Essential

CREDIT CARDS
AE, DC, MC, V

À LA CARTE
25.82–41.32€

MENÙ TURISTICO
None

COVER & SERVICE CHARGES
Cover 2.07€, service discretionary

ENGLISH
Yes

TELEPHONE
06 686 4018

OPEN
Mon–Sat: dinner 5–11 P.M.

CLOSED
Sun; Aug, Dec 24–Jan 3

RESERVATIONS
Not accepted

CREDIT CARDS
None

À LA CARTE
5.16€

MENÙ TURISTICO
None

COVER & SERVICE CHARGES
Cover 0.77€, service included

ENGLISH
Limited

TELEPHONE
06 687 1626

OPEN
Mon: dinner 8–11 P.M.; Tues–Sun: lunch 1–3:30 P.M., dinner 8–11 P.M.

CLOSED
Mon lunch; Aug

RESERVATIONS
Absolutely essential
CREDIT CARDS
MC, V
À LA CARTE
58.41–33.57€
MENÙ TURISTICO
None
COVER & SERVICE CHARGES
Cover 1.03€, service included
ENGLISH
Yes, and English menu

and desserts are made here by two women who do nothing else. If you look in before lunch, or in the afternoon, you will probably see them working in the front room, rolling and cutting the pasta, or putting the finishing touches on a sublime dessert. The menu changes often, and almost everything on it works—with the notable exception of the bread pasta with a pecorino and pesto sauce. The rubbery pasta tastes like uncooked dough balls and lands like wet laundry in your stomach, but the sauce is sensational. A better choice is red chicory ravioli. For a second course, skip the odd cabbage and cuttlefish rolls and think instead of venison stew with prunes or the *pollo alla marengo,* chicken cooked with white wine, tomatoes, and mushrooms. Vegetarians are offered three or four main courses that might include a shallot flan with pumpkin sauce or a carrot flan with a cheese fondu. The best salad is the spinach with walnuts, fresh pears and moliterno cheese.

You cannot possibly consider leaving without dessert . . . remember those two hardworking ladies I mentioned? Their sweet finales will not let you down, especially their rich and unusual apple tart swirled with a dark chocolate sauce or the wild cherry and ricotta cake. Locals place Ditirambo high on their list of favorites, so arrive with reservations or be prepared to go elsewhere.

HOSTARIA FARNESE (65)
Via dei Baullari, 109

TELEPHONE
06-6880 1595
OPEN
Mon–Wed, Fri–Sun: lunch noon–3 P.M., dinner 7 P.M.–midnight
CLOSED
Thur; Aug
RESERVATIONS
Advised
CREDIT CARDS
AE, DC, MC, V
À LA CARTE
20.66–23.24€
MENÙ TURISTICO
None
COVER & SERVICE CHARGES
Cover 1.03€, service discretionary
ENGLISH
Yes

At the Hostaria Farnese, you will enjoy homemade food served in a pleasant family atmosphere. The inside hasn't many froufrous, just black bentwood chairs, tables with green tablecloths, and a few outside tables during the summer months.

Everyone gets into the act with the food and service: Mama cooks while Papa and their three daughters and one son serve. The menu is one of utmost simplicity, featuring healthy minestrone, spinach ravioli, eggplant Parmesan, roast lamb, grilled meats, veal scaloppine, pizza for lunch and dinner, and a few desserts. The portions will not overwhelm you, and neither will your bill.

HOSTARIA GIULIO (63)
Via della Barchetta, 19

Hostaria Giulio is in a wonderful old building that dates back to the early 1400s. Fiorella and Giulio, the friendly owners, are into their fourth decade of serving and pleasing their guests. The small dining room has arched ceilings, a beautifully tiled floor, and stone walls lined with black-and-white prints of old Rome and an interesting collection of Sicilian provincial plates. The fifteen tables are covered with light yellow linens and bouquets of fresh flowers. During the steaming summer-time, be sure to reserve one of the tables on the sought-after streetside terrace.

The menu features a parade of seasonal dishes. De-pending on the time of your visit, you will find good renditions of homemade ravioli filled with spinach and ricotta cheese, fettuccine with garlicky pesto or topped with truffles in a white sauce, and *orecchiette* (ear-shaped semolina pasta) tossed in winter with broccoli and in summer with fresh tomatoes and mozzarella cheese. Gnocchi is homemade and served daily. Veal and fresh fish are always on, along with vegetables, assorted cheeses, and the usual desserts, including wild strawber-ries in season. When all is said and done, you will not have spent much more than 24 or 25€ per person, including a glass or two of the drinkable house wine.

TELEPHONE
06 6880 6466

OPEN
Mon–Sat: lunch 12:30–3 P.M., dinner 7 P.M.–midnight

CLOSED
Sun; Aug (dates vary)

RESERVATIONS
Advised for terrace

CREDIT CARDS
AE, DC, MC, V

À LA CARTE
25.82€, beverage included

MENÙ TURISTICO
18.08€, 2 courses; cover and service included, beverage extra

COVER & SERVICE CHARGES
Cover 1.55€, service included

ENGLISH
Yes, also Spanish and Portu-guese

L'INSALATA RICCA (62)
Largo del Chiavari, 85/86

L'Insalata Ricca is a small chain of popular, almost-fast-food trattorias strategically located around Rome. Several are in the tourist boonies and not listed here, but in addition to this one, you will find another not far away, near Piazza Navona (see page 127), and another close to the Vatican (see page 163).

All are bustling with Italian families and foreign residents and offer great value and variety, admirably conforming to the budget and quality concerns of Great Eaters. For both lunch and dinner, plan to arrive early, because within ten minutes of opening, there is a crowd standing outside waiting for a seat. Once in, everyone sits at closely packed tables or on the outside terraces, delighting in the mammoth helpings of their specialties: antipasti, pastas, pizzas, and huge salads that are meals in themselves. Dense chocolate cake, fruit tarts, mousses, and *tartufo* round out the successful meal. The house

TELEPHONE
06 6880 3656

INTERNET
www.linsalataricca.com

OPEN
Daily: lunch noon–4 P.M., dinner 6 P.M.–midnight

CLOSED
Christmas

RESERVATIONS
Advised

CREDIT CARDS
AE, DC, MC, V

À LA CARTE
12.91–15.49€

MENÙ TURISTICO
None

COVER & SERVICE CHARGES
Cover 1.03€, service included

ENGLISH
Yes, and menu in English

wines, including organic varieties, are good. Other pluses included an English menu and a nonsmoking policy that is enforced.

OSTARIA AR GALLETTO (64)
Vicolo del Gallo, 1 at Piazza Farnese, 102

TELEPHONE
06 686 1714

OPEN
Mon–Sat: lunch 12:30–3 P.M., dinner 7–11:30 P.M.

CLOSED
Sun; 1 week mid-Aug (dates vary), Dec 23–Jan 14

RESERVATIONS
Advised, especially for outside tables

CREDIT CARDS
AE, DC, MC, V

À LA CARTE
20.66–25.82€

MENÙ TURISTICO
None

COVER & SERVICE CHARGES
Cover 1.03€, service included

ENGLISH
Yes

Ostaria ar Galletto is a perennial favorite because it is a family-owned place where every member plays a part. Mama, the *real* boss, runs the kitchen. Papa holds court in the dining room while seating and serving guests, who swap stories about their favorite soccer teams. One of the sons-in-law, a colonel in the Italian army, jokes that he ate here as a young man and loved the restaurant so much he married the owner's youngest daughter. After one meal you will understand his enthusiasm. The inside is charming, with its wood-beamed ceiling festooned with hanging hams, hunting murals, and bright orange linens on well-spaced tables. On warm days, reserve a table outside on the Piazza Farnese, a beautiful Baroque square that's an ideal place to forget everything but what is on your plate and who is across the table.

A full meal can creep into the Big Splurge category if you are not watchful, but with a little care and a liter of the house wine you should be fine. I recommend going easy on the appetizers, thus saving room for a bowl of Mama's homemade ravioli, gnocchi, or fettuccine noodles tossed with zucchini. If you like fish, be sure to order the special *fritto misto Italiano* when you reserve your table. Meat eaters lean toward the *saltimbocca alla romana,* thin slices of veal seasoned with fresh sage, covered with ham, and sautéed in butter with a splash of white wine. The beef, slowly cooked in red wine with carrots and fresh mushrooms, and the osso buco with mushrooms are other favorites. The desserts are all homemade, but I have never had any room for more than the *fragole con gelato,* fresh strawberries spooned over vanilla ice cream.

RISTORANTE DER PALLARO (67)
Largo del Pallaro, 15

TELEPHONE
06 6880 1488

OPEN
Tues–Sun: lunch 12:30–3:30 P.M., dinner 7:30 P.M.–12:30 A.M.

CLOSED
Mon; Aug 10–25

Ristorante der Pallaro will not thrill you with a glitzy location or a snappy interior design, but it reflects the loving attention of a chef-owner husband-and-wife team who really care about what is put on your plate—and, after all, that is the bottom line. The cast of characters in the knotty-pine *ristorante* usually includes a lively mix of families, spry senior citizens, a yuppie or two, and anyone else on the prowl for a satisfying budget Great Eat in Rome.

When you arrive, look a little to the right of the beaded curtains covering the entry, and you will see Paolo Fazi busily working in her tiny kitchen. Her husband, Mario, and Carlo, the waiter (who has been here a decade and is considered "almost a son"), help out front. They offer no à la carte menu . . . whatever Paolo cooks is what you eat, and the portions are so large that even a veteran coal miner after a ten-hour shift would have trouble finishing. You will start with an antipasto, then be served the pasta of the day, which might be spaghetti or pappardelle with tomato sauce and cheese. Next comes the main course, which is usually beef or veal served with potatoes. Finally, there is a piece of cheese and the house sweet—homemade peach marmalade cake—all washed down with tangerine juice, mineral water, *and* wine. Coffee is not available.

RESERVATIONS
Advised, especially on Sun and holidays

CREDIT CARDS
None

À LA CARTE
None

MENÙ TURISTICO
18.08€, 4 courses; beverages, cover, and service included

COVER & SERVICE CHARGES
All included

ENGLISH
Enough

Colosseum and Forum

The main archaeological ruins are concentrated south of Piazza Venezia, down Via dei Fori Imperiali to the Forum, around the Colosseum to the Circus Maximus, and south toward the Baths of Caracalla.

RESTAURANTS

GOURMET FOOD AND WINE SHOPS

Restaurants

ENOTECA CAVOUR 313 (116)
Via Cavour, 313

TELEPHONE & FAX
06 678 5496
OPEN
Mon–Sat: lunch 12:30–
2:30 P.M., dinner 7:30 P.M.–
12:30 A.M.; Sun: dinner
7:30 P.M.–12:30 A.M.
CLOSED
Sun lunch; every Sun in Aug
RESERVATIONS
Advised in the evening
CREDIT CARDS
AE, DC, MC, V
À LA CARTE
12.91€
MENÙ TURISTICO
None
COVER & SERVICE CHARGES
Cover 0.77€, service included
ENGLISH
Yes

For a light lunch or dinner accompanied by a few glasses of fine wine, it would be hard to beat the Enoteca Cavour 313, one of the most complete wine bars in Rome. This appealing location features more than six hundred different wines and champagnes from every wine-growing region in Italy, as well as wines from France, California, and Australia. The casual atmosphere, with wooden tables and booths, draws everyone from construction workers in dusty shoes on their way home from the job site to socialites dressed to the nines. Angelo, one of the owners, speaks English and knows his wines. He and his partner, Marco, will be happy to make suggestions about what to drink, or to discuss whatever special wines are being featured at the time. Lingering is encouraged, and you are free to order as much or as little as you want to eat. Don't expect pizza, pasta, or three-course meals. Instead, they serve tempting salads, smoked fish, cold meats, cheeses, pâtés, rich desserts, and fruits filled with special ice cream from Southern Italy.

HOSTERIA ULDERICO A SAN CLEMENTE (121)
Via San Giovanni in Laterano, 106

TELEPHONE
06 7045 0935
OPEN
Mon–Fri: lunch noon–3 P.M.,
dinner 7:45–10:30 P.M.; Sat:
lunch noon–3 P.M.
CLOSED
Sat dinner, Sun; NAC
RESERVATIONS
Not necessary
CREDIT CARDS
None
À LA CARTE
15.49–18.08€
MENÙ TURISTICO
15.49€, 3 courses, including
wine or mineral water, cover
and service charges
COVER & SERVICE CHARGES
Cover 1.03€, service included
ENGLISH
Limited, menu in English

White walls, hard chairs, bright lights, and ersatz Trevi Fountain frescoes define this homespun cheap eat two blocks east of the Colosseum. While hardly destination dining, it is a good place to remember if you are here around lunch, whether you just want a bowl of pasta or feel ready to do justice to a big set-price meal. The no-frills *menù turistico* offers a choice of soup or pasta, roast chicken or pork, or an omelette, plus potatoes, veggies or a salad, fruit or cheese for dessert, and wine or mineral water to wash it all down. The owner and his family have been cooking and serving here for more than fifty years, so you know that they have the formula for pleasing the neighborhood down pat.

IL RE DEL TRAMEZZINO (118)
Via Mecenate, 18A

Management does not stand on ceremony at this residential neighborhood bar within walking distance of the Colosseum and Forum. They only care about providing good food and lots of it to hungry diners searching for a decent value. When you go, check the menu written on a board by the bar or in the front window. You can sit at the bar that wraps around an antipasti display or, in summer, nab one of the sidewalk tables.

The typical lunch-only menu should put you in fine spirits; it contains such dependable standbys as gnocchi, eggplant *alla parmigiana,* and pasta *all'amatriciana* (bacon, garlic, tomatoes, hot red peppers, and onion). In addition to the daily hot specials, they offer different salads, cold meat plates, sandwiches, and a homemade dessert. Because it is a bargain eat in a pricey area, it is a very popular destination. Time your visit to beat the rush because they often run out of the best dishes early.

TELEPHONE
06 487 2360

OPEN
Mon–Fri: bar 7:30 A.M.–8 P.M., lunch 12:30–3 P.M.; Sat: bar 7:30 A.M.–3 P.M., lunch 12:30–3 P.M.

CLOSED
Sun; Aug

RESERVATIONS
Not accepted

CREDIT CARDS
AE, V

À LA CARTE
Sandwiches 2.07–2.58€; full meal 7.75–10.33€, beverage extra

MENÙ TURISTICO
None

COVER & SERVICE CHARGES
No cover charge at the bar, 0.26€ for each roll consummed at a table; service included at bar and indoor tables, 10% added at tables outside

ENGLISH
Minimal

LA PIAZZETTA (117)
Vicolo del Buon Consiglio, 23/a (at the Forum end of Via Cavour)

Quietly hidden on a little street mere minutes from the Forum and Colosseum is La Piazzetta, a charming respite from the usual tourist-clogged choices in the heart of historic Rome. At the entrance is an inviting display of the house antipasti and lovely desserts, and the small, off-white dining room is decorated with formally set tables and a properly dressed staff, headed by Franco, the owner. Because the restaurant is so secluded, on warm days or evenings you can enjoy dining alfresco on the shaded terrace blissfully free of automobile fumes and sidewalk crowds. Service is not hurried, which is all the more reason to order a nice bottle of wine and settle in for a relaxed Roman meal that is pleasing from beginning to end. I like to start with an assortment of the chef's antipasti accompanied by a basket of herb focaccia bread. For a first course I look for a creamy risotto, perhaps perfumed with a touch of ginger and zucchini flowers, or *pasta alla norma,* made with tomatoes, mozzarella, and eggplant. Next I might order grilled fish, or if I didn't have a pasta course, a hearty *saltimbocca a la*

TELEPHONE
06 699 1640

OPEN
Mon–Sat: lunch noon–3 P.M. dinner 7–11 P.M.

CLOSED
Sun; 10 days in Aug (dates vary)

RESERVATIONS
Advised

CREDIT CARDS
MC, V

À LA CARTE
25.82–30.99€

MENÙ TURISTICO
None

COVER & SERVICE CHARGES
No cover, 10% service added

ENGLISH
Yes

romana—slices of tender veal with ham and sage, cooked in butter and white wine. The only problem with dessert is the number of choices: fresh fruit tarts, creamy custards, a dense chocolate slice, and these are just for openers. Just let your eyes and your appetite be your guide.

OSTARIA DA NERONE (120)
Via delle Terme di Tito, 96

TELEPHONE & FAX
06 481 7952

OPEN
Mon–Sat: lunch noon–3 P.M.,
dinner 7–11 P.M.

CLOSED
Sun; Aug

RESERVATIONS
Advised

CREDIT CARDS
AE, DC, MC, V

À LA CARTE
23.24–25.82€

MENÙ TURISTICO
None

COVER & SERVICE CHARGES
Cover 1.29€, 10% service
added

ENGLISH
Enough, and menu in English

This classic restaurant is a smart choice for a leisurely lunch between sightseeing rounds near the Colosseum and the Forum. The emphasis is firmly on old-fashioned value, as is evidenced by its many longtime patrons, some of whom have been eating here for decades. In addition, I have had readers tell me that once they found this restaurant, they didn't eat anyplace else during their stay in Rome. I think that is because no matter who you are or how many times you visit, you receive the same genuinely friendly service. The interior is mighty basic: whitewashed walls with a picture or two, white linens on the tables, uniformed waiters who came with the building, hard chairs, and a pay phone by the front door. In warm weather, tables are set up outside so you can dine with a view of the Colosseum.

Before ordering, be sure to take a long look at the beautiful antipasti display and the lovely desserts and plan the rest of your meal accordingly. For lunch, you may want to concentrate solely on these two courses. Otherwise, for the first course, hope that the homemade ravioli stuffed with ricotta cheese and sage in a butter sauce is on the menu. On Thursday, you can depend on gnocchi, and every day you can order their specialty, *fettuccine alla Nerone,* a creamy dish with salami, ham, peas, mushrooms, and eggs. As your main course, try the chicken with tomatoes and peppers in a wine sauce or the roast rabbit. The desserts are worth every calorie. To ease your pangs of guilt, remember, you can walk back to your hotel or spend the afternoon strolling around Rome's ancient sites.

PIZZERIA LEONINA (115)
Via Leonina, 84

TELEPHONE & FAX
06 482 7744

OPEN
Mon–Fri: 8:30 A.M.–9 P.M.,
continuous service

One of the best slices of pizza you will have in Rome will be at the Werner family stand-up pizza bar, which is within walking distance of the Colosseum and the Forum. It is run by Pietro Werner, his two daughters, Barbara and Marta, and perhaps by now his smiling little grandson, Lorenzo. They make a total of seventy-eight pizzas. Every week they feature one kind of pizza at a special price in addition to the twenty-five or thirty other varieties available each day. If you still don't see what you want, ask; they will try to accommodate any order. The biggest selection of pizza is available at lunch—which is a mob scene. The wait for your number to be called can seem endless, and the crowd ahead of you will seem to multiply, not dwindle. The big trays of piping-hot pizzas are brought from the oven every ten to fifteen minutes. The pizzas are cut into pieces as big or as small as you want, and sold by weight. I suggest trying two or three varieties, saving plenty of room for a healthy sampling of their dessert pizzas, such as the apple (replete with warm apple slices and raisins under a light dusting of cinnamon) or the double-crusted chocolate pizza. If you want to order a whole pizza, save yourself some waiting time and order ahead by phone.

CLOSED
Sat–Sun; last half of July, Aug, Dec 23–Jan 6

RESERVATIONS
Not accepted

CREDIT CARDS
None

À LA CARTE
Sold by weight, from 1.55€ per slice

MENÙ TURISTICO
None

COVER & SERVICE CHARGES
None

ENGLISH
Yes

Jewish Quarter

It is said that when St. Peter came to Rome, he stayed in the Jewish Quarter in Trastevere, where there were some thirty thousand fellow Greek-speaking Jews and fifteen synagogues. Europe's oldest surviving Jewish community was moved in 1555 to its present location by Pope Paul IV, who ruled that the Jewish Quarter was the only place where all Rome's Jews could live and work. Today, the Jewish population in all of Italy is what it was in Nero's time, and the Rome community is the largest. The Via del Portico di Ottavia, behind the synagogue, is the Jewish Quarter's main street and has some of the best Jewish restaurants in Rome.

RESTAURANTS

PASTRY SHOPS AND BAKERIES

($) indicates a Big Splurge

Restaurants

DA GIGGETTO AL PORTICO D'OTTAVIA ($, 73)
Via del Portico di'Ottavia, 21/a

TELEPHONE
06 686 1105

FAX
06 683 2106

OPEN
Tues–Sun: lunch 12:30–3 P.M.,
dinner 7:30–11 P.M.

CLOSED
Mon; last week of July, first
week Aug

RESERVATIONS
Advised, especially on
weekends

CREDIT CARDS
AE, DC, MC, V

À LA CARTE
28.41–33.57€

MENÙ TURISTICO
None

COVER & SERVICE CHARGES
Bread 1.55€, service included

ENGLISH
Enough, and menu in English

Any trip to Rome would be incomplete without sampling Roman-Jewish cuisine. Nowhere will it be more authentic than in this family-owned trattoria next to the ruins of the Theater of Marcellus. Out front is a large seating area shaded by umbrellas. Inside are four rooms done in the usual rustic style with terra-cotta floors and ropes of garlic and dried herbs hanging from the ceiling. The ambitious menu is thankfully translated into English.

For your appetizer course, you must try one of their specialties: crisp, tender fried artichokes, fried zucchini flowers filled with mozzarella and anchovies, fried codfish fillets, rice balls filled with mozzarella and covered with tomato sauce, or potato croquettes. If I order meat, I usually like to stay light on the *primo* course, selecting a simple spaghetti with butter and Parmesan cheese. When I skip the meat and fish dishes, I order something more substantial, say the *spaghetti carbonara* or the *spaghetti con vongole veraci* (with fresh clams). If you are having meat, the osso buco with mushrooms and peas is a filling choice, as is the roast lamb or veal. True to Roman tradition, many unusual cuts of meat are featured. If you're not careful, the beef tongue in parsley sauce, lamb sweetbreads, or the fried brains with mushrooms, artichokes, and zucchini will make a convert out of you. The pace doesn't let up with dessert, which includes fresh fruit, ice cream, or a sinfully fattening delicacy from La Dolceroma, an American-Austrian bakery next door run by the owner's son (see page 108).

DAL POMPIERE ($, 70)
Via S. Maria del Calderari, 38 (off Via Arenula)

TELEPHONE
06 686 8377, 06 6880 3142

OPEN
Mon–Sat: lunch 12:30–3 P.M.,
dinner 7:30–11:30 P.M.

CLOSED
Sun; July 20–Aug 31

RESERVATIONS
Advised

CREDIT CARDS
AE, MC, V

The Jewish Quarter in Rome is a maze of tiny piazzas, cobblestone streets, small shops, restaurants, and ancient ruins. In the heart of this you will find Dal Pompiere, a charming restaurant located on the second floor of the Cenci Bolognetti Palace, which dates from the 1600s. The three simple dining rooms have dark ceilings, frescoes, rustic wooden tables and chairs, and not much else. The emphasis here is on Roman-Jewish cooking at its best.

For the antipasti, *do not miss* the *carciofo alla giudia,* a flattened, fried artichoke that looks like a pressed flower.

Another must, whenever they are in season, is the *fiori di zucca ripieni,* zucchini blossoms stuffed with mozzarella and anchovies, then deep-fried. Other house specialties include daily homemade pastas, succulent roast baby lamb, *baccalà* (salt-dried cod), and *fritto vegetale,* a plate of crisply fried vegetables. The desserts to order include ricotta cheesecake and three types of *crostata:* cherry-cheese, cherry-almond, and chestnut-cheese.

L'ENOTECA DI ANACLETO BLEVE (69)
Via S. Maria del Pianto, 9A/11/12

Rising prices for food and services have forced many small restaurants and trattorias out of business in Italy. Coming along in their place are *enoteche* (wine shops) that sell wine by the case, bottle, or glass. In addition, many of these places offer lunch and light snacks geared to complement the wines as well as your budget.

Whenever I am in the Jewish Quarter in Rome, I head for this *enoteca,* where I can depend on having a nice lunch and a glass of good wine. On display in a glass buffet case are artistically arranged salads and vegetables, assorted cheeses and cold meats, and several hot daily specials. No one speaks much English on the food side, but it won't matter because you can let your eyes guide you to whatever looks most appealing, and then take your food to a place at one of the scattered tables.

TELEPHONE & FAX
06 686 5970

OPEN
Mon–Sat: *enoteca* 10 A.M.–3 P.M., 5–8 P.M.; lunch 1–3 P.M.

CLOSED
Sun; Aug 5–30

RESERVATIONS
Advised for lunch

CREDIT CARDS
AE, MC, V

À LA CARTE
12.91€

MENÙ TURISTICO
None

COVER & SERVICE CHARGES
No cover charge, service included

ENGLISH
Limited

SORA MARGHERITA (71)
Piazza della Cinque Scole, 30

To the designer sunglasses and cellular phone glitterati, Sora Margherita has little appeal. But for Great Eaters searching for good value in unexpected places, this basement hideaway (behind a green door with no sign) is very appealing. The menu is handwritten in red and black felt-tip pen on a piece of grid paper ripped out of a notebook. Wine is served in juice glasses, which are placed on paper overlays covering formica tables. Despite the humble setting, chef Margherita Tomassini turns out some of the heartiest and best Jewish cooking in the Quarter. She wears slippers to work and stands on tradition, never changing her time-worn menu, which is served only for lunch.

She always fixes fettuccine with cheese, black pepper, and tomatoes or cream sauce, as well as her specialty—*agnolotti*—a type of meat ravioli. On Monday, anchovies

TELEPHONE
06 686 4002

OPEN
Mon–Fri: lunch noon–3 P.M.

CLOSED
Sat–Sun, Aug 7–Sept 15

RESERVATIONS
Not accepted

CREDIT CARDS
None

À LA CARTE
12.91–15.49€

MENÙ TURISTICO
None

COVER & SERVICE CHARGES
Bread 0.52€, service included

ENGLISH
None

À LA CARTE
23.24–30.99€

MENÙ TURISTICO
None

COVER & SERVICE CHARGES
Cover 1.55€, service included

ENGLISH
Yes

with endives make an appearance. On Thursday she dishes up gnocchi with tomato sauce. Grilled fish is the Tuesday and Friday highlight, but before ordering, be sure you check the price: is it sold by the gram or the piece? Meatballs are a daily dish, as are the fried artichokes, beef stew, and the veal chops. However, Margherita doesn't bother with dessert.

Pastry Shops and Bakeries

LA DOLCEROMA (72)
Via del Portico di' Ottavia, 20/B

TELEPHONE
06 689 2196

OPEN
Tues–Sat, 8 A.M.–1:30 P.M., 3:30–8 P.M.; Sun, 10 A.M.– 1 P.M.

CLOSED
Mon; July and Aug

CREDIT CARDS
None

PRICES
From 1.55€ per pastry

ENGLISH
Yes

Stefano Ceccarelli's family has owned the restaurant next door for generations (see Da Giggetto al Portico d'Ottavia, page 106). But Stefano wanted to do something on his own. Since he has always been interested in baking, it was natural for him to open La Dolceroma, which sells American and Austrian delicacies and is now one of Rome's most popular and well-known bakeries.

The tiny place, which has a display case and a table with two chairs, allows you to see directly into the kitchen. Stefano does all of the baking himself, listing the ingredients so you will know exactly what you are eating. And what will you be eating? The choices are endless: perhaps chocolate or blueberry muffins, scones, plain bagels, or one of several types of cookies, including chocolate chip and oatmeal raisin. He makes brownies, cheesecake, carrot cake, chestnut cake, pecan pie, and *Sacher torte.* At Christmastime you will find *stollen* and *Linzer torte.* Once your order has been pulled together, it will be impossible to leave without trying one of his hand-dipped chocolates or ice cream. Everything is sold by weight and packaged to go. From late spring until October, American coffee and cappuccino are served.

Piazza del Popolo

The Piazza del Popolo, which means the "people's square," is at the northern entrance to the city. Today the piazza serves as a general meeting and assembly place for celebrations, strikes, and political demonstrations. Standing here you can see the Piazza Venezia at the end of Via del Corso; the Via di Ripetta, which served as a throughway to the Vatican; and Via del Babuino leading to the Spanish Steps. In the center of the piazza is the 3,200-year-old obelisk of Pharaoh Ramses II, the largest in Rome, brought by Augustus from Egypt around 10 B.C.

RESTAURANTS

GOURMET FOOD AND WINE SHOPS

($) indicates a Big Splurge

Restaurants

AL 59 RISTORANTE DA GIUSEPPE ($, 14)
Via Angelo Brunetti, 59

The food at Al 59 Ristorante da Guiseppe is a triumph of Bolognese cooking and a good reason to make a pilgrimage across Rome. If you can stretch your budget only once or twice for a special meal in Rome, this is a worthy choice. The clean and classic interior is elegant, and so is the superb food, passionately prepared by master chef and owner Giuseppe, who is, naturally, from Bologna. Everything from start to finish is made in-house. If you walk by before lunch, you will see several gray-haired men sitting around a large table hand-rolling the tortellini, which is the trademark pasta of Bologna. The meal could begin with antipasto or soup, but I always start with the tortellini with pumpkin or the heaven-sent spinach ravioli filled with ricotta cheese and lightly sauced with fresh tomatoes. Next consider the *bolliti misti* (boiled meats), which is served from a

TELEPHONE
06 321 9019

OPEN
Mon–Sat: lunch 1–3 P.M., dinner 8–11 P.M.

CLOSED
Sun; Aug

RESERVATIONS
Essential for dinner, recommended for lunch

CREDIT CARDS
AE, MC, V

À LA CARTE
30.99–33.57€

MENÙ TURISTICO
None

COVER & SERVICE CHARGES
Cover 2.07€, service included

ENGLISH
Yes

special cart rolled to your table. With a side of vegetables or a mixed salad, you will have a very filling meal. The sheer culinary bliss continues with the desserts, whether it be the plump baked apple or the *crostata* filled with jam.

Because this restaurant is so popular with the locals, reservations are absolutely essential, especially for dinner, which is still humming at 10:30 P.M.

AL VANTAGGIO (16)
Via del Vantaggio, 34

An interesting mixture of neighborhood locals and smart Great Eating visitors has been filling this family-run restaurant for more than forty years because it consistently offers good food and good value. During one of my research trips to Rome, my flat was just around the corner, so I grew to know and enjoy this homespun spot whether I was eating there—again and again—or merely walking by, observing. The tables in the two rooms inside or on the streetside terrace are always busy because the owner, Luigi, keeps everyone well served and well fed.

The six *menù turisticos* are dependable Great Eats that include two courses, fruit or lemon *sorbetto*, wine, and mineral water. If you are going à la carte, the menu has all the popular icons of Roman cuisine, served in generous portions, and always includes pizza and a dozen or more pastas. No matter what you order for your meal, be sure to ask for an order of the house pizza bread, which comes to the table in a puffy and hot round; if you are not careful, it will be gone before your first course appears. The house wine is fine.

TELEPHONE
06 323 6848

OPEN
Daily: lunch noon–3 P.M.,
dinner 7–11 P.M.

CLOSED
Never

RESERVATIONS
Advised, especially if you want
to sit outside

CREDIT CARDS
AE, DC, MC, V

À LA CARTE
Pizza and pasta from 6.20€,
3-course meal 18.08€,
beverage extra

MENÙ TURISTICO
15.49€, 3 courses, including
wine or mineral water

COVER & SERVICE CHARGES
Cover 0.77€, service included

ENGLISH
Yes, and menu in English

BUCCONE (17)
Via di Rippeta, 19

The modest business card says, "Buccone sells wine, liquors, champagnes, and regional foods"—which is true enough in fact but not in spirit. Inside this seventeenth-century *palazzo* is a fabulous *enoteca* filled with wines and spirits all clearly organized by region and at prices to fit every pocketbook. In addition, they stock an amazing selection of olive oils and balsamic vinegars, and they now serve lunch daily and dinner on Thursday, Friday, and Saturday nights. Their delicious buffet menu always includes soup, two or three pastas, vegetables, salads, cold meats and cheeses, and tortes, strudels, and lemon

TELEPHONE & FAX
06 361 2154

OPEN
Daily: wine shop 9 A.M.–
8:30 P.M. (till midnight Thur–
Sat, till 5 P.M. Sunday); lunch
12:30–3 P.M.; dinner Thur–Sat
7:30 P.M.–midnight;

CLOSED
3 weeks in Aug

RESERVATIONS
Advised

CREDIT CARDS
AE, DC, MC, V

cake for dessert. Wine is served by the bottle or glass, enabling you to sample as you go, and if all you want is a glass or two of wine, you can stop in at the bar at any time during the day. Francesco and Vincenzo Buccone speak English and are very knowledgeable and proud of their wines, which can be shipped *only* in Italy, not abroad. You will recognize their mother, Maddalena, sitting at the cash register, simultaneously holding court and keeping an eagle eye on the proceedings.

À LA CARTE
10.33–15.49€, beverage extra

MENÙ TURISTICO
None

COVER & SERVICE CHARGES
None

ENGLISH
Yes

PIZZA RÉ (15)
Via di Ripetta, 14

Pizza Ré has been a hit from the get-go because it delivers what Romans adore: huge Neapolitan wood-fired pizzas with enough toppings to keep things interesting time and again. The location, a block or so from Piazza del Popolo, is open, airy, and pleasant. The floors are tiled with turquoise and yellow inserts, the yellow walls have murals and blue light accents, the tabletops are plain marble, and the food is served with dispatch. Even though every table is crowded to the point of sharing, and the waiting crowd spills ten deep into the street almost every night, you never feel squeezed in or given the bum's rush. On Sunday you will share your Pizza Ré experience with happy, boisterous families, while on the weekends after 10 P.M., the scene gets decidedly trendy—women will feel out of place unless they can fit into a strappy size-two minidress, but men will only need a dark shirt and a cellphone glued to their ear to feel part of the action.

If you decide to start your meal with a salad, I advise you to share it; they arrive on a platter big enough for three. Two of the best are the *caprese*, made with *mozzarella di bufala,* and the *insalate mista,* with three types of greens, tomatoes, and carrots. All of the thirty-six pizzas almost fall off the plate—you will think you can't finish more than a slice or two, but you will be surprised. They are light and oh so easy to eat. You can also get grilled meats, including a hamburger, but for best results, stick with the pizza program.

There are two other Pizza Ré locations in Rome; one is not far from the American Embassy and Via Veneto (see page 145), and the other is on the outskirts of the city.

TELEPHONE
06 3211 4468

OPEN
Mon–Sat: lunch 12:30–3 P.M., dinner 7:30 P.M.–midnight; Sun: dinner 7:30 P.M.–midnight

CLOSED
Sun lunch; Aug 15–30

RESERVATIONS
Essential for dinner

CREDIT CARDS
AE, DC, MC, V

À LA CARTE
Pizza from 7.23€, salads 7.23€, desserts from 3.63€

MENÙ TURISTICO
Lunch only, 8.26€, either pizza, the daily special, grilled meat, or salad and beverage

COVER & SERVICE CHARGES
None

ENGLISH
Yes

Piazza di Spagna (Spanish Steps) and Via Condotti

The 138 steps in the Piazza di Spagna were built from 1723 to 1725 to join the piazza with the important places above it, including the Villa Medici and the Church of Santa Trinità dei Monti. In May the steps are banked by potted azaleas, and throughout the year, they serve as resting grounds for an international collection of lounge lizards, who hang out here hoping for some action. The view from the top over the roofs of Rome is worth the climb, but the view from Via Condotti looking up the steps is equally beautiful. The streets leading to the piazza are lined with expensive boutique shopping, especially the Via Condotti, the city's premier shopping street.

RESTAURANTS

INDOOR/OUTDOOR MARKETS

($) indicates a Big Splurge

Restaurants

AL 34 ($, 20)
Via Mario de' Fiori, 34

Popular, crowded, and romantic, Al 34 was voted Best Value Trattoria in its price category by American Express cardholders in Rome. I am not surprised . . . it is a wonderful restaurant. Reservations are essential for dinner; the best time to make them are for 9 or 9:30 P.M. If you eat much earlier, you will be dining with other tourists, and any later could put you standing in the aisles waiting for your table to clear. The cozy, wood-beamed interior is illuminated at night with ceramic table lights. Both dried and fresh flowers add a nice touch, as does the collection of soup tureens and lids displayed near the entrance to the kitchen. The food is typically Roman, and for variety and the sheer elegance of dishes offered, the three fixed-price menus are, without question, the best high-class Great Eating deals in Rome.

Waiters in bow ties and black vests serve guests big bowls of soup, the best spinach salad in the area, pastas with imaginative toppings, well-executed meat dishes (including Argentine Angus beef), and fresh seasonal vegetables. For dessert, any of the homemade cakes can be recommended, especially the chocolate almond torte or the lemon cream, and the tiramisù.

TELEPHONE
06 679 5091

OPEN
Tues–Sun: lunch 12:30–3 P.M., dinner 7–11 P.M.

CLOSED
Mon; Aug 6–28

RESERVATIONS
Essential, especially for dinner

CREDIT CARDS
AE, DC, MC, V

À LA CARTE
28.41–33.57€

MENÙ TURISTICO
Menu "Oscar" del Gambero Rosso and Menu "Roma": 30.99€, includes appetizer, 3 courses, salad, wine, water, coffee, and cover charge; Menu "Syrenuse": 36.15€, features fish for every course, salad, sorbet, wine, water, coffee, and cover charge

COVER & SERVICE CHARGES
Cover 1.03€, service included

ENGLISH
Yes, and menu in English

ARANCIO D'ORO (25)
Via Monte d'Oro, 17

Located near the small daily antiques market on the Piazza Borghese, this typical trattoria is a popular lunch-time rendezvous for the area's many businesspeople. In the evening, the mood slows down, and it fills with residents and a stray tourist or two. Arancio d'Oro and its cousins, Settimio all'Arancio (see page 119) and Piccolo Arancio (see page 157), are owned by the Cialfi family and are equally well known for their friendly hospitality and good food at realistic prices. The only time I have seen them fall a little short is on major holidays (such as Christmas or New Year's Day), when other restaurants are closed but they choose to stay open. The help and the kitchen staff operate on a limited basis during these holiday times, and it is reflected in the food and service, which can be mediocre. At all other times, the cooking tempts you with pastas in creamy sauces,

TELEPHONE
06 686 5026

OPEN
Tues–Sun: lunch 12:30–3:30 P.M., dinner 7 P.M.–midnight

CLOSED
Mon; July–Aug

RESERVATIONS
Advised

CREDIT CARDS
AE, DC, MC, V

À LA CARTE
23.24–25.82€

MENÙ TURISTICO
None

COVER & SERVICE CHARGES
Cover 1.03€, service included

ENGLISH
Yes, and menu in English

sizzling platters of grilled meats, fresh fish every day, and a lemon mousse dessert you wish was double in size. Pizzas are served in the evenings only.

BELTRAMME DA CESARETTO FIASCHETTERIA (22)
Via della Croce, 39

TELEPHONE
None

OPEN
Daily: lunch 12:30–3 P.M., dinner 7:30–11 P.M.

CLOSED
Never

RESERVATIONS
Advised, but they don't have a phone number!

CREDIT CARDS
AE

À LA CARTE
28.25–28.41€

MENÙ TURISTICO
None

COVER & SERVICE CHARGES
Cover 2.58€ (includes bread and a bottle of mineral water), service included, but tips appreciated

ENGLISH
Yes

I cannot claim to have discovered this uncut gem because it has been a household name for more than a century. It is now a national monument, and not much has changed since it opened in 1879. There are still just seven tables with forty place settings. In the 1960s, it was the hangout of important painters, actors, and poets, as well as for the scriptwriters for *La Dolce Vita,* which was conceived over long lunches at the back tables. The restaurant is located on an interesting shopping street that has everything from fishmongers, flower stalls, and fancy bakeries to luxurious lingerie shops and trendy leather boutiques. It doesn't stand out as a flashy spot; in fact, the only name you will see at this address is the word *Fiaschetteria* positioned at the top of the building. The present mix of diners figures into the restaurant's continuing success. At lunchtime, regulars sit at shared tables with napkins around their necks, downing their food and wine with earnestness. At night, it is mostly couples who live nearby and a few smart visitors who have been tipped off to some of the only affordable food in this expensive enclave of Rome. All is presided over by a young, humorless owner who sits in the back, chain smokes, and gets up only to serve an occasional plate of food.

While it is a national monument, it is no health-food sanctuary for the calorie conscious. Rather, put all puritan thoughts aside and delve uninhibited into an outrageously rich fettuccine with veal or mushroom sauce, a rabbit in white wine, or a filling pork chop. The basic menu stays about the same, but watch for the daily handwritten specials, which reflect seasonally fresh choices. Desserts are entirely forgettable.

CENTRO MACROBIOTO ITALIANO (30)
Via della Vite, 14 (third floor)

TELEPHONE
06 679 2509

OPEN
Mon–Sat: lunch 12:30–3 P.M., dinner 7–11 P.M.

CLOSED
Sun; Aug

Serious vegetarians in Rome all know about the Centro Macrobioto Italiano, the first macrobiotic center in Italy, which is reached by four long flights of steep stairs or via a white-knuckle trip in a creaking elevator. At lunchtime, you can either eat here or take your meal with you. At dinner, it becomes a fish restaurant, and there is no takeout.

The center is run by Aloma, a dedicated vegetarian who believes that it is not only what you eat but how you eat that is important. She is assisted by her mother, who makes the desserts. All their food is made with organic products and uses no animal fats or eggs. The lunch menu offers something for every type of vegetarian, including vegans. You can have macrobiotic grain casseroles, steamed veggie plates, a variety of salads and interesting breads, yogurt shakes, natural ice creams (made here between May and September), and fresh fruit, plus vegetable juices, biologic wines, and organic beer. In the evening, only fresh fish and vegetable plates are served.

Because the center is a private organization, membership is required. Normally it costs 15.49€ per year to "belong." Visitors are allowed to eat here for lunch by paying a 1.03 € surcharge and showing their passport; however, at dinner the fee is waived. If you plan to be in Rome for an extended period and think you will be a regular, show your copy of *Great Eats Italy,* and the 15.49€ annual fee will be dropped.

LA FONTANELLA ($, 27)
Largo della Fontanella Borghese, 86

La Fontanella is a beautiful choice, whether you sit inside in the main room, with its shimmering gold mosaic tiled mural, or outside on the tree- and umbrella-shaded terrace. Heavy pink damask table coverings, gleaming silver, and pretty china further enhance the appeal, as do the lighted hurricane candles and fresh flowers. A formal and dignified tone is set by owners Nicola and Bruno and their polite staff, who wear maroon vests and black bow ties. Service is unobtrusive, and the clientele attractive. Even though you are a visitor in Rome, the staff at La Fontanella never makes you feel that way. Everyone is treated with respect and great dignity.

Dinner begins with a flute of champagne and a plate of nibbles to enjoy while you read the menu. Be sure to ask about the daily specials, which reflect the season. As you decide on your courses, keep in mind that the Abruzzo-inspired food is rich and the portions generous. Bruno is exceptionally proud of his wines, and is ready to help you make the right choices. For a light antipasto,

RESERVATIONS
Preferred for dinner

CREDIT CARDS
None

À LA CARTE
7.75–10.33€

MENÙ TURISTICO
None

COVER & SERVICE CHARGES
No cover or service charges, 1.03€ lunch surcharge for nonmembers

ENGLISH
Yes

TELEPHONE
06 687 1582

FAX
06 687 1092

OPEN
Tues–Sun: lunch 12:30–3 P.M., dinner 7:30 P.M.–midnight

CLOSED
Mon; Aug 7–21

RESERVATIONS
Advised

CREDIT CARDS
AE, DC, MC, V

À LA CARTE
33.57–41.32€

MENÙ TURISTICO
None

COVER & SERVICE CHARGES
Cover 2.07€, service included

ENGLISH
Yes

consider the fried artichoke, served slightly warm and crisply tender—not woody and greasy like the "pine-cones," as I call them, that you often get. Another nice beginning is one of their salads, each of which is a little different. The *insalata Fontanella* has arugula, cheese, mushrooms, and prosciutto tossed in a light mustard vinaigrette. Serious mushroom lovers will like the raw mushrooms mixed with fresh slices of Parmesan cheese. There is also a baby leaf spinach salad and one made with hearts of palm.

The pastas recall the days when we did not feverishly count calories and fat grams. I found both the spinach and ricotta and the zucchini ravioli to be divine, as were the crepes filled with black truffles. Then there is the spaghetti with seafood and the gamey *paparadelle al sugo di lepre,* wide noodles in a robust hare sauce. Decisions, decisions. Perfectly roasted and grilled Danish and Chianti beef, game and truffles in season, tender veal, baby Abruzzo lamb, and fresh fish follow. The fish is expensive, but it is fresh and delicious, usually plainly grilled and served smelling fragrantly of olive oil and lemon.

For the dessert of your dreams, treat yourself to the chef's signature creation: a warm vanilla soufflé draped in rich chocolate sauce and gilded with whipped cream. There is also a beautiful dessert trolley, and if it is available, one of you might try the fresh fruit tart, a lovely mixture of fresh raspberries, boysenberries, and cranberries with a layer of cream placed on a crisp cookie crust. The house wine is good and served by the bottle. You pay only for as much as you drink. While the final bill makes this a Big Splurge, it will be a special meal you will long remember.

NOTE: If you go for lunch, be sure to take a few minutes to wander through the small antiques market held in the square in front of the restaurant.

MARIO ($, 29)
Via della Vite, 55

TELEPHONE
06 678 3818

OPEN
Mon–Sat: lunch 12:30–3 P.M., dinner 7–11 P.M.

CLOSED
Sun; Aug

No one ever comes to pick and nibble at Mario's, a typical Tuscan-style trattoria with whitewashed walls, raffia-covered chairs, bottles of Chianti on the tables, and service that ranges from friendly and attentive to rather slow . . . but with a trusty Chianti at hand, who cares? For more than forty years it has been run by the

Mariani family, and it's a popular eating destination for both Romans and visitors. I think it is fine for lunch but best for dinner, when there is a crowded, happy atmosphere. Because of the crunch during this prime time, always arrive with a dinner reservation.

This is definitely the place to sample classic Tuscan fare, including *ribollita,* a heavy bread-thickened soup, and the famous *bistecca alla fiorentina,* a big steak rubbed with olive oil and herbs and grilled until just pink. Other dishes to consider are the braised beef with polenta, any of the daily specials, and, when in season, the wild boar and pheasant. Your wine, of course, should be a bottle of the house Chianti Classico. For dessert, I recommend zeroing in on the tiramisù, a liqueur-soaked layering of cake, marsala wine, espresso, and creamy mascarpone cheese.

RESERVATIONS
Strongly advised

CREDIT CARDS
AE, DC, MC, V

À LA CARTE
25.82–30€

MENÙ TURISTICO
None

COVER & SERVICE CHARGES
Cover 1.55€, service included

ENGLISH
Yes, and menu in English

PASTICCERIA D'ANGELO (19)
Via della Croce, 30

For power snacking or lunching, the Pasticceria d'Angelo in the heart of Rome's premier shopping district is a *must.* It is open from 7:30 A.M. until 9 P.M., with continuous service from the bar and pastry counter and lunch service from 12:30 P.M. until 3 P.M. It's a good place to start the day with a quick cappuccino and warm roll or other tantalizing sugary pastry made in their kitchen. Later on, between shopping sprints, you can order lunch from the cafeteria line, where the daily offerings include assorted antipasti, salads, soups, pastas, and meats. The nice thing about eating here is that you can have just a bowl of soup or indulge in a four-course blowout if you are stoking up for heavy-duty afternoon shopping. Freshly made sandwiches are also available, but these must be eaten standing at one of the bar tables in front. If you are on the run, ask to have your order wrapped to go: *da portare via.*

TELEPHONE
06 678 2556, 06 678 3924

OPEN
Daily: bar 7:30 A.M.–9 P.M.; lunch 12:30–3 P.M.

CLOSED
Never

RESERVATIONS
Not necessary

CREDIT CARDS
AE, DC, MC, V

À LA CARTE
5.16–10.33€, pastries from 1.03€, sandwiches from 1.81€

MENÙ TURISTICO
None

COVER & SERVICE CHARGES
None

ENGLISH
Limited

PIZZERIA AL LEONCINO (28)
Via del Leoncino, 28

Look for pizza, pizza, and more pizza at Al Leoncino, a knotty-pine pizzeria with formica tabletops and hooks around the walls to hold winter coats. The service is fast, the pizzas inexpensive, the ambience as informal as it gets, and the place popular. What more can any Great

TELEPHONE
06 687 6306

OPEN
Mon–Tues, Thur–Fri: lunch 1–2:30 P.M., dinner 7 P.M.– midnight; Sat–Sun: dinner 7 P.M.–midnight

CLOSED
Wed, Sat–Sun for lunch; Aug

RESERVATIONS
Not necessary

CREDIT CARDS
None

À LA CARTE
Pizzas from 5.16–8.26€

MENÙ TURISTICO
None

COVER & SERVICE CHARGES
None

ENGLISH
No, but menu in English

Eater ask? The hardworking pizza chefs cook crisp-crust creations in the wood-fired oven in full view of the diners. Romans know their pizza, so when it is good and cheap, expect to wait, especially here, as few other pizzerias in the area are open for lunch. The drinkable house wine sells for around 4.13€ a half-liter.

RE DEGLI AMICI (21)
Via della Croce, 33B

TELEPHONE
06 679 5380, 06 678 2555

OPEN
Daily: lunch 12:30–2:30 P.M.,
dinner 7:30–10:30 P.M.

CLOSED
Never

RESERVATIONS
Advised for dinner

CREDIT CARDS
AE, DC, MC, V

À LA CARTE
28.41€, pizza from 7.75€

MENÙ TURISTICO
None

COVER & SERVICE CHARGES
Cover 1.55€, service included

ENGLISH
Yes

This five-room restaurant, run by friendly Luigi for twenty-seven years, is a Roman institution with orange-and-white tablecloths, murals on the ceiling, local artists' works lining the walls, and brash waiters racing about madly. The classic trattoria cooking offers multiple-choice self-service antipasti, a full complement of pastas, succulent grilled meats, and wood-fired pizzas (for both lunch and dinner) to hungry audiences. Re Degli Amici also upholds the long-standing Roman tradition of serving a particular dish on certain days of the week. On Tuesday and Friday fresh fish are the specials. On Thursday, you can count on gnocchi; Saturday is tripe. Sometimes these dishes and other daily specials are not on the menu, so be sure and ask about them. Lasagna is baked daily. A big bonus for many Great Eaters is that you can select your entire meal from the beautiful antipasti buffet, or order only a first or second plate, along with maybe a salad to start or a dessert to finish, and not suffer from a grumpy waiter who expects you to order the works.

RISTORANTE NINO ($, 23)
Via Borgognona, 11

TELEPHONE
06 678 6752

OPEN
Mon–Sat: lunch 12:30–3 P.M.,
dinner 7:30–11 P.M.

CLOSED
Sun; Aug (dates vary)

RESERVATIONS
Essential

CREDIT CARDS
AE, DC, MC, V

Despite its prime location in boutique central, Nino is a fashion-resistant restaurant that has not changed its interior, staff, or traditional Roman cooking . . . nor, by the looks of things, has any intention of ever doing so. You can easily recognize the owner, dressed in a coat and tie and sitting by the cash register, often reading a newspaper, but always keeping an eagle eye on the hourly take. Patrons are seated at white draped tables in a dark wood-paneled room with wrought-iron coat hooks along the walls. If possible, consult the Italian menu, because the one in English leaves out the daily specials, and these are definitely the dishes to order. Here you will find such dishes as risotto loaded with shellfish, fettuccini with truffles or fresh artichokes, *orecchiette* with a light, buttery broccoli sauce, roast chicken with potatoes, wild hare, wild boar, liver with polenta, grilled scampi, and stewed cod with tomatoes and sliced potatoes. The house dessert is *castagnaccio,* a cake made with chestnut flour, pine nuts, almonds, raisins, and candied fruits. The final tally? The service is professional and correct, the food consistently well-prepared, and the bill fair . . . all vital ingredients for a Great Eat in Rome.

À LA CARTE
28.41–33.57€

MENÙ TURISTICO
None

COVER & SERVICE CHARGES
Cover 1.55€, service discretionary

ENGLISH
Yes

SETTIMIO ALL'ARANCIO (26)
Via dell' Arancio, 50

Settimio all'Arancio is part of a trio of trattorias run by the Cialfi family. The other two are Arancio d'Oro (see page 113) and Piccolo Arancio (see page 154). The mood here is exactly right for a neighborhood dining establishment, with wholesome, well-prepared food served in two small whitewashed dining rooms with green-and-white table linens. In summer the dining moves to one of the tables on the street, shielded from traffic by a wall of planter boxes filled with trees and shrubs.

Go for the *misto fritto* of fried zucchini, olives, and artichokes for your appetizer, the *fusilli alla melanzana* (fusilli with eggplant) or *farfalle ai fiori di zucca* (butterfly pasta with zucchini flowers) for your pasta dish, and the grilled fish. Popular desserts include the lemon mousse or tiramisù. The menus at all three places are virtually the same, and the number of interesting wines impressive.

TELEPHONE
06 687 6119

OPEN
Mon–Sat: lunch 12:30–3 P.M., dinner 7–11:30 P.M.

CLOSED
Sun; NAC

RESERVATIONS
Advised

CREDIT CARDS
AE, DC, MC, V

À LA CARTE
23.22–25.82€

MENÙ TURISTICO
None

COVER & SERVICE CHARGES
Cover 1.03€, service included

ENGLISH
Yes, and menu in English

TRATTORIA OTELLO ALLA CONCORDIA (18)
Via della Croce, 81

The off-street Otello alla Concordia includes a vine-covered garden with a dramatic vegetable display. The family-run restaurant has long been a favorite because of its reliable, good-value food. The wide-ranging menu embodies Roman cuisine nicely and includes a series of handwritten seasonal and daily specials. Unfortunately, the person writing the specials on the daily menu flunked penmanship, but you should be able to decipher most of it. In early spring, start with prosciutto and fresh melon or a linguine tossed with shrimp and arugula. The daily

TELEPHONE
06 689 1178

OPEN
Mon–Sat: lunch 12:30–3 P.M., dinner 7:30–11 P.M.

CLOSED
Sun; 2 weeks in Jan or Feb (dates vary)

RESERVATIONS
Recommended

CREDIT CARDS
AE, DC, MC, V

À LA CARTE
23.24–30.99€

MENÙ TURISTICO
20.66€, 2 courses, potato or
salad, fruit or cheese, wine or
water

COVER & SERVICE CHARGES
Cover 1.55€, service included

ENGLISH
Enough, and menu in English

main courses include tripe, roast pork, veal, lamb, and sausage all fixed almost any way you want. Fresh fish is served on Tuesday, Wednesday, Friday, and Saturday, and wines from Castelli Romani and Tuscany are poured with your meal.

NOTE: There is a nonsmoking section.

VINI E BUFFET (31)
Piazza della Toretta, 60

TELEPHONE
06 687 1445

OPEN
Mon–Sat: lunch 12:30–3 P.M.,
dinner 7:30–11 P.M.

CLOSED
Sun; 4–5 days around Aug 15

RESERVATIONS
Dinner only

CREDIT CARDS
None

À LA CARTE
10.33–12.91€

MENÙ TURISTICO
None

COVER & SERVICE CHARGES
Cover 1.55€, service included

ENGLISH
Yes, and menu in English

"This is a place for people; I am here for the neighborhood," states Victorio, the hospitable owner of this trattoria, and he has indeed been here for his loyalists for better than a decade. Inside, the twelve white-tiled tables have grape-accented centers, and prints on the stark white walls carry the grape theme further. A seasonal menu changes four times a year and lists appetizers, *crostini,* main-course salads, cheeses, and cold plates. Wine is sold by the bottle, and you pay only for what you drink, or if you want to experiment with several of Victorio's regional Italian wines, you can order by the glass. This is a good watering hole to keep in mind if you are between the Spanish Steps and Piazza Navona and want to escape from the more touristy wine bars in the area.

Piazza Navona and the Pantheon

Piazza Navona is the most theatrical square of Baroque Rome. It is where the aristocracy rubbed shoulders with the populace at the games and where celebrations were held on the site of Roman Domitian's stadium. In the center is Bernini's towering Fountain of the Rivers, and on the west side, Borromini's masterpiece, the Church of S. Agnese in Agone. Now the impressive piazza serves as Rome's center stage, ringed with cafés and filled night and day with residents, tourists, and hawkers.

The Pantheon, with its majestic marble columns, original bronze doors, and domed interior, is unchanged from two thousand years ago, when it was erected by Hadrian. It is the only perfectly preserved ancient building in Rome, and a reminder of the city's glorious past.

RESTAURANTS

GELATERIAS

($) indicates a Big Splurge

Restaurants

ANTICA TAVERNA (46)
Via Monte Giordano, 12

Antica Taverna is just what you expect in a Roman trattoria: mildly uncomfortable seating, closely packed tables, a lively crowd of regulars, and a laid-back waitstaff sporting Levi's and T-shirts. Don't bother with the plasticized menu; concentrate on the two hand-scribbled specials written on white notepaper and stuck inside. The gently robust food is meant to be enjoyed, and you are expected to keep the orders rolling. Start by sharing a plate of *crostini* or a caprese salad (tomato, mozzarella, and basil) and a pasta, perhaps penne with salmon or ravioli with ricotta cheese and nuts. This leaves room for a succulent roast chicken or rabbit served with potatoes and a plate of grilled vegetables with razor-thin slices of eggplant, zucchini, peppers, and radicchio. If you can entertain dessert thoughts, think *torta della nonna* (a

TELEPHONE
06 6880 1053

OPEN
Daily: noon–midnight, continuous service

CLOSED
Never

RESERVATIONS
Essential for dinner

CREDIT CARDS
V

À LA CARTE
23.24–28.41€

MENÙ TURISTICO
None

COVER & SERVICE CHARGES
None

light, cream cake), or walk over to Piazza Navona and indulge in a *tartufo* at I Tre Scalini (see page 124).

DA FRANCESCO (47)
Piazza del Fico, 29 (corner of Via della Fossa and Via del Corallo)

TELEPHONE
06 686 4009

OPEN
Mon–Tues, Thur–Sun:
lunch noon–3 P.M.,
dinner 7 P.M.–1 A.M.; Wed:
dinner 7 P.M.–1 A.M.

CLOSED
Wed lunch; NAC

RESERVATIONS
Preferred for dinner

CREDIT CARDS
None

À LA CARTE
18.08–20.66€, pizza 6.20–
9.30€

MENÙ TURISTICO
None

COVER & SERVICE CHARGES
Cover 1.03€, service included

ENGLISH
Limited

"What are they giving away?" my friend asked as we strolled by this local favorite across the narrow street from a heavy-duty biker bar. At lunchtime it boasted wall-to-wall people inside and almost as many milling outside waiting to get in. The chef, who is also the owner, prepares huge portions of food at fair prices in a lively atmosphere—proving that the public will support a good thing. His food packs a punch, starting with fettuccine covered in a mushroom cream sauce, *penne all'arrabbiata*, or *tonnarelli* with artichokes. Meatballs in tangy tomato sauce, pork stewed in white wine, or ham and beans will keep you going for hours. At night, everyone is back for the self-service antipasti table and the pizza, bursting with tomatoes, mozzarella, and the usual toppings. It is all very informal, with paper table covers and wine poured into drinking glasses by prompt, if inelegant, waiters. Note that pizza is served for dinner only.

ENOTECA IL GOCCETTO (51)
Via dei Banchi Vecchi, 14

TELEPHONE
06 686 4268

OPEN
Mon–Sat: lunch 11 A.M.–2 P.M.,
dinner 5:30–11 P.M.

CLOSED
Sun; 3 weeks in Aug (dates vary)

RESERVATIONS
Not accepted

CREDIT CARDS
MC, V

À LA CARTE
7.75–12.91€, wines from
2.58€ per glass

MENÙ TURISTICO
None

COVER & SERVICE CHARGES
Included

ENGLISH
Yes

The original, hand-painted ceiling dates from the sixteenth century when this was a medieval bishop's home. Today it is a friendly *enoteca* serving international wines by the glass, accompanied by plates of cheeses and meat, marinated mushrooms, and other appropriate nibbles. It is a good place to come several times, schmooze at the bar with the regulars, and before you know it, feel like one yourself.

FIAMMETTA (44)
Piazza Fiammetta, 10 (off Via Zanardelli)

The pizza chef in his white undershirt has the ovens stoked and ready to go before every mealtime; during dinner, there is not an empty seat by 9:30 P.M. at this all-purpose pick near Piazza Navona, run since 1960 by members of the Christiani family. The rustic rooms have "Old West–style" chandeliers with wine carafes as lampshades. There is a wall mural of the Ponte Vecchio in Florence, a collection of hanging pots, and the mandatory table displaying antipasti and desserts. When you order, look for the daily specials attached to the corner of the menu. Skip the boring salads and focus on one of the pizzas or a grilled meat or fish accompanied by a seasonal vegetable. For dessert, I would suggest the *cantuccini con vin santo* (a glass of sweet wine with *biscotti* to dip into it), or in the winter and early spring, the *castagnaccio,* a chestnut flour cake.

TELEPHONE
06 687 5777

OPEN
Mon, Thur–Sun: lunch 12:45–3 P.M., dinner 7–11:15 P.M.; Wed: dinner 7–11:15 P.M.

CLOSED
Tues; Wed lunch; July 15–Aug 1 (dates can vary)

RESERVATIONS
Advised for dinner

CREDIT CARDS
AE, DC

À LA CARTE
20.66–23.24€, pizza 6.20–8.78€

MENÙ TURISTICO
None

COVER & SERVICE CHARGES
Bread 1.03€, service included

ENGLISH
Limited

FRATERNA DOMUS (38)
Via dell' Cancello, 9 (at Via di Monte Brianzo, 62; close to Piazza Nicosia)

For an inspiring Great Eat in Rome, consider communal dining, family style, at Fraterna Domus, a Holy Hotel run by nuns. In addition to providing very nice Great Sleep accommodations (see *Great Sleeps Italy*), the exceptionally friendly and welcoming nuns serve lunch and dinner to both guests and nonguests every day but Thursday. Reservations are required, since each meal has only a single seating. The smells coming from the spotless kitchen are the first signal that the simply prepared food is going to be wonderful, and you can trust me that it is. There is only one set-price menu, so make sure you ask what they are serving if you have dietary restrictions. The menu includes a pasta or soup, main course, garnish, salad, and dessert or fruit. Wine is extra. They also offer special student prices.

If you have time, attend mass in their lovely, thousand-year-old chapel. Even though the sisters received church funds to expand and improve their bed and breakfast and dining operations for the 2000 Holy Year Jubilee, no money has been forthcoming for the badly needed restoration of this magnificent chapel. The sisters told me they are praying for a miracle . . . maybe you can help.

TELEPHONE
06 688 2727

OPEN
Mon–Wed, Fri–Sun: lunch seating 1 P.M., dinner seating 7:30 P.M.

CLOSED
Thur; NAC

RESERVATIONS
Required

CREDIT CARDS
MC, V

À LA CARTE
None

MENÙ TURISTICO
12.91€, 3 courses; cover and service included, beverage extra

COVER & SERVICE CHARGES
Included

ENGLISH
Yes

IL BACARO ($, 42)
Via degli Spagnoli, 27

TELEPHONE
06 686 4110
OPEN
Mon–Fri: lunch 12:30–
2:45 P.M., dinner, two seatings
at 8 and 10 P.M.; Sat dinner,
two seatings at 8 and 10 P.M.
CLOSED
Sat lunch, Sun; Aug, a few days
at Christmas, last half of Jan–
first week in Feb
RESERVATIONS
Required
CREDIT CARDS
AE, DC, MC, V
À LA CARTE
30.99–36.15€
MENÙ TURISTICO
Menù degustazione, 28.41€ and
36.15€, 4 courses, beverage
extra
COVER & SERVICE CHARGES
Included
ENGLISH
Limited, but menu in English

I am always happy to stumble upon places like Il Bacaro. Hidden on a back street, just far enough from tourist central to keep it locally based, it caters to a well-dressed, sophisticated clientele who know and appreciate good food. It is open for lunch and dinner, with two reservation-only seatings for dinner at either 8 or 10 P.M. Inside is a small, understated room with a bar in one corner and rather loud music playing over it all, while outside is an umbrella-shaded terrace.

No matter what time of the year you are here, or where you sit, you can depend on an imaginative meal, well-executed and politely served. There are two tasting menus that offer daily and seasonal dishes, but no choices or beverages. They are interesting only if you want a large meal and are satisfied with the chef's choices. I recommend staying with the more varied à la carte menu. Start with the house salad, which is a pretty array of thin slices of zucchini and fresh Parmesan on a bed of fancy greens, garnished with finely chopped carrots and fennel and dressed with a light vinaigrette. The pastas are all made here and presented in different combinations. I thought the *rigatoncini* with Stilton cheese and brussel sprouts was an odd mix that worked well, and that the fusilli with pumpkin, broccoli, and fresh Parmesan was a creamy delight. The meat and fish dishes are prepared with simple respect and without sauces to mask the real flavor of the food. Try the *carpaccio alto di manzo,* tender beef slices cooked on one side and served with chicory and white truffle oil. Also delicious are the veal medallions cooked with apples and flavored with Calvados. The fish is as innovatively conceived as the rest of the menu. If you like salmon, try their smoked Canadian salmon with a spicy salsa.

And don't forget dessert! The winner here is the warm pear tart, dusted with powdered sugar and drizzled with hot dark chocolate sauce. The house wine is realistically priced by the bottle, or you can order other vintages by the glass.

I TRE SCALINI (49)
Piazza Navona, 28/32

TELEPHONE
06 6880 1996
OPEN
Mon–Tues, Thur–Sun: 9 A.M.–
midnight

For a *tartufo* to die for, I Tre Scalini is *the* place. It is big and barnlike, with a long bar, a dreary tearoom upstairs, and lots of tables on the Piazza Navona. For the uninitiated, *tartufo* is chocolate ice cream and cherries covered with a bittersweet chocolate casing and swathed in whipped cream. Smart Great Eaters will order theirs standing at the bar, or nab a bench seat on the piazza and people-watch while eating, since it will cost double to have it served at a table. If you do sit outside, tell whoever seats you that you are just having a *tartufo,* or you could be seated in the dining section, where ordering just dessert would not be acceptable. Indeed, full lunches and dinners are served, but they are basically high-priced tourist fare that I cannot recommend.

A word of warning: Don't be fooled by imitations and mistakenly go to Al Tre Tartufi next door.

CLOSED
Wed; Jan 8–Feb 20 (dates vary)

RESERVATIONS
Not necessary

CREDIT CARDS
None

À LA CARTE
Tartufo at the bar 3.87€, at a table 6.46€

MENÙ TURISTICO
Not recommended

COVER & SERVICE CHARGES
None for *tartufo* ordered at the bar or to go

ENGLISH
Limited

LA CAMPANA ($, 39)
Vicolo della Campana, 18

It is nice occasionally to have starched linen tablecloths with proper table settings and polite service by an accomplished Italian waitstaff in rooms filled with up-market diners. You will find this, along with excellent-value-for-money food, at La Campana, one of Rome's oldest restaurants.

The servings are big and the food robust, so I suggest following the lead of the regulars and ordering as you go along. When ordering, pay attention to the paper menu with its daily and seasonal specials, not the plasticized one. Start with either the house red or white to sip with the *antipasti misti,* which is big enough to share. Next, try the spicy *spaghetti alla puttanesca* or the fettuccine with butter and mushrooms if you plan on ordering a second meat or fish course. Otherwise, the *pappardelle con salsa lepre* (wide noodles with hare sauce) or the Thursday special of gnocchi are heavy-duty enough to require only a salad or vegetable accompaniment.

The important thing is to save room for dessert. La Campana also wants to make sure you do not miss this course, and they display most of their seductive offerings on tables by the entrance, resulting in oohs and aahs of anticipation. Their version of *tarte Tatin* has a spongy base covered with glazed apples. It is not too sweet and is laced with just enough cream to give it an interesting edge. If that does not speak to you, surely one of the cakes, tarts, puddings, abundant fruit creations, or a simple dish of gelato topped with wild strawberries will.

TELEPHONE
06 686 7820, 06 687 5273

OPEN
Tues–Sun: lunch 12:30–3 P.M., dinner 7:30–11 P.M.

CLOSED
Mon; last 2 weeks in Aug

RESERVATIONS
Advised

CREDIT CARDS
AE, DC, MC, V

À LA CARTE
28.41–33.57€

MENÙ TURISTICO
None

COVER & SERVICE CHARGES
Cover 1.55€, service included

ENGLISH
Limited

LA SCALETTA DEGLI ARTISTI (48)
Via di Santa Maria dell'Anima, 56

TELEPHONE
06 6880 1872

OPEN
Mon–Tues, Thur–Sun: lunch
noon–3:30 P.M., dinner
7–11:30 P.M.

CLOSED
Wed; NAC

RESERVATIONS
Advised for dinner

CREDIT CARDS
AE, MC, V

À LA CARTE
25.28–28.41€

MENÙ TURISTICO
None

COVER & SERVICE CHARGES
Cover 1.03€, service included

ENGLISH
Limited, but menu in English

Around the corner from the tourist glare surrounding Piazza Navona is La Scaletta degli Artisti, a pretty trattoria where the food is gently robust and surprisingly well priced. In typical trattoria style, the rather small inside is decorated with a mix of Roman photos, tromp l'oeil paintings, and a mural or two. On warm days, the prime tables are those under big umbrellas on the sidewalk terrace. As always, try to order from the daily specials found taped to the menu. Otherwise, traditional starters of prosciutto and melon or dried beef with arugula lead the way to a choice of sixteen pastas, including gnocchi and lasagne. Skip the tripe and order the homemade meatballs in a tomato and basil cream sauce along with fresh artichokes or roast potatoes for a filling main course. Desserts are limited in number but not in quality. The tiramisù, creme caramel, and *panna cotta* are all made here and worthwhile endings to a filling, Great Eat in Rome.

LILLI (41)
Via Tor di Nona, 23

TELEPHONE
06 686 1916

OPEN
Mon–Sat: lunch 1–2:45 P.M.,
dinner 8–11 P.M.

CLOSED
Sun; Dec 20–Jan 1, one week
mid-Aug (dates vary)

RESERVATIONS
Not accepted

CREDIT CARDS
AE, MC, V

À LA CARTE
20.66€

MENÙ TURISTICO
None

COVER & SERVICE CHARGES
Cover 1.03€, no service
charged

ENGLISH
Yes

The Ceramicola family runs this Great Eat pick nestled alongside the river not too far from Piazza Navona. This small, modest restaurant caters to locals as well as tourists, and in warm weather, everyone wants a seat on their pleasant, umbrella-shaded terrace. The stone-tiled, beamed interior has well-spaced tables draped in brown cloths with white overlays. The homespun food is delicious, there is always more than enough on your plate, and the bottom line is reasonable—all of which make it a compelling Great Eat. Depending on the time of year, the daily menu features pasta laced with clams, *penne all'arrabbiata* (short, thick pasta with a hot red sauce), several meat dishes, and the usual salads and veggies. Anytime, you can count on their signature pasta, *rigatoni alla Lilli,* made with tomatoes, Parmesan cheese, black pepper, basil, and butter . . . oh, so rich and good. For dessert, why have an orange or an apple when you can dig into their own *torta al cioccolato* (chocolate cake) or *crostata di ricotta,* their version of cheesecake.

L'INSALATA RICCA (54)
Piazza Pasquino, 72

For a description of this restaurant, see page 99. All other information is the same.

TELEPHONE: 06 6830 7881

L'ORSO '80 ($, 40)
Via dell' Orso, 33

The same is true every year—all I want for Christmas besides world peace and a week at my favorite spa is another great meal at this wonderful trattoria in the heart of old Rome. The restaurant has been owned for years by brothers Alfredo and Memmo and their long-time friend Antonio, the talented chef. They prepare truly memorable food that is guaranteed to ignite even the most jaded palate, and they serve it with gusto. Aside from the pizza (which is served only for dinner), the prices tend to be high, so you may want to reserve this dining experience for a Big Splurge.

The restaurant is justly famous for its fabulous antipasti table, and I agree—it is one of the best I have sampled in Italy. You name it and it is here, from seasonal vegetables prepared six different ways to dozens of bowls of fish and shellfish. If you are not careful, you could make this your entire meal. But save room, please, for one of the homemade pastas, such as the *papparadelle al salmone,* wide buttery noodles smothered in a creamy salmon sauce, or the spaghetti with fresh clams. Grilled meats are another specialty, as is the impressive lineup of fresh fish. In the evenings, the wood-fired pizza oven is roaring, turning out a limited but delicious selection of crisp-crusted pizzas. After a meal such as this one, dessert hardly seems possible, but I do recommend a bowl of sweet strawberries as the perfect finish.

TELEPHONE
06 686 4904, 06 686 1710

OPEN
Tues–Sun: lunch 1–3:30 P.M., dinner 7:30–11:30 P.M.

CLOSED
Mon; Aug

RESERVATIONS
Essential, especially for dinner

CREDIT CARDS
AE, DC, MC, V

À LA CARTE
Pizza from 5.16€, full meals from 30.99–33.57€

MENÙ TURISTICO
None

COVER & SERVICE CHARGES
Included

ENGLISH
Yes

PALLADINI (53)
Via del Governo Vecchio, 29

There is no sign outside, no seating inside, positively no charm, and definitely no English spoken in this spartan deli, which is a great place for those whose cash supplies are in danger of running out . . . or for anyone who appreciates a really great sandwich. That's all they make, and all they need to make: freshly baked chunks of *pizza bianca* (pizza bread) are brushed with olive oil and stuffed with fillings of your choice by cute girls wearing white caps. But don't take my word for it—the six-deep crowd at lunchtime tells you these are sensational sandwiches,

TELEPHONE
06 686 1237

OPEN
Mon–Sat: 7 A.M.–7 P.M. (Thur till 3 P.M.), continuous service

CLOSED
Thur afternoon, Sun; Aug

RESERVATIONS
Not accepted

CREDIT CARDS
None

À LA CARTE
Sandwiches from 2.32€

MENÙ TURISTICO
None

COVER & SERVICE CHARGES
None

ENGLISH
Very limited

especially the *bresaola e rughetta,* smoked meat and arugula sprinkled with Parmesan and lemon juice. You can either have your creation wrapped to go or join the lunch bunch, grab the offered paper towel in lieu of a napkin, and eat standing against the back wall.

PIZZERIA DA BAFFETTO (50)
Via del Governo Vecchio, 114

TELEPHONE
06 686 1617

OPEN
Daily: dinner 6:30 P.M.–1 A.M.

CLOSED
2 weeks in Aug (dates vary)

RESERVATIONS
Not necessary

CREDIT CARDS
None

À LA CARTE
6.20–10.33€

MENÙ TURISTICO
None

COVER & SERVICE CHARGES
Included

ENGLISH
Limited

In Rome, Pizzeria da Baffetto is synonymous with good pizza, and the line that forms nightly at the front door of this matchbook-size spot attests to this. Seats are hard, long stays are discouraged, and you can expect to share your table. The tiny room isn't much to look at either: it is dominated by a pizza oven, a menu board on one wall, and a small cash desk. Besides the sizzling pizzas, the only other things on the menu are *bruschette,* the traditional preparation of grilled bread covered with garlic, basil, and ripe red tomatoes, and *crostini,* toasted bread with mozzarella cheese and a variety of simple toppings.

PIZZERIA LA MONTECARLO (55)
Vicolo Savelli, 12

TELEPHONE
06 686 1877, 06 687 2200

OPEN
Daily: lunch noon–3 P.M.,
dinner 7 P.M.–midnight

CLOSED
Mon for dinner in the winter,
Aug 1–15

RESERVATIONS
Not accepted

CREDIT CARDS
None

À LA CARTE
4.13–10.33€

MENÙ TURISTICO
None

COVER & SERVICE CHARGES
None

ENGLISH
Yes

It's a continuous scrimmage to snag a seat at this pizzeria near Piazza Navona. Unless you arrive when the doors open, be prepared to stand in line until a spot opens. Is it worth the wait? I think so, and obviously so does the huge contingent of locals who mix and mingle until they can order the *tonnarelli anna* (topped with mushrooms, zucchini flowers, and sweet peppers) or the works, otherwise known as the *montecarlo,* laden with artichokes, sausages, egg, pepperoni, onions, and olives. Aside from pizzas, you will find a few salads, a handful of pastas, and *bruschette.*

TRATTORIA DA GINO E PIETRO (52)
Corner of Via del Governo Vecchio, 108, and Vicolo Savelli, 3

Your fellow diners will be a mix of visitors and neighborhood regulars at this venerable trattoria, where the service is welcoming and the food consistently dependable. Good luck on wedging your way in for Sunday lunch if you have not called ahead for your table. At other times, play it safe, make a reservation, and get ready for a meal that eschews anything remotely trendy, but always epitomizes quality. The eye-popping vegetable antipasti display is a good place to begin your meal planning. Add a pasta, *scamorza al prosciutto* (cheese melted over thin slices of prosciutto), or whatever fresh fish is being served, plus *tiramisù della casa,* and you will have had a fairly priced Great Eat, Roman style.

TELEPHONE
06 686 1576

OPEN
Mon–Wed, Fri–Sun: lunch noon–3 P.M., dinner 6:30–11 P.M.

CLOSED
Thur; Aug 1–15

RESERVATIONS
Advised, especially for Sun lunch

CREDIT CARDS
MC, V

À LA CARTE
20.66–25.82€

MENÙ TURISTICO
None

COVER & SERVICE CHARGES
Cover 0.77€, service discretionary

ENGLISH
Yes

TRE ARCHI DA LORETO (45)
Via dei Coronari, 233

Tre Archi is the sort of folksy place people frequent when no one is in the mood to cook, and as such it provides a glimpse into the life of the average Roman citizen. The clientele ranges from families with noisy children to gray-haired couples who have staked out regular tables. The inside is neat and utilitarian, with orange tablecloths, a few green plants, and a mural on one wall. The sole waiter is a study in efficiency and grace under pressure. The food is simple, standard fare: minestrone soup, pastas with the familiar *ragù,* daily specials, above-average salads, and desserts in the never-mind column. The *menù turistico* is filling and fattening, the house wine is perfectly adequate, and prices are firmly in the pennywise category.

TELEPHONE
06 686 5890

OPEN
Mon–Sat: lunch 12:15–3 P.M., dinner 7 P.M.–midnight

CLOSED
Sun; Aug

RESERVATIONS
Advised for dinner

CREDIT CARDS
AE, MC, V

À LA CARTE
15.49–18.08€

MENÙ TURISTICO
12.91€, 3 courses; beverage, cover, and service included

COVER & SERVICE CHARGES
Cover 0.52€, service included

ENGLISH
Limited

Gelaterias

CREMERIA MONEFORTE (56)
Via Della Rotunda, 22

TELEPHONE
06 686 7720
OPEN
Tues–Sun: 10 A.M.–10 P.M.,
sometimes later
CLOSED
Mon; NAC
CREDIT CARDS
None
PRICES
From 2.07€
ENGLISH
Enough

No matter what the weather, everyone in Rome eats ice cream, and plenty of it. I would too if I lived in the same city as Cremeria Monteforte, which dispenses its delicious, natural flavors every day but Monday from a storefront by the Pantheon. It is owned by Pina, who has been making ice cream for thirty years and scooping in this location for the last two decades. If you can't decide between chocolate or walnut *semifreddo,* white chocolate, caramel, or pistachio ice cream, or melon *sorbetto,* you can order a "tasting cone" with little bites of several flavors to see which one you like best. If you really want to gild the lily, ask to have your cone or cup topped with a scoop of real whipped cream, or dipped in dark chocolate.

GIOLITTI (43)
Via Uffici del Vicario, 40

TELEPHONE
06 699 1243
OPEN
Daily: *gelateria* 7 A.M.–2 A.M.;
Mon–Fri: lunch noon–2 P.M.
CLOSED
Sat–Sun lunch; NAC
CREDIT CARDS
AE, DC, MC, V
PRICES
Ice cream from 1.81–7.75€;
lunch: sandwiches from 1.55€,
hot and cold dishes from
7.75–10.33€
ENGLISH
Yes

Giolitti is an always-crowded Art Nouveau *gelateria* near the Pantheon where generations of the same family have been selling gelato since 1900. It is admittedly not an easy address to find: the best strategy, once you are within a two-block radius, is to look for people eating ice cream and just head in the direction from which they are coming, and you will soon be there. In the early morning, fifteen flavors of ice cream are available, along with cappuccino and a counter full of waist-expanding pastries. On Tuesday through Saturday, light lunches of salads, omelettes, and a few hot dishes are served. Standing at the bar you can order a quick sandwich or more pastries. By 2:30 in the afternoon, there is a three-deep crowd ordering cones or dishes from more than fifty-seven revolving varieties of pure gelato. First you pay for the size you want, then you take your order to the counter. There is no real place to sit while eating your ice cream, but it is fun to join the throng standing outside and indulging in the premier people-watching this place always affords.

Piazza Venezia

The majestic Via dei Fori Imperiali links Piazza Venezia to the Colosseum in a six-way traffic circle that is a spectacle of insane Roman driving. The commanding white Vittoriale was built to honor the first king of united Italy, and it now houses a permanent museum of tapestries, medieval sculpture, silver, and ceramic works. In the front is an equestrian statue of Vittorio Emanuele, whose moustache is three meters long. This is also the home of the eternal flame, Italy's memorial to the unknown soldier.

RESTAURANTS

Restaurants

BIRRERIA PERONI (57)
Via di San Marcello, 19

There is no spa cuisine at Birreria Peroni—only hearty, stick-to-your-ribs plates of sausage and beans, beef, pork, and veal that appeal to strong-hearted souls who have put in a hard day's work. Pasta is relegated to a bit player in this cast. With the unbeatable combination of enormous portions and reliable prices, all washed down with tall mugs of beer or prosecco wine, it is no wonder that this restaurant has such a following. Unless you arrive early, or go late and run the risk of your favorite dish being sold out, you can expect to stand and wait for a table during the crowded lunch hour. The service is hectic at best, with waiters shouting orders to a harried cashier who somehow keeps it all straight while ringing up everyone's order. Things calm down somewhat at night, but you can still count on sitting mighty close to your neighbor or sharing a table in one of Rome's oldest restaurants.

TELEPHONE
06 679 5310

OPEN
Mon–Sat: noon–midnight (Fri–Sat till 1:30 A.M.); lunch noon–3:30 P.M., dinner 7 P.M.–midnight; cold food 4–6:30 P.M.

CLOSED
Sun, 2 weeks in mid-Aug (dates vary)

RESERVATIONS
Accepted for dinner only

CREDIT CARDS
AE, DC, MC, V

À LA CARTE
15.49€

MENÙ TURISTICO
None

COVER & SERVICE CHARGES
None

ENGLISH
Yes, and menu in English

ENOTECA CORSI (59)
Via del Gesù, 87–88 (off Via del Plebescito)

TELEPHONE & FAX
06 679 0821
OPEN
Mon–Fri: lunch noon–3:30 P.M.
CLOSED
Sat–Sun; Aug
RESERVATIONS
Advised
CREDIT CARDS
AE, DC, MC, V
À LA CARTE
15.49€
MENÙ TURISTICO
None
COVER & SERVICE CHARGES
Cover 1.03€, service
discretionary
ENGLISH
Yes

Enoteca Corsi is a good roll-up-your-sleeves *enoteca* where patrons have been eating and drinking since 1937. It is packed for lunch, which means if you want a seat, you may have to share a table. The waiter tells you what the specials are, but in addition, a daily chalkboard menu is posted inside the front door. The choices are limited and very traditional. Three starters always include a pasta and a soup; mains feature meaty dishes of roast pork or veal with potatoes, zucchini flowers stuffed with meat or cheese, and *saltimbocca*. Add a salad or fresh vegetable, a few glasses of the house wine, and you will round out this satisfying good-value meal. Everyone orders the *limoncello* (lemon liqueur) or *cantucci con vin santo* for a light ending.

L'ARCHETTO (58)
Via dell' Archetto, 26

TELEPHONE
06 6789 064
OPEN
Daily: lunch noon–3 P.M.,
dinner 7 P.M.–midnight
(Fri–Sat till 1 A.M.)
CLOSED
Never
RESERVATIONS
Advised for dinner
CREDIT CARDS
AE, DC, MC, V
À LA CARTE
15.49–18.08€
MENÙ TURISTICO
None
COVER & SERVICE CHARGES
No cover charge, 15% service
added
ENGLISH
Yes, and menu in English

An impressive selection of pastas served in mammoth portions, along with a full complement of pizzas, *crostini, bruschette,* and meat dishes, make L'Archetto one of the restaurants most frequented by Great Eaters when they are between Piazza Venezia and the Trevi Fountain.

By all means, try not to be seated upstairs, a small area that's a jumble of posters, fringed lamp shades, garlic braids, dried peppers, and a display of aging postcards sent by customers. There is just too much going on here, with waiters zipping around as if they were in training for the next Olympics and diners wandering by en route to better seating downstairs (the best tables are in the second room of the basement).

The *only* things to consider ordering are the pastas and pizzas; for antipasti, stick to *bruschette* or *crostini.* Pasta aficionados will have a delicious meal with any of the sixty-seven varieties. There is everything from a simple rendition of garlic, olive oil, and parsley to fresh seafood (Tuesday and Friday only) and the "Chanel," topped with tomato, garlic, lobster, brandy, cream, and pepper. Pizza eaters have twenty-five choices. If you can make it to dessert, the temptations include homemade cakes, *torte,* gelato, tiramisù, or *panna cotta.*

San Lorenzo

San Lorenzo is in the center of the sprawling University of Rome; it is about a ten-minute bus ride east of the train station. The streets, named for ancient tribes of the Italian peninsula, are undergoing renewed vigor, and the area, once entirely blue-collar, is now considered a contemporary place to live. The restaurants here cater mostly to students, and are heavy on the pizza, but there are some notable Great Eat exceptions.

RESTAURANTS

($) indicates a Big Splurge

Restaurants

DA FRANCO AR VICOLETTO (111)
Via dei Falisci, 1A

Da Franco ar Vicoletto is destination dining if you love fresh fish. Yes, they have steak and veal offerings, but they are unremarkable. Here, stay with fish for every course from appetizer through main. Start by ordering the fish *antipasto misto*. My pick for pasta goes to the fettuccine with shrimp and artichokes or to the spaghetti with fresh mussels and clams. For the second course, order the mixed grilled seafood platter or whatever is touted on the daily special list. Most of the fish is priced by each 100 grams, so watch out or your bill will climb. The way around this is to order one of the three *menù turistico*s, all featuring fish in varying quantities, depending on the price. The desserts are mundane, so there's no need to save room for the end.

NOTE: If you arrive around noon, take a few minutes to check the local outdoor market at the corner of Via dei Falisci and Via dei Latini.

TELEPHONE
06 495 7675

OPEN
Tues–Sun: lunch 12:30–3:30 P.M., dinner 7:30–11:30 P.M.

CLOSED
Mon; last 3 weeks of Aug

RESERVATIONS
Advised

CREDIT CARDS
None

À LA CARTE
23.24–25.82€

MENÙ TURISTICO
Three menus: 18.08€, 20.66€, 23.24€, all include 3 fish courses, wine, and mineral water

COVER & SERVICE CHARGES
Cover 1.03€, service included

ENGLISH
Yes, and menu in English

PIZZERIA L'ECONOMICA (110)
Via Tiburtina, 46

TELEPHONE
06 445 6669

OPEN
Mon–Sat: dinner 6:30–
11:30 P.M.

CLOSED
Sun; Aug

RESERVATIONS
Not accepted

CREDIT CARDS
None

À LA CARTE
5.16–8.78€

MENÙ TURISTICO
None

COVER & SERVICE CHARGES
No cover charge, 10% service
added

ENGLISH
Yes

The name says it all. Pizzeria L'Economica is a bare-bones, family-run place with zero decor. Its wide-ranging claim to fame is that it serves the least expensive (and its fans claim the best variety of) pizzas in the San Lorenzo area of Rome. The giant wood-burning pizza fires are lit in the evening only from 6:30 to 11:30 P.M. If you don't want one of their super pizzas, the only other options are *crostini* or an unbeatable antipasti selection. The desserts are definitely in the ho-hum category, so pass them up for another time, another place.

POMMIDORO ($, 108)
Piazza d. Sanniti, 44

TELEPHONE
06 445 2692, 06 445 2652

OPEN
Mon–Sat: lunch 12:30–3 P.M.,
dinner 7:30 P.M.–midnight

CLOSED
Sun; Aug

RESERVATIONS
Advised

CREDIT CARDS
AE, DC, MC, V

À LA CARTE
23.24–30.99€

MENÙ TURISTICO
None

COVER & SERVICE CHARGES
Cover and service included

ENGLISH
Yes

Anna and Aldo Bravi run a remarkable trattoria in the university district of San Lorenzo. Opened by Aldo's grandmother, Clementine, as a wine shop, it was expanded into a restaurant by his father. Aldo has been on the payroll since he was seven, and now his sons and daughters and their spouses all work here. The wonderful food is the creation of his wife, Anna. The clientele is a wide sampling of locals—professors and students, intellectuals and artists, workers in overalls, ladies draped in mink, businessmen making deals—all of whom are welcomed by Aldo with the same degree of warmth and friendliness.

In the main room, with its arched brick ceilings, is a large open-fire oven and grill where seasonal game and other meats are cooked to perfection. Tables set with yellow linens are crowded into several rooms, as well as outside on a glass-enclosed raised terrace that is used year-round. The value-packed menu is astonishing in its versatility, offering the kind of quality that inspires repeat visits. Order a liter of the house wine and a plate of the thinly sliced prosciutto with figs. Don't miss Anna's own fettuccini tossed with wild mushrooms or her pappardelle with wild boar sauce. If you appreciate wild game, nowhere in Rome is it prepared with more skill. The culinary curious can try another of their specialties, offal cooked over the open fire, which they claim removes most of the fat and "gamey" taste. Otherwise, the mutton stew is a tasty alternative, as are any of the grilled chops or fresh fish selections. The desserts are all by Anna, and her repertoire is long and the items delicious. Just ask what she has made that day, and whatever you pick will be sweet and perfect.

TRAM TRAM (109)
Via dei Reti, 46

Tram Tram is named after the tram that goes by on Via dei Reti, and this popular San Lorenzo trattoria is filled with tram memorabilia. The banquettes are tram seats, and the wine racks above were once coat racks. In the bathroom the soap dispenser is a tram original, and so are the collection of old photos taken from a book on the history of trams in Rome. It is all happily presided over by the Divittorio sisters, Antonella and Fabiola, and their mother, Rosanna. They make their own organic bread, and their pastas are a leap above the mundane, especially *pappardelle tram tram*, large egg fettuccini with a lamb, peppers, and tomato sauce; the *orecchiette* with clams and cauliflower; and *cavatelli alla siciliana*—short pasta with swordfish, eggplant, and tomato sauce. It is always acceptable to order only a main course, perhaps *involtini di verza* (cabbage rolls stuffed with minced lamb), or for a more Roman experience, a tort made with anchovies, endive, tomatoes, cheese, and topped with pine nuts. Desserts are made by Mama, so you can depend on a wonderful *zabaione,* chocolate mousse, or lemon cream with fresh strawberries. One room is nonsmoking.

TELEPHONE
06 490 416

OPEN
Tues–Sun: lunch 12:30–3:30 P.M., dinner 7:30–11:30 P.M.

CLOSED
Mon; Aug 15–22

RESERVATIONS
Advised for dinner

CREDIT CARDS
AE, DC, MC, V

À LA CARTE
18.08–20.66€

MENÙ TURISTICO
None

COVER & SERVICE CHARGES
Cover 1.55€, service discretionary

ENGLISH
Limited

Testaccio

The Testaccio is not known for its designer boutiques, dainty tearooms, or matrons who lunch. This was once the slaughterhouse area of Rome, and many butcher shops are still in full swing. As you can imagine, food was, and still is, geared toward burly workers who do not worry about cholesterol or their waistline, but it well worth a meal foray, especially for those eager to add another unusual cuisine experience to their roster. In addition, the area has risen higher on the trendy nightlife index. The morning market in Piazza Testaccio is one of Rome's best, and it provides a good view of what the locals are eating at any time of year.

Restaurants

BUCATINO (86)
Via Luca della Robbia, 84/86

TELEPHONE
06 574 6886

OPEN
Tues–Sun: lunch 12:30–3 P.M., dinner 7:30–11:30 P.M.

CLOSED
Mon; end of July to Aug 20

RESERVATIONS
Advised

CREDIT CARDS
AC, DC, MC, V

À LA CARTE
18.08–20.66€, pizza 5.16–7.75€

MENÙ TURISTICO
None

COVER & SERVICE CHARGES
Cover 1.03€, service discretionary

ENGLISH
Yes, and menu in English

Bucatino is a popular tavern with three main dining areas: two upstairs and a large one downstairs. I like to sit in the big room upstairs because it is more central to the interesting action and not as claustrophobic or stuffy as the room downstairs. Avoid at all costs the closet-size anteroom to your left as you walk in the door.

For the most inexpensive meal in the evening, have a pizza or pasta with a salad and the house specialty dessert, *millefoglie*—a cream-filled puff pastry. On Fridays, the *pasta e ceci*—pasta with garbanzo beans in an onion, garlic, and tomato sauce—is a wonderful choice, and so is the gnocchi with tomato sauce served only on Thursday. At anytime you can order a heaping plate of *bucatini all'amatriciana,* spaghetti covered in a thick tomato, pecorino cheese, and bacon sauce. Main-course standbys are the *trippa alla romana, coda alla vaccinara* (oxtail stew), roast veal with potatoes, or any fresh fish. Those eager to engage in off-beat dining should be satisfied for a *long* time with the *coratella alla Veneta:* lamb's heart, lung, liver, and spleen cooked in olive oil and seasoned with lots of pepper and onion. You will need a strong red wine to get you through this one, so if you go for lunch and have this lusty meal, don't plan on an active afternoon.

CHECCHINO DAL 1887 ($, 91)
Via Monte Testaccio, 30

I urge you: *Please* do not be turned off by the location or the many unusual specialty dishes this restaurant is famous for. Checchino dal 1887 is one of Rome's most elegant and sophisticated dining choices. When it opened in 1887, it was a place to drink wine. Today, the original wine license hangs on the wall next to a picture of the great-great-grandfather and -grandmother of the Mariani family, which is still firmly in command in the hands of Ninetta Mariani and her sons, Elio and Francesco. In addition to its fine food, the restaurant is known for its diversity of wines, with more than five hundred varieties housed in a naturally temperature controlled underground *cave* that dates back to 75 B.C. You can pay up to 413.17€ for a museum-quality wine, but there are also scores of wines available for 10.33€ to15.49€, as well as monthly featured wines that are affordably priced.

The dining room is beautiful, with original marble tables now covered with linen cloths, embroidered napkins, and fresh yellow roses, the favorite flower of the owner's mother, who can usually be found sitting behind the cash register at the entrance. During warm weather, tables are placed outside on the front terrace.

The menu is not only translated into English, but each dish is explained so you will know exactly what you are eating—and here more than most places, this is *very* important. The Testaccio location means an emphasis on meats of all kinds, especially entrails, which most Americans never even consider trying. I can promise you that even though you think you would never *taste*, let alone *like*, veal kidneys, lamb's brains, oxtail stew, or pig's trotters . . . here they are raised to a gourmet level and are quite delicious. I was wary at first, but after one meal, I was impressed and eager to return. To begin, there is head cheese, macaroni with calf's intestines, rendered pig's cheeks in ewe's milk cheese, and veal foot, which is boiled, boned, and served in salad with carrots, beans, celery, and dressing. Any one of these is wonderful, I promise you. To follow, there is oxtail stew, which is cooked for five hours with tomato sauce, celery, pine nuts, raisins, and bitter chocolate; the recipe is said to have originated here in the 1890s. There is also tripe, veal intestines stewed or grilled, and the jackpot offal entrée: *arrosto misto,* which offers a sampling of roasted sweetbreads, calf's small intestines, and marrow. Tamer

TELEPHONE
06 574 6318

FAX
06 574 3816

EMAIL
checchino_roma@tin.it;
checchino@usa.net

INTERNET
www.checchino-dal-1887.com

OPEN
Tues–Sat: lunch 12:30–3 P.M., dinner 8–11 P.M.; Oct–May, also Sun lunch

CLOSED
Mon; Sun from June–Sept; Aug, 1 week at Christmas

RESERVATIONS
Required

CREDIT CARDS
AE, DC, MC, V

À LA CARTE
41.32–49.06€

MENÙ TURISTICO
None

COVER & SERVICE CHARGES
Included

ENGLISH
Yes, and menu in English

tastes will find many other safer but still satisfying choices, including *bue garofolato*—beef studded with cloves, garlic, and pancetta, then seared and braised in a light tomato sauce—and their specialty lamb dish: *abbacchio alla cacciatora,* bite-size pieces of leg and shoulder of lamb sautéed with garlic, vinegar, olive oil, anchovies, and chili. If you order this, you get a bonus: a pretty ceramic plate from the restaurant to take home as a souvenir.

To finish your meal, you can order from a long list of interesting cheeses or homemade sweets, each served with a glass of an appropriate wine. From beginning to end, the service is impeccable, the food delicious, and the time memorable. Please do yourself a favor and try it as a special Big Splurge.

NOTE: The restaurant has a no-smoking section. At night, especially, the best way to arrive is by taxi.

DA FELICE (90)
Via Mastro Giorgio, 29

TELEPHONE
06 574 6800

OPEN
Mon–Sat: lunch 12:30–2:30 P.M., dinner 8–10:30 P.M.

CLOSED
Sun; Aug

RESERVATIONS
Not accepted

CREDIT CARDS
None

À LA CARTE
18.08€

MENÙ TURISTICO
None

COVER & SERVICE CHARGES
Cover 1.03€, service included

ENGLISH
None

What a place! What a find! Don't look for a sign outside, English to be spoken, coffee to be served, credit cards to be accepted, or much charm, other than the megadose of local color provided by the other patrons. The simple room is filled with roughcast laborers, rotund men mopping their plates with chunks of bread, and perhaps a teased bleached blond in spike heels who keeps the mix interesting. The gruff, eighty-year-old owner (assisted by his pretty blond daughter, son, and grandson) keeps a *riservato* sign on all the tables, not that anyone has booked them—it is just his way of looking you over and deciding if he wants to bother with you. The daily menu is written in Italian heiroglyphics and of course always depends on the mood of the chef and what the market has to offer. The waiters also rattle off the selections in rapid-fire Italian, and you are expected to select from the first reciting, so if your Italian is rudimentary, this may not be your ideal Great Eat. There is nothing dainty about the recipes or the servings. It is all he-man fare guaranteed to put hair on your chest regardless of your gender. When you are through, you will have wined and dined for around 25.82€.

VOLPETTI PIÚ (89)
Via Alessandro Volta, 8/10

Volpetti Piú is a wonderful deli and self-service restaurant around the corner from the gourmet shop, bakery, and cheese shop of the same name (see "Food Shopping in Rome," page 168). At the restaurant, the service is swift and simple, as in most cafeterias: you look, select, pay, have your dish warmed if necessary, and then take it to your seat. The *pizza bianca* is divine, and so are the daily dishes featuring the foods and fabulous cheeses from the gourmet shop. Everything you see can be packaged to go. Smoking is not allowed.

TELEPHONE
06 574 4306

OPEN
Mon–Sat: 10 A.M.– 9:30 P.M., continuous service

CLOSED
Sun; NAC

RESERVATIONS
Not necessary

CREDIT CARDS
AE, MC, V

À LA CARTE
Most dishes sold by 100 grams; 3-course meal 9.30–12.39€, beverage extra

MENÙ TURISTICO
None

COVER & SERVICE CHARGES
None

ENGLISH
Limited, but you won't need it

Train Station Area

From a Great Eating standpoint, most of the immediate area around the train station (Termini Station) should be considered Tourist Trap Central. There are, however, always exceptions, and of course *Great Eats* has found them, though some entail a moderate walk from the train station itself. In anticipation of the multitudes arriving for the 2000 Holy Year Jubilee, the train station had a complete makeover. In addition to the usual news kiosks and greasy pizza joints, there are bars, restaurants (even two McDonalds and Dunken Donut franchises), countless mid-line clothing stores, and a twenty-four-hour supermarket. It is a virtual city unto itself.

Four blocks southwest of the railroad station on top of the Esquilino, one of the seven hills of Rome, is the Basilica of Santa Maria Maggiore, one of the major basilicas of Rome and officially part of Vatican City. The bell tower, built in 1377, is Rome's highest *campanile*. This area is home to Rome's largest immigrant population, which is concentrated around Piazza Vittorio Emanuele II, the city's largest square.

North of the train station is Villa Borghese, a magnificent Baroque park with walking and jogging trails, a children's cinema, Rome's zoo, romantic beautiful views of Rome, and three important art museums: Galleria Borghese, Galleria Nazionale d'Arte Moderna e Contemporanea, and Villa Giulia. A number of Great Eat selections are about halfway between the train station and the park.

RESTAURANTS

GELATERIAS

GOURMET FOOD AND WINE SHOPS

GROCERY STORES AND SUPERMARKETS

INDOOR/OUTDOOR MARKETS

($) indicates a Big Splurge

Restaurants

AL FAGIANETTO (106)
Via Filippo Turati, 21

Restaurants near train stations tend to be overpriced tourist traps with uninspired chefs and bored waiters. Al Fagianetto is not in this category, and it gets my vote for serving satisfying fare in this difficult area.

The comfortable dining room is hospitable and justifiably busy, especially at lunch. For both the first and second courses, there are more than twenty options, plus pizza. I like to start with the *tonnarelli alla ciociara* (pasta with mushrooms, ham, and tomatoes) or the *risotto con funghi porcini*. Popular main courses include the house specialty: *fiagiano alla casareccia,* pheasant cooked with olives and mushrooms. They also do roast lamb and veal marsala well, and serve pizza (at night only). For a light, easy-on-the-wallet evening meal, try one of these pizzas and a salad. With the exception of the ice cream, all the desserts are made here, so go ahead and indulge in one of their cakes or a seasonal fruit tart.

TELEPHONE
06 446 7306

OPEN
Tues–Sun: lunch 12:30–3:30 P.M., dinner 7–11 P.M.

CLOSED
Mon; Aug

RESERVATIONS
Advised for four or more

CREDIT CARDS
AE, DC, MC, V

À LA CARTE
15.47–23.24€, pizza (dinner only) 6.20–7.23€

MENÙ TURISTICO
None

COVER & SERVICE CHARGES
Cover 1.03€, 10% service added

ENGLISH
Limited, but menu in English

DA GIOVANNI (99)
Via Antonio Salandra, 1 (off Via XX Settembre)

Da Giovanni was founded more than forty years ago by the Vittucci family, which continues to run it today. Seating is downstairs in two pine-paneled rooms lined with coat hooks; the entrance is graced with hanging meats, and fresh flowers accent the dessert and appetizer table. Sunny yellow damask linens complete the picture.

The chef really struts his stuff when it comes to the pastas. One of his best is the *fettuccine alla Giovanni,* a combination of butter, cheese, mushrooms, tomatoes, and peas; this dish will go directly to your arteries, but what a delicious journey. Another one in the same category is their homemade *agnelotti*—egg ravioli filled with ground meat and vegetables and served with a meat sauce. The main-course plates range from *abbacchio alla cacciatora con funghi* (lamb served with a dressing of olive oil, vinegar, sage, rosemary, garlic, anchovies, and mushrooms) to grilled veal chops, roast chicken, fresh fish, and eggplant Parmesan. In addition to these regulars, there are daily pastas, main courses, and a vegetable special. For a finale, the top choices are a heady version of tiramisù or whole baked pears (in season). A very light

TELEPHONE
06 485 950

OPEN
Mon–Sat: lunch noon–3 P.M., dinner 7–10 P.M.

CLOSED
Sun; Aug

RESERVATIONS
Not necessary

CREDIT CARDS
MC, V

À LA CARTE
18.08–20.66€

MENÙ TURISTICO
15.49€, 3 courses; wine, water, cover, and service included

COVER & SERVICE CHARGES
Cover 1.03€, service included

ENGLISH
Yes

alternative is the *frutta secca*, a serving of dried fruit and nuts that goes well with an after-dinner espresso.

DAGNINO (100)
Galleria Esedra, Via Vittorio Emanuele Orlando, 75

TELEPHONE
06 481 6660

OPEN
Daily: 7 A.M.–10 P.M., hot food noon–10 P.M., continuous service

CLOSED
1 week mid-Aug

RESERVATIONS
Not accepted

CREDIT CARDS
AE, MC, V

À LA CARTE
Pastries 1.55–3.10€, ice cream 2.58–4.13€, hot food 5.16–10.33€

MENÙ TURISTICO
15.49€, 2 courses include vegetable, fruit or pastry, and coffee

COVER & SERVICE CHARGES
None

ENGLISH
Yes

When I first looked for this cafeteria/pastry shop in the Galleria Esedra arcade (near Piazza della Repubblica and the train station), I was pessimistic. Most restaurants in this area are simply terrible: either overpriced greasy spoons, dirty ethnic joints, or total tourist traps serving lousy food to the unsuspecting. What a surprise was in store when I reached Dagnino, which bills itself as a bar, *pasticceria, gelateria,* and a cafeteria specializing in Sicilian pastries and ice cream.

Time stopped somewhere in the fifties in this two-level monument to mirrors, marble, fat grams, and sweets. You can stop in during the early morning cappuccino and *cornetto* rush; hit the cafeteria line around noon before the hot choices get too picked over; or drop by later in the day for a snack. I like to go in the late afternoon, look over the magnificent pastries displayed along one wall, pick several, and retire to a quiet table with a pot of tea. I always think I will take a few of the pastries home with me, but I usually end up devouring them all right on the spot. If you have children in tow, the ice creams are wonderful, and the *granita di limone* (lemonade) is the best I have tasted.

FIASCHETTERIA MARINI (92)
Via Rafaele Cadorna, 9 (north of Termini Station off Via Piave)

TELEPHONE
06 474 5534

OPEN
Mon–Sat: bar 9 A.M.–8 P.M., lunch 12:15–2:45 P.M.

CLOSED
Sun; last 3 weeks of Aug

RESERVATIONS
Groups of 10 or more

CREDIT CARDS
None

À LA CARTE
7.75–12.91€

MENÙ TURISTICO
None

COVER & SERVICE CHARGES
Cover 0.77€, service included

ENGLISH
Enough

Eating at an *enoteca,* or wine bar, is a smart Great Eating tactic in Rome, not only because of the lower cost but because the wine is good and the food choices lighter. From Monday through Friday, the Fiaschetteria Marini serves lunch to a packed house. In the afternoon you can always drop in for a ham and cheese sandwich along with a glass or two of wine.

The setting is casual, with paper covers on tiny marble-topped tables set both inside amid crates of wine bottles and outside on the sidewalk when weather permits. The menu hangs on a hook by the cash register. The daily-changing choices are limited, but all are absolutely delicious, especially the *pasta e fagioli* or any of the special German dishes that appear when the owner's mother, who is Austrian, gets busy in the kitchen.

NOTE: Dinner for ten or more is by reservation only.

GRAN CAFFÈ STREGA (105)
Piazza del Viminale, 27/31

Huge, brightly lit, and packed with animated Italians—that is Gran Caffè Strega, a combination cafeteria, restaurant, and pizzeria catering to Ministry of the Interior workers and tourists at lunch and an eclectic crowd in the evening.

At lunch, skip the ready-made sandwiches and head straight for the self-service cafeteria counter. Also bypass the diet-destroying display of desserts and concentrate on one of the twenty salads and ten or twelve hot daily specials. Seating is either in a room with the pizza ovens or on a large outdoor lighted terrace shielded from traffic and street noise by a ring of bushes and trees. Along the back wall is a waterfall with a picture in the middle of it of a woman wearing (depending on your age and point of view) either a black slip or an old-fashioned 1920's-style bathing suit.

If you want to avoid the sometimes frustratingly long cafeteria line, you can opt for a pizza, which is served for both lunch and dinner. The twenty-three wood-fired varieties run the gamut from a simple topping of tomato and cheese to "the works" with a fried egg on top. In the evening, a waitstaff serving *only* pizzas and salads replaces the cafeteria line.

TELEPHONE
06 485 670

FAX
06 486 770

OPEN
Daily: bar 7 A.M.–midnight; lunch noon–3:30 P.M., dinner 7 P.M.–midnight

CLOSED
Never

RESERVATIONS
Not necessary

CREDIT CARDS
AE, DC, MC, V

À LA CARTE
Cafeteria 10.33–15.49€, pizza 7.75–10.33€

MENÙ TURISTICO
None

COVER & SERVICE CHARGES
Cover 0.77€, service included at lunch, 10% service added at dinner

ENGLISH
Yes

IL RISTORANTINO (93)
Via Servio Tullio, 9 (between Termini Station and Villa Borghese)

In its earlier life, Mario Paziani's Il Ristorantino was known as Bottigliera Reali, a chummy Lilliputian place with six tables and an endless line to fill them. Now he has expanded ten-fold and the setting has lost its quirky charm, but the locals seem to love the new look: well-spaced tables under arched ceilings and a staff of waiters wearing black pants with T-shirts sporting the restaurant's logo.

Daily pastas, hearty soups, fresh fish, and a wide selection of meaty main courses headline a daily menu that brings back the tastes and smells of Mom's kitchen. The food is not delicate or approaching gourmet, but there is plenty of it, and the prices are still budget-friendly. A word of caution: Be sure to ask for the list of specials, handwritten in Italian, but not given out with the English menu.

TELEPHONE
06 487 2027

OPEN
Mon–Fri: lunch 12:30–3 P.M.; dinner 7:30–10 P.M.; Sat: dinner 7:30–10 P.M.

CLOSED
Sat lunch, Sun; 1 week in Aug

RESERVATIONS
Not necessary

CREDIT CARDS
AE, DC, MC

À LA CARTE
15.49–20.66€

MENÙ TURISTICO
None

COVER & SERVICE CHARGES
Cover 0.77€, service included

ENGLISH
Limited

LA REATINA (98)
Via S. Martino della Battaglia, 17

TELEPHONE
06 494 0768

OPEN
Mon–Fri, Sun: lunch noon–
3 P.M., dinner 7:30–11 P.M.

CLOSED
Sat; Aug 15–30, 10 days at
Christmas

RESERVATIONS
Not necessary

CREDIT CARDS
None

À LA CARTE
12.91–15.49€, including house
wine; pizzas from 4.65–6.20€,
beverage extra

MENÙ TURISTICO
None

COVER & SERVICE CHARGES
Cover 0.77€, service included

ENGLISH
Not much

Sunday night is never easy for dining out in Rome, but you can solve that problem easily at La Reatina, where the promise of cheap eats packs them in. For thirty-five years, five brothers and their wives and children have cooked for and served a weathered-looking neighborhood clientele at this typical *trattoria di quatiere* near the train station. Neither the exterior nor interior have any panache, but you are here for the inexpensive food; nothing else matters. Ask for the handwritten Italian *menu del giorno,* which lists all the good stuff; it is placed in a plastic cover and tacked to a wall outside, so you can check it to see if something appeals. The house pasta specialty is *farfalle impazzite,* a homemade bow-tie pasta tossed with cream and spinach that is a kissing cousin to fettuccine Alfredo.

Fresh fish is not on the kitchen's shopping list, but meat and potatoes, veal, and seasonal vegetables are. In the evenings they serve a few pizzas. I have never been able to do dessert, but if you can, be sure it is made here.

MONTE CARUSO ($, 107)
Via Farini, 12 (near Santa Maria Maggiore)

TELEPHONE
06 483 549

OPEN
Mon: dinner 7:30 P.M.–
midnight; Tues–Sat: lunch
noon–3 P.M., dinner 7:30 P.M.–
midnight

CLOSED
Mon lunch, Sun; Aug

RESERVATIONS
Required; no admittance
without them

CREDIT CARDS
AE, DC, MC, V

À LA CARTE
36.15–38.73€

MENÙ TURISTICO
Two tasting menus: *menù
dell'amicizia,* 30.99€, 3 courses,
beverage extra; *gran menù
degustazione,* 38.73€, 4 courses,
wine and coffee included; both
menus must be ordered by
everyone at the table

COVER & SERVICE CHARGES
Cover 2.58€, service included

ENGLISH
Yes, and menu in English

The menu states that the chef does everything with love, and it will take but one meal at Monte Caruso to convince you that this is true. Reservations are required not just for a table, but even to get in: the front door is always locked and you will not be admitted unless your reservation is confirmed. The restaurant's several dining areas have well-spaced tables set with Richard Ginori china and attractive glassware; a display of your grand dessert finale is to the right of the entrance.

The atmosphere is pleasant and unhurried, allowing you to relax and enjoy all courses, which lean heavily on the food from Lucana, in the south of Italy. A glass of prosecco, a bowl of black olives, and a plate of bite-sized *crostini* will keep you occupied while you order and wait for your first course. If everyone at your table can agree, the two tasting menus offer a good sampling of the chef's specialties. One offers an assortment of first and second courses, plus dessert; the other covers all courses from antipasto to coffee and includes wine. I loved both the *orecchitelle,* small, homemade ear-shaped pasta served with meat sauce and grated Parmesan cheese, and *cautarogni,* a hot mix of broccoli, olive oil, garlic, and chili peppers; both are accompanied by a basket of fresh bread from the kitchen's oven. I thought *glu'glu',* which is white turkey in an orange sauce, to be an overpowering, cloyingly sweet main course, especially after a hearty pasta first course. Better choices are *babette,* roast veal with truffle cream; zucchini flowers stuffed with mozzarella cheese and stewed in a fragrant tomato sauce; or a simple lemon veal escalope. Dessert is important: plan on either the *profitterol fatto al momento*—cream puffs with warm chocolate sauce and whipped cream—or a plate of *frappe,* quickly fried pieces of pastry dough dusted with powdered sugar, which are melt-in-your-mouth wonderful.

PIZZA RÉ (95)
Via Lucullo, 22 (between Termini Station and Villa Borghese)

The second location of this popular pizza restaurant is close to the Via Veneto. Please see page 111 for details. All other information is the same.

TELEPHONE: 06 4201 3075

RISTORANTE DA VINCENZO ($, 94)
Via Castelfidardo, 4/6 (off Via XX Settembre)

Even though the menu is translated into English, German, French, and Japanese, the clientele is usually local. The setting is simple, the service friendly yet professional, the plates warmed when they should be, and the food delicious. From appetizers to dessert, there are fifty-six possibilities. Still, if you do not see what you want, just ask, and chances are it can be prepared for you. Fresh fish is the kitchen's strong suit, and it is cooked and served with pride. My dinner guests all agreed that it was one of the best fish meals they had had in Rome.

If you are going all the way with fish, the sautéed clams or mussels and the smoked swordfish are nice starters. The spaghetti with clams and prawns or the rice with seafood are well-executed first courses. Besides fish, the *penne all'arrabbiata* (a hot combination of peppers, tomatoes, and garlic) is a reliable first course. The baked sea bass or flounder are served with potatoes and can be topped with a zesty tomato sauce. The *saltimbocca alla romana* (veal and ham cooked in a wine sauce), grilled pork chops, or roast chicken will keep the carnivores in your party pleased. Fresh fruit tarts, gelatos, and lemon-flavored *sorbetto* splashed with vodka will not lead you too far astray from your dieting resolutions, but the house specialty, *millefoglie*—thin sheets of pastry layered with cream, chocolate cream, and chocolate—will break

TELEPHONE
06 484 596

FAX
06 487 0092

OPEN
Mon–Sat: lunch 12:30–3 P.M., dinner 7–11 P.M.

CLOSED
Sun; Aug

RESERVATIONS
Advised

CREDIT CARDS
AE, DC, MC, V

À LA CARTE
28.41–38.73€

MENÙ TURISTICO
None

COVER & SERVICE CHARGES
Cover 1.03€, service discretionary

ENGLISH
Yes, and menu in English

them down every time. A shot of Sambuca, served if you order a full meal, will add to your desire to dine again at this wonderful Roman restaurant.

TRATTORIA ABRUZZESE (104)
Via Napoli, 3a/4

TELEPHONE
06 465 505

OPEN
Mon–Sat: lunch noon–
3:30 P.M., dinner 7–11 P.M.

CLOSED
Sun; NAC

RESERVATIONS
Not necessary

CREDIT CARDS
AE, DC, MC, V

À LA CARTE
23.24€

MENÙ TURISTICO
18.08€, 3 courses; beverage, bread, and service included

COVER & SERVICE CHARGES
Cover 1.03€, service included

ENGLISH
Yes, and *menù turistico* in English

The generous cooking at this two-room trattoria, located in the shadow of the opera and near an interesting morning produce market, is more likely to please a hungry gourmand than a finicky gourmet. Still, the food is prepared with the best ingredients, and the red-coated waiters in black pants and bow ties serve a reliable crew of regular locals.

The best wallet-watching meal is certainly the *menù turistico,* which includes everything from soup to service. The choices for each course are varied and include daily specials. The meat dishes are better than the fish, especially the soul-soothing osso buco or the roast lamb. Typical Roman specialties of tripe or brains fried with artichokes offer different choices you can't get back home. If you stray from the set-price meal, you will pay more, but you will be able to indulge in the house pasta—*rigatoni bohème,* a cholesterol festival of cream cheese and sausage blanketed with Parmesan cheese. For dessert, skip the prunes and the baked pears and go for the *mont blanc,* a meringue of cream, whipped cream, and custard that's covered with even more cream. Oh well, you won't have it every day!

TRATTORIA DA BRUNO & ROMANA (101)
Via Varese, 29

TELEPHONE
06 490 403

OPEN
Mon–Sat: lunch noon–
2:30 P.M., dinner 7–10:30 P.M.

CLOSED
Sun; 2 weeks Aug (dates vary)

RESERVATIONS
Advised for dinner

CREDIT CARDS
MC, V

À LA CARTE
15.49–18.08€

MENÙ TURISTICO
None

COVER & SERVICE CHARGES
None

ENGLISH
Some, but menu in English

Well thought of by locals, Trattoria da Bruno & Romana is a safe bet for back-burner home cooking if you are in this neck of the woods, which is not known for gourmet anything. The Santarelli family has been in this spot a half century, when Bruno's parents operated it as an *osteria;* then, the regulars ate on one side, and on the other, folks would come for a glass of *vino,* play cards, and catch up on the local gossip. The food is plain but fresh. I know because on my last research trip my flat in Rome was nearby, and I would often see Bruno or Romana shopping at the morning market on Via Milazzo for the food prepared and served that day. That is why you don't need to consult the menu. Just ask Bruno what he would recommend.

I was also interested to learn that Bruno is quite an artist known for his wood-carved nativity scenes, which he displays at Christmastime. If you look carefully, you will see a framed photo hanging in the restaurant of Bruno with Pope John Paul II admiring one of his nativity scenes.

TRATTORIA MONTE (112)
Via San Vito, 13a (near Santa Maria Maggiore)

Everyone who eats here returns. I know I did, despite a few dishes that missed their mark. The three dining areas are defined by brick arches and bright, modern versions of Tiffany lamps. The best seats are somewhere in the middle, away from the kitchen in the back and the door traffic at the entrance. Vegetarians will be in seventh heaven trying to decide between the four vegetable flans (similar to a silky quiche): zucchini with carrot sauce, potato with arugula, Parmesan, or just plain artichoke. Carnivores will be curious about the olives, stuffed with artichokes and sausage, and then fried. Let's just say it is an acquired taste. Everyone loves the spinach and cheese ravioli, the green pasta tossed with colorful vegetables, and the rich eggplant Parmesan. The braised pork and sweet onions was a soothing, wintery choice, and so was the roasted rabbit, served with sauteed potatoes. The desserts seemed to be works in progress, with no successful endings. The only other downside to Trattoria Monte is the snail-paced service that only picked up when waiters wanted to score with patrons. There is no house red wine, but reasonably priced bottles are available.

TELEPHONE & FAX
06 446 6573

OPEN
Mon, Wed-Sun: lunch 12:30–2:45 P.M., dinner 7:30–10:45 P.M.

CLOSED
Tues; 2 weeks Aug (dates vary)

RESERVATIONS
Essential

CREDIT CARDS
AE, DC, MC, V

À LA CARTE
20.66–25.82€

MENÙ TURISTICO
None

COVER & SERVICE CHARGES
Cover 1.03€, service discretionary

ENGLISH
Enough, and menu in English

TRIMANI (96)
Via Cernaia, 37b (between Termini Station and Villa Borghese)

The name Trimani is synonymous in Rome with fine wines, which are sold in their shop around the corner on Via Goito (see page 168). Twelve years ago the Trimani family opened this wine bar, where more than six hundred labels are available, fifty or more of them by the glass. As you can imagine, the wine list looks and feels like the telephone book, but don't feel intimidated—the knowledgable staff is patient with neophytes. From Monday to Saturday, the dining room is filled with an attractive mix of Romans who are dressed for success and enjoying the well-prepared food. The *piatti del giorno* always include a pasta, cheese plate, something fishy, and a hot meat dish. Quiche, *crostini,* salads, and assorted cured and smoked meat plates round out the choices. The chocolate mousse is definitely the dessert of choice.

TELEPHONE
06 446 9630

OPEN
Mon–Sat: lunch 11:30 A.M.–3 P.M., dinner 6 P.M.–12:30 A.M., happy hour 5:30–7:30 P.M.

CLOSED
Sun; middle 2 weeks in Aug

RESERVATIONS
Advised

CREDIT CARDS
AE, DC, MC, V

À LA CARTE
12.91–15.49€

MENÙ TURISTICO
None

COVER & SERVICE CHARGES
None

ENGLISH
Yes

Gelaterias

GIOVANNI FASSI/PALAZZO DEL FREDDO (119)

TELEPHONE
06 446 4740

OPEN
Tues–Sun: noon–midnight (till 1 A.M. Fri–Sat, from 10 A.M. Sun)

CLOSED
Mon; holidays

CREDIT CARDS
None

PRICES
Gelato from 1.55€

ENGLISH
Depends on server

Via Principe Eugenio, 65/67A (south of Termini Station near Piazza Vittorio Emanuele II)

It is said that modern-day Romans hold the nation's gelato consumption record at more than five gallons per person per year. Judging from the amount I saw consumed at this century-old *gelateria* near the train station, I think that is an extremely low estimate. Giovanni Fassi began in 1816 as a little shop in Piazza Navona, and in 1880 moved to its present location. It has been run by the same family since the beginning and is considered one of Rome's gelato meccas.

The ice cream is displayed in glass cases with signs in English. Decide what size *cono* (cone) or *coppa* (cup) you want, pay the cashier, and give your receipt to a server. You can take your treat to one of the tables scattered around the cavernous room or eat it on the run. Prices start at around 1.81€ and climb according to how elaborate and involved your order gets.

NOTE: Now there is a second location not too far from the Vatican (see page 164).

Trastevere

Trastevere means "across the Tiber," and this colorful and vibrant neighborhood is on the other side of the Ponte Sisto from the Jewish Quarter. It is famous for its nightlife, authentic neighborhood atmosphere, and many restaurants, bars, and most especially, pizza palaces. Purists insist that one has not been to Rome until one has had a baptism by pizza in Trastevere.

RESTAURANTS

($) indicates a Big Splurge

Restaurants

AL FONTANONE IN TRASTEVERE (76)
Piazza Trilussa, 46 (as you cross Ponte Sisto)

Naturally, I recommend every entry in this book. I have been to them all, and in many cases, more than a few times. Still, some stand out more than others, and Al Fontanone in Trastevere remains one of my favorites in Rome. I am not alone; the locals swear by it, and many readers have told me that when in Rome, this is their virtual canteen.

Joseph Pino (or Pino, as everyone calls him), his wife, Marisa, her sister Mariela, and her husband, Luciano, have been greeting guests at their popular restaurant for more than thirty years, treating everyone who arrives as a friend, whether they are here for the first time or the fiftieth. The family's heartfelt hospitality and good food are nicely complemented by the rustic interior, which has dried herbs and flowers hanging from the wooden beams, comfortable chairs, well-spaced yellow-clad tables, and a gaily lit summer terrace.

I like to start my meal with a small sampling from the antipasti table or the *fritto all'italiana,* a plate of quickly deep-fried vegetables. Then I move on to the specialty of the house, *fettuccine alla Fontanone,* a rich pasta with mushrooms, tuna, garlic, tomato, and fresh parsley. The simple fettuccine with *funghi porcini* (wild mushrooms) and a liberal lacing of garlic, fresh parsley,

TELEPHONE
06 581 7312

OPEN
Mon, Thur–Sun: lunch 12:30–2:45 P.M., dinner 7:15–11:15 P.M.; Wed: dinner 7:15–11:15 P.M.

CLOSED
Tues; Wed lunch; Aug 20–Sept 18, 1 week at Christmas

RESERVATIONS
Advised

CREDIT CARDS
AE, DC, MC, V

À LA CARTE
20.66€

MENÙ TURISTICO
None

COVER & SERVICE CHARGES
Cover 1.03€, service included

ENGLISH
Yes, and menu in English

and extra-virgin olive oil is another simple yet very satisfying first course (served only from May through November, when the mushrooms are fresh). The noodles in all their pastas are made here, and the ingredients for most of the dishes come from their own vegetable gardens or from local producers near their country home outside Rome. If you are going for a meat course, stellar choices are the *abbacchio al forno* (pink roasted baby lamb), the strapping osso buco (veal shank with mushrooms or peas), and on a cold day, polenta served with spicy sausage or pork ribs with pecorino cheese and tomato. In the late spring through summer, try *vignarola,* a dish made with new potatoes, artichokes, fava beans, and green peas cooked with ham, butter, and onion. Demand for this preparation is so high that they offer it for both lunch and dinner. In addition to the regular menu, wood-fired pizzas, *crostini,* and *bruschette* are available each evening. For dessert order Marisa's tiramisù or a plate of her nut-filled *cantucci* to dip in a glass of *vin santo.*

CHECCO ER CARETTIERE ($, 75)
Via Benedetta, 10

TELEPHONE
06 581 7018, 06 580 0985

FAX
06 588 4282

OPEN
Mon–Sat: lunch 12:30–3 P.M., dinner 7:30–11 P.M.; Sun: lunch 12:30–3 P.M.

CLOSED
Sun dinner; NAC

RESERVATIONS
Advised

CREDIT CARDS
AE, DC, MC, V

À LA CARTE
38.73–43.90€

MENÙ TURISTICO
None

COVER & SERVICE CHARGES
Cover 2.07€, service discretionary

ENGLISH
Yes

Checco er Carettiere is a long-standing family-run restaurant that deserves its fine reputation. It is a big place, with a large, rustic main dining room festooned with dried herbs, garlic and pepper braids, and signed photos of the great and near-great who have eaten here. Beyond this is a secluded summer terrace where diners are spared the usual exaust fumes and noise that come with sidewalk dining. Now in the skillful hands of Stefania Porcelli, the daughter of the owner, it is a great place to go, especially with a voracious appetite. The mixed antipasti is a festival of fried zucchini flowers, artichokes, meat, and rice balls, and it makes a nice transition to the rest of the meal. You can try *bombolotti,* short pasta with a hearty tomato and bacon sauce, or spaghetti with garlicky shrimp. Carnivores can celebrate with grilled steak, lamb chops, or tender oxtail simmered in a celery broth. Fish fanciers only have to remember what they saw in the iced fish display to know if they want seabass, turbot, or sole, just to name a few of the seasonal offerings. The ice cream, the zabaglione, and all the cakes are made here.

Down the street at Via Benedetta, 7, is their bar, *pasticceria,* and *gelateria,* which is open every day but Monday.

DA GIOVANNI OSTERIA E CUCINA (74)
Via della Lungara, 41A

For local color, cheap eats, and few other tourists, check out this hole-in-the-wall on Via della Lungara, which runs along the Tiber River. It is definitely a family-run show. The *padrone,* Giovanni de Blasio, is a neighborhood fixture (his sister runs the *tabaccheria* next door). Before the restaurant opens at noon, grandchildren occupy some of the tables, while their mothers hurry about getting ready and writing out the daily menu.

There are two rooms. The front one squeezes in fifteen tables and is "decorated" with coat hooks, a clock, some dusty wine bottles, and copper pots with dried pasta sticking out of them. The green-and-white tablecloths are covered with butcher paper. The small room in back is where the many regulars come in early to get their favorite table and catch up on local news. For lunch or dinner, you will be almost elbow-to-elbow with your neighbors, who might be a young student couple falling in love, a table full of boisterous workers in paint-spotted overalls downing their fourth glass of Chianti, or relatives of inmates from the Regina Coeli prison, which is down the street.

No one is here for inspirational cuisine, but for the kind of simple, satisfying peasant food their grandmothers used to make. The handwritten menu is *almost* possible to decipher. On Monday, everyone starts with a bowl of homemade egg noodle or chicken soup, and on Tuesday, the bean soup. Thursday, it is gnocchi, and on Saturday, the loyalists come for *agnolotti* (meat-and-cheese-stuffed pasta with tomato sauce) or zucchini flowers, also filled with minced meat. Ambitious portions of roast veal, chicken, fresh fish, and boiled beef follow, with the usual seasonal vegetables and salads available as extras. The dessert choices are narrow, so it is best to stay with the fresh fruit or a slice of the chocolate cake if your sweet tooth insists.

TELEPHONE
06 686 1514

OPEN
Mon–Sat: lunch noon–3 P.M., dinner 7:30–10 P.M.

CLOSED
Sun; Aug

RESERVATIONS
Not accepted

CREDIT CARDS
None

À LA CARTE
10.33€

MENÙ TURISTICO
None

COVER & SERVICE CHARGES
Cover 0.62€, service included

ENGLISH
Minimal

DA LUCIA (78)
Vicolo del Mattonato

Four generations of the Bizzarri family have been cooking here since 1938. What is their key to ongoing success? Dependable meals that remind everyone of slower, less complicated times when friends and family gathered around a big table eating comfort food *all'italiana*. In places like this, some things never change, mainly because the regulars would rise up in rebellion.

TELEPHONE
06 580 3601

OPEN
Tues–Sun: lunch 12:30–3:30 P.M., dinner 7:30 P.M.–12:30 A.M.

CLOSED
Mon; 15 days in Aug (dates vary)

So you can count on a short list of pastas highlighted by *spaghetti alla gricia* (tossed with sausage, pecorino cheese, and black pepper); beef stew laced with onions; rabbit cooked with a touch of vinegar, white wine, rosemary, and garlic; seasonal vegetables; and without fail, gnocchi on Thursdays, and *baccalà* on Fridays. No one skips desserts because they are all made here: crème caramel, chocolate mousse, *panna cotta,* and tiramisù.

RESERVATIONS
Advised

CREDIT CARDS
None

À LA CARTE
18.08–20.66€

MENÙ TURISTICO
None

COVER & SERVICE CHARGES
Cover 1.55€, service discretionary

ENGLISH
Yes

DAR POETA (77)
Vicolo del Bologna, 45/46 (near Piazza della Scala)

TELEPHONE
06 588 0516

OPEN
Daily: dinner 8 P.M.–midnight

CLOSED
NAC

RESERVATIONS
Advised

CREDIT CARDS
AE, DC, MC, V

À LA CARTE
Pizza 5.16–9.30€

MENÙ TURISTICO
None

COVER & SERVICE CHARGES
None

ENGLISH
Sometimes

Take your pick at this pizzeria: crusts are either thin or thick and puffy. Either way, both are covered with the usual mix of toppings, plus a few off-beat combinations such as apples and Grand Marnier. Also unusual is the calzone filled with Nutella (a chocolate and hazelnut spread) and ricotta cheese. Open nightly for dinner only, it is perpetually crowded, a good value, and a great pizza eat in Trastevere. It is run by three men and Mama, who makes the desserts. If you haven't reserved, arrive when the doors open, or very late. Otherwise, expect to get to know the people standing in line with you.

MARIO'S (80)
Via del Moro, 53/55

TELEPHONE
06 580 3809

OPEN
Mon–Sat: lunch noon–4 P.M., dinner 7 P.M.–midnight

CLOSED
Sun; Aug 10–31

RESERVATIONS
Not necessary

CREDIT CARDS
AE, DC, MC, V

À LA CARTE
10.33–15.49€

MENÙ TURISTICO
11.36€, 3 courses; beverages, cover, and service included

For serious bottom-of-the-budget dining in Trastevere, Mario's has long been the place; it's a haven for hard-core cheap eating desperados of all nationalities. Forget all about imaginative dishes, exotic sauces, elegant surroundings, or lines of beautiful people clamoring to get in. Mario's is a remarkably plain family-run restaurant where the waitresses wear slippers and the cook hasn't had a new idea in years. The prices not only reflect this, but they have barely kept pace with Italy's spiraling inflation.

For those still struggling to master the Italian menu, it is printed in English. The *menù turistico* is a deal when you consider that it includes three courses, wine, mineral water, and the bread and service charges. For not much more, you can select from uncomplicated à la carte dishes such as spaghetti with ricotta cheese and black pepper, osso buco, *scamorza ai ferri con prosciutto* (fried cheese with ham), or daily specials of gnocchi on Thursday, *baccalà* on Friday, and tripe on Saturday. In winter, look for the apple cake made by Mario's sister-in-law. Otherwise, forget this course. And always avoid the dishes on the menu marked with an asterisk (*); this indicates frozen food.

COVER & SERVICE CHARGES
Cover 0.77€, service included

ENGLISH
Yes, and menu in English

PIZZERIA AI MARMI (84)
Viale di Trastevere, 53/59

The place may not look like much, but despite the drab interior, it is one of the loudest, most crowded, and above all, cheapest pizzerias in Trastevere. If you time it right on a weekend night, you will witness the pizza chefs turning out more than a hundred pizzas per hour to a loyal corps of young-at-heart diners. As you can guess, service is casual, and the tables are smashed together in the interest of squeezing in as many people as possible. If you want some variety with your pizza, there are several very good bean dishes. Try the *fagioli di fiasco* (beans cooked in wine over an open fire) or the white beans with tuna, onions, and cabbage. Here is all the fiber and roughage you will need for a week! Otherwise, take a pass on the uninspired antipasti and the tired desserts.

TELEPHONE
06 580 0919

OPEN
Daily: dinner 6:30 P.M.–2:30 A.M.

CLOSED
Aug 8–28 (dates vary)

RESERVATIONS
Not accepted

CREDIT CARDS
None

À LA CARTE
Pizzas from 5.16–7.23€

MENÙ TURISTICO
None

COVER & SERVICE CHARGES
None

ENGLISH
Yes, and menu in English

TRATTORIA DA AUGUSTO (79)
Piazza de' Renzi, 15

Trattoria da Augusto, a Trastevere icon, has been serving basic Roman food to legions of committed penny-pinchers for decades. The spirited place has been owned for fifty-plus years by Augusto; his wife, Leda, who is in charge of desserts; their daughter, Anna, who cooks; and their son, Sandro. It has no sign outside, absolutely no decor inside, and certainly no pretense anywhere. The menu is handwritten in an Italian script that takes only a little detective work to decode. The locals know it by heart and thrive on the filling and predictable fare—big bowls of lentil soup on Monday, bean or vegetable soup on Wednesday, gnocchi on Thursday, and fish on Tuesday and Friday. Everything is washed down with large amounts of the rough house wine, and a good time is had by all.

TELEPHONE
06 580 3798

OPEN
Mon–Fri: lunch 12:30–3 P.M., dinner 8–11 P.M.; Sat: lunch 12:30–3 P.M.

CLOSED
Sat dinner, Sun; Aug

RESERVATIONS
Not accepted

CREDIT CARDS
None

À LA CARTE
12.91–18.08€

MENÙ TURISTICO
None

COVER & SERVICE CHARGES
Cover 0.77€, service included

ENGLISH
Yes

Gelaterias

FONTE DELLA SALUTE (85)
Via Cardinale Marmaggi, 2/4

TELEPHONE
06 589 7471
OPEN
Daily: 10 A.M.–2 A.M.,
continuous service
CLOSED
Never
CREDIT CARDS
None
PRICES
From 1.55€
ENGLISH
Depends on server

If you are in Trastevere, you are probably planning on pizza for dinner. For dessert, I can think of no better choice than a creamy gelato from Fonte della Salute. You can order yours in a cup, but I think the ice cream, especially their "After Eight," a minty rendition of the candy, tastes wonderful in a chocolate-dipped cone. Of course, you can also follow the lead of the gelato-loving Romans around you and gild the lily by asking for *panna* (whipped cream) on top, or any of the other two dozen toppings that range from cornflakes, rice crispies, and crumbled brownies to fruit and candies. Dieters can order frozen yogurt, fruity *sorbettos,* or a soy-based sugar- and milk-free ice cream—and of course, skip the *panna*— but if you do, you will miss the real experience of gelato in Rome.

Pastry Shops and Bakeries

PANIFICIO ARNESE (81)
Via del Moro, 15/16

TELEPHONE
06 581 7265
OPEN
Daily: 9 A.M.–9 P.M. (Fri–Sat
till midnight)
CLOSED
Never
CREDIT CARDS
None
PRICES
From 1.03€ per 100 grams
ENGLISH
Depends on server

You are going to have to use your nose to find this insider bakery in Trastevere. Even though there is an address, there is no sign outside. As you are walking along Via del Moro, look for the Corner Bookshop, which is across the street at number 48.

Any bakery that sells one thousand loaves of bread and five hundred pizzas *daily* is a rousing success. The breads and pizzas are baked in a 150-year-old wood-fired oven. When you go, take a number and you will eventually be called to the counter. Waiting a few minutes to be served works in your favor, allowing you time to look and decide what you want—but there is not much room for dallying once your number is up! If you are buying a slice of zucchini and cheese, potato rosemary, or plain tomato pizza to eat here, ask to have it heated; it will then be handed to you wrapped in wax paper and sitting on a tray. Other eat-in choices are big pieces of focaccia bread, slit, and then filled with tomato, mozzarella, and arugula, and dashed with pure olive oil. They cannot make these wonderful sandwiches fast enough to keep up with demand. Once you have been served, take your tray to a stool at the bar along the wall, buy a soft drink from the machine nearby, and enjoy one of the best Great Eating snacks in Rome.

Trevi Fountain

To ensure a return visit to Rome, Frank Sinatra advised in song that all visitors toss a coin into the Trevi Fountain—that is, of course, if they can get close enough to hit the water. The most famous fountain in Rome seems to be at the top of everyone's list, and it is jam-packed day and night. The fountain, a magnificent white marble rococo of sea horses, craggy rocks, and Tritons, is worthy of the attention and the hundreds of rolls of film used every day by those wishing to preserve their trips in a scrapbook of memories.

RESTAURANTS

GELATERIAS

($) indicates a Big Splurge

Restaurants

COLLINE EMILIANE ($, 32)
Via degli Avignonesi, 22

In Rome, as in any world-famous city, quality has its price. To enjoy a fine meal in subtly stylish surroundings during your stay in the Eternal City, follow the lead of savvy Romans and reserve a table at Colline Emiliane.

The decor takes its cue from the countryside, pairing yellow walls with yellow floral tablecloths, and accenting the two rooms with food posters and fruit and vegetable prints. The Bolognese food is hearty and served with style. All of the pastas are made by the owner's

TELEPHONE
06 481 7538

OPEN
Mon–Thur, Sat–Sun: lunch 12:45–2:45 P.M., dinner 7:45–10:45 P.M.

CLOSED
Fri; Aug

RESERVATIONS
Essential

CREDIT CARDS
MC, V

À LA CARTE
28.41–33.57€, house wine
included

MENÙ TURISTICO
None

COVER & SERVICE CHARGES
Cover 1.55€, service included

ENGLISH
Yes, and menu in English

wife, and I'm sure you will agree that they are superb. The springtime *tagliatelle con asparagi e prosciutto* (home-made noodles with asparagus and ham) and the *tortelli di zucca* (pumpkin dumplings) are both worth a trip across town. To go all out, treat yourself to one of their truffle specialties, which range from a salad with truffles to veal and cheese fondue. All is fit for a king and priced accordingly. For the *secondi piatti* (main course) stay with any veal preparation or the mixed boiled meats served with green sauce. Don't leave without trying the pear tart with raisins and pine nuts or the *budino al cioccolato,* a chocolate custard.

GIOIA MIA (33)
Via degli Avignonesi, 34

TELEPHONE
06 488 2784

OPEN
Mon–Sat: lunch 12:30–3 P.M.,
dinner 6:30–11:30 P.M.

CLOSED
Sun; Aug

RESERVATIONS
Advised

CREDIT CARDS
AE, DC, MC, V

À LA CARTE
18.08€, pizza 6.20–7.23€

MENÙ TURISTICO
None

COVER & SERVICE CHARGES
Cover 0.52€, 15% service added

ENGLISH
Yes, and menu in English

Gioia Mia has a well-deserved reputation for consistently good food, service, and prices—as is evident from the tantalizing smells and the always happy crowd. The inside is typical trattoria, with hanging sausages and peppers, bowls of seasonally fresh fruits and vegetables in the window, wines displayed on high shelves, and for fun, a clothesline with baby clothes clipped to it.

Smart diners start light by ordering a vegetable antipasto misto and then one of the twenty wood-fired pizzas, ranging from a *margherita* (with tomato sauce, mozzarella, and basil) to the *super televisione,* topped with peas, mushrooms, sausages, and an egg. A number of meat-based main dishes also vie for attention, and you may be hard-pressed to choose between the beautifully grilled baby lamb chops and the *cuscinetto alla Gioia Mia,* veal and ham wrapped around cheese and served in a white wine cream sauce topped with mushrooms. Those with trencherman appetites can attack the one-pound *bistecca alla fiorentina,* an enormous grilled steak that is almost enough for three people.

The two desserts to keep in mind are the *millefoglie della casa* (a flaky pastry layered with thick cream, chocolate, and whipped cream) and the *pera alla Gioia* (a pear cake covered with whipped cream and chocolate). No one said this would be a meal for someone on Weight Watchers!

IL CHIANTI VINERIA (35)
Via del Lavatore, 81/82

A stylishly rustic wine bar, Il Chianti celebrates the bountious food and wine of Tuscany from Monday to Saturday nonstop from noon until the wee hours. Lunch and dinner are both packed with an attractive crowd who appreciate the well-prepared Tuscan fare, and the pretty front terrace is perfect for people-watching or sharing a bottle of wine with a favorite person. The special house pasta made with tomatoes, mushrooms, and pecorino cheese or the oversized spinach and ricotta ravioli bursting with the flavor of truffles will remind you of why you are in Italy. Il Chianti is also popular because you don't have to order a huge meal here. In addition to daily lunch specials, the menu lists a handful of pizzas, some beautiful salads, a selection of *crostini*, cold meat and cheese plates, plus their own *biscotti* to dip into *vin santo*. Also under the same ownership is the more formal restaurant next door, but I think the Great Eats are in this wine bar.

TELEPHONE
06 678 7550

OPEN
Mon–Sat: 12:30 P.M.-2:30 A.M., continuous service

CLOSED
Sun; Aug

RESERVATIONS
Advised

CREDIT CARDS
AE, MC, V

À LA CARTE
12.91–20.66€

MENÙ TURISTICO
None

COVER & SERVICE CHARGES
Cover 1.03€, service discretionary

ENGLISH
Yes

PICCOLO ARANCIO (36)
Vicolo Scanderbeg, 112

Many restaurants near the Trevi Fountain have given in to the temptation to feed as many tourists as possible, serving barely adequate food at prices as high as the traffic will bear. You will find none of this at Piccolo Arancio, a popular location off Via del Lavatore where Romans mix happily with visitors. The Cialfi family also owns Settimio all'Arancio (see page 119) and Arancio d'Oro (see page 113). The menus are almost the same at all three locations, but for my Great Eating in Rome, this is the most friendly of the three, and it has the edge on food as well.

From the outside, it looks just like dozens of other establishments: white walls, beamed ceilings, a bouquet or two of flowers, and a posted menu. If you arrive early, you will see the family in action. One of the daughters-in-law will be minding a baby or two, while another will be helping in the kitchen. Grandfather usually sits at a table shelling peas or stuffing zucchini flowers with mozzarella and anchovies, which will later be dipped in bread dough and deep-fried to order. If you have never had one of these appetizers, they are especially well done here.

TELEPHONE
06 678 6139, 06 678 0766

OPEN
Tues–Sun: lunch noon–3 P.M., dinner 7 P.M.–midnight

CLOSED
Mon; 2 weeks in mid-Aug

RESERVATIONS
Advised for dinner and holidays

CREDIT CARDS
AE, DC, MC, V

À LA CARTE
18.08–23.24€

MENÙ TURISTICO
None

COVER & SERVICE CHARGES
Cover 1.03€, service included

ENGLISH
Yes, and menu in English

The food is substantial, and fresh fish is always featured. As I find best in so many places, ignore the compendium-style printed menu and turn to the colored, one-page version entitled *lo chef consiglia*—the chef recommends. Depending on the season, you might start with a melt-in-your-mouth fried artichoke, the stuffed zucchini flowers, or *insalata del polpo*—octopus salad. The tagliatelle with swordfish, eggplant, and tomato or the *tonnarelli* with fat lemony prawns are real winners in the seafood category. The delicate sole with a lemon and wine sauce is also a sure bet. If you are going vegetarian, look for *orecchiette* with broccoli or their own pasta tossed with fresh tomatoes and basil . . . a simple dish they do very well. Popular meat dishes are roast baby lamb and a heavy-duty serving of spare ribs, sausage, and polenta. You might think you need a light dessert at this point. However, their *millefoglie*—layers of thin pastry with chocolate, raspberry, and cream—is positively addictive. The couple seated next to me ordered one to share. Soon they *each* ordered another with no intention of sharing. Don't say I didn't warn you.

TRATTORIA SCAVOLINO (34)
Vicolo Scavolino, 72/74

Tucked away on Vicolo Scavolino near the Trevi Fountain, this typical trattoria is owned by a hardworking couple, Antonio and Epifani, who open early for dinner year-around. If you are here during the summer months, there is music on the terrace starting at 8:30 P.M.

When you arrive, look for the daily specials written on a blackboard by the door. A plus for many is that you can feel free to order as little as you want from this daily menu or the regular one without incurring the wrath of snooty waiters or grumbling management. The *fettuccine con funghi porcini* or the ravioli *di ricotta e spinaci* are two reliable beginnings. An almost guilt-free meal is the vegetable antipasti plate or any of the fresh fish served daily. For a change of dessert pace, the assortment of typical Italian cheeses is a good choice. When accompanied by a basket of fresh bread, a glass of wine, and your favorite person across the table . . . what else could you ask for on a Roman holiday?

TELEPHONE
06 679 0974

OPEN
Daily: lunch noon–3 P.M., dinner 6 P.M.–midnight

CLOSED
Sat from Oct–May; NAC

RESERVATIONS
Recommended for dinner

CREDIT CARDS
AE, MC, V

À LA CARTE
15.49–18.08€

MENÙ TURISTICO
None

COVER & SERVICE CHARGES
No cover charge, 10% service added

ENGLISH
Yes

Gelaterias

IL GELATO DI SAN CRISPINO (37)
Via della Panetteria, 42 (off Via del Lavatore)

For an unforgettable taste of what gelato connoisseurs consider the absolute best in Rome, come to this *gelateria* not far from the Trevi Fountain. Il Gelato di San Crispino is run by the Giuseppe and Pasquale Alongi, who are meticulous about using only the highest quality ingredients in all of their flavors, which of course they make themselves. Put butter fat grams, cholesterol concerns, and dietary worries aside, if only for a moment, so you can try without guilt their *gelato di San Crispino* (a heavenly combination of heavy cream and honey), zabaglione (a rich mixture of marsala wine and egg yolks), or dark chocolate. Don't ask for a cone . . . the brothers only serve their manna-from-heaven in cups because they believe cones interfere with the purity of the ice cream flavors.

TELEPHONE
06 679 3924

OPEN
Mon, Wed–Sun: noon–12:30 A.M. (Fri–Sat till 1:30 A.M.)

CLOSED
Tues, Jan 15–Feb 15

CREDIT CARDS
None

PRICES
Cups 1.55–6.20€

ENGLISH
Yes

The Vatican and Piazza Cavour

St. Peter's Basilica, the Sistine Chapel, and the Vatican Museums and Gardens are all within a 108-acre area known as Vatican City in the Vatican State, the world's smallest independent sovereign state. No one leaves Rome without seeing these sites: there are the splendors of St. Peter's Basilica, the world's largest church and the holiest shrine of Roman Catholicism; the Sistine Chapel with its magnificent Michelangelo ceiling; and one of the world's greatest art collections housed in the Vatican museums. An important side note is that mail sent from Vatican City goes much faster than from any other location in Rome.

Piazza Cavour holds nothing much for a visitor other than its proximity to Castel Sant' Angelo. The Castel was originally built by Emperor Hadrian in A.D. 135 as his tomb, and it was used as a fortress in A.D. 271 during the building of the Aurelian Wall. Now visitors can see a chapel designed by Michelangelo for Pope Leo X, military paraphernalia, beautiful frescoes, and tromp l'oeil paintings. The views from the top of the Vatican to the heart of Rome are wonderful.

($) indicates a Big Splurge

Restaurants

DAL TOSCANO ($, 1)
Via Germanico 58/60

TELEPHONE
06 3972 5717, 06 3972 3373

INTERNET
www.girarrostotoscano.it

OPEN
Tues–Sun: lunch 1–3 P.M., dinner 8–11:15 P.M.

CLOSED
Mon; Aug 10–31

RESERVATIONS
Essential, as far in advance as possible

CREDIT CARDS
AE, DC, MC, V

À LA CARTE
25.82–33.57€

MENÙ TURISTICO
None

Dal Toscano, which specializes in the foods and wines of Tuscany, is a truly Great Eat that is always packed with boisterous, gesticulating Italians, many of whom look like they have been firmly planted at the same tables, eating the same rich food, and discussing the same gossip or politics for years. The restaurant is so popular that reservations are required at least one day in advance. Seating is in a large two-room space dominated by a huge exhibition kitchen and open grill.

I think it is best to get started by ordering the hand-cut prosciutto or a light soup to save room for a bracing veal or beef steak grilled over the coals. As a garnish, consider forgoing the usual vegetables and ordering the *fagioli toscani all'olio,* white beans cooked in olive oil with a liberal lacing of garlic. They are so creamy and wonderful . . . I dream of having them right this minute.

If you add a small salad and a bottle of Chianti Classico, you will set sail on the winds of happiness. Another strong recommendation is the house dessert, which has been served since the day they opened. It is, simply, a cream cake with hot chocolate sauce poured over it at the last minute, but it provides the perfect finish on this Big Splurge in Rome.

DA MARCO E FABIO FORMICHELLA (2)
Via Silla, 26

The sign in front says, "Ristorante Ragno d'Oro," but this establishment is really Da Marco e Fabio Formichella. It is just one of those go-figure oddities so common in Rome. Because it is far enough from the mainstream tourist beat, it has remained a genuine neighborhood trattoria catering to regular diners who know that the food, from first to last course, seldom disappoints. The white interior is decorated with a dizzying collection of lighted Greek and Roman busts, mirrors, and paintings, including one of Rosie's Diner and a Hindu god. Black-panted servers zoom from one table to another, never missing an order.

The food is a bracing blend of Roman favorites. Start by sharing the *antipasti assortiti,* a plate of quickly fried zucchini, shrimp, salt cod, stuffed olives, and cheese and potato puffs. Lighter eaters may want to start with the tossed tomatoes and salad greens, but frankly, it is not as interesting as the antipasti mix. There are sixteen pastas, ranging from a plain spaghetti with *ragù* to a heady *linguine all'astice* (with lobster), several risottos, and, for the undecided, a sampling of several pastas. A smattering of pizzas is available as well as a full roster of meats and vegetable sides. The best dessert is not listed; ask for the dessert *misto,* a large assortment of bite-size pieces of cheesecake, macaroons, various *biscotti,* and shelled nuts. It is just the right ending, leaving you wishing you could keep this restaurant to yourself so that it would be just the same every time you return.

HOSTARIA DEI BASTIONI (5)
Via Leone IV, 29

Due to the constant influx of tourists to the Vatican, finding a decent meal at a fair price can begin to feel almost like a mission here. All Great Eating hope is not lost, however, thanks to the Hostaria dei Bastioni, which is through a tiny doorway below street level on the busy Via Leone IV. Inside, the basement dining room is

---

COVER & SERVICE CHARGES
Cover 1.55€, 10% service added

ENGLISH
Yes

TELEPHONE
06 321 2362

OPEN
Mon–Sat: lunch 12:30–3:30 P.M., dinner 7:30 P.M.–midnight

CLOSED
Sun; Aug, Christmas, New Year's

RESERVATIONS
Advised, especially for dinner

CREDIT CARDS
AE, DC, MC, V

À LA CARTE
20.66–23.24€

MENÙ TURISTICO
None

COVER & SERVICE CHARGES
Cover 1.03€, service discretionary

ENGLISH
Limited

TELEPHONE
06 3972 3034

OPEN
Mon–Sat: lunch noon–3 P.M., dinner 7–11:30 P.M.

CLOSED
Sun; July 15–31

RESERVATIONS
Advised for dinner

CREDIT CARDS
AE, DC, MC, V

À LA CARTE
18.08–20.66€

MENÙ TURISTICO
None

COVER & SERVICE CHARGES
Cover 1.03€, service included;
note that cover charge is waived
if you show your copy of
Great Eats Italy

ENGLISH
Yes, and menu in English

nicely turned out with black and red chairs and linen-covered tables. There is also a sidewalk dining terrace where you can relax in comfort and thank your lucky stars that you are not standing in the queue across the street, which wraps itself around the block with pilgrims waiting to get into the Vatican museums.

The appreciative diners are made up largely of businesspeople, neighborhood regulars, and smart visitors. At this homey, hospitable eatery, you will find moderately priced seafood and a host of other familiar Roman dishes. The antipasti selection is limited. Just have a peek at the display and see what looks best—it changes constantly—or ask Antonio, the hands-on owner who never seems to stop meeting, greeting, and serving his guests. You can't go wrong with the house specialty—*fettuccine alla Bastioni,* made with cream, bacon, fresh tomato, and a hint of orange. The risotto with seafood, the veal with potatoes, or the assorted roast meats, also served with potatoes, are safe bets if you do not go for the other house specialty—fish. The house *panna cotta* or a seasonal fruit make the best ending.

L'ABRUZZESE (8)
Via Catone, 18 (at Via dei Gracchi)

TELEPHONE
06 3973 3290

OPEN
Tues–Sun: lunch noon–4 P.M.,
dinner 7 P.M.–1 A.M.

CLOSED
Mon; Aug 15–26

RESERVATIONS
Advised

CREDIT CARDS
AE, MC, V

À LA CARTE
18.08–20.66€, pizzas from
5.68€

MENÙ TURISTICO
None

COVER & SERVICE CHARGES
Cover 1.03€, service included

ENGLISH
Yes, and menu in English

At this plain neighborhood restaurant, all the tables are filled by 12:45 P.M. for Saturday lunch with a mix of regulars and visitors. On one wall is a bulletin board with photos and appreciative postcards from the many international guests who consider themselves part of this place's extended family. Run by the Carloni clan, the restaurant's specialty is hearty Abruzzi dishes, and the menu holds something for everyone, from the daring to the daunted.

To the uninitiated, Abruzzi dishes are based on the pig and its interiors. A safe choice but one you will probably not see on the menu of your favorite Italian restaurant back home is *papparadelle con cinghiale,* long, fat noodles with a dense and savory wild boar sauce. Another, their *tagliatelle all'abruzzese,* flat ribbon pasta with mushrooms, cream, ham, and peas, is as soothing a soul-food dish as you could hope for. The ravioli pillows stuffed with ricotta and spinach and blanketed with a tomato sauce is another comforting choice.

Fresh fish is served daily, wood-fired pizzas come out only at night, and the cream-based desserts are probably sinful enough to give your cardiologist a heart attack. As a compromise, you could always split a *charlotte* (cream-filled cake laced with liqueur) or the *dolce* darling of the last decade, tiramisù.

L'INSALATA RICCA (6)
Piazza Risorgimento, 5/6

For a complete description of this restaurant, see page 99. All other information is the same.

TELEPHONE: 06 3973 0387

PIZZA RUSTICA AI GRACCHI (7)
Via dei Gracchi, 7

The pizza joint across the street is usually empty, with the waiters standing at the door and watching all the customers crowding into Pizza Rustica ai Gracchi. At this takeout pizza stand, the pizza chefs and ovens work overtime turning out big trays of lip-smacking pizza as fast as they can sell it. Also available are rotisserie chicken and soft drinks. The food prices along this strip of real estate near the Vatican tend to reach the outer limits, so it is nice to find a convenient pit stop for refueling before or after tackling the Vatican's "D" plan: a five-hour walking tour. When you order, you choose the type and size of your slice from twelve to fifteen varieties, which are then cut and sold by the weight. You will probably not snag either of their two red plastic chairs, so plan to take this one with you.

TELEPHONE
06 372 3733

OPEN
Mon–Sat: 10 A.M.–8 P.M., continuous service

CLOSED
Sun; Aug

RESERVATIONS
Not accepted

CREDIT CARDS
None

À LA CARTE
1.29–1.55€ per 100 grams

MENÙ TURISTICO
None

COVER & SERVICE CHARGES
None

ENGLISH
Depends on server, but generally very limited

TRATTORIA DINO (12)
Via Tacito, 80

If you're hungry, cash strapped, and yearning for homecooking near the Vatican and Piazza Cavour, the Marrocu's family-run jewel is a smart choice. I knew immediately upon seeing the eight-table room and smelling the wonderful aromas floating from the tiny kitchen in back that I would have my lunch here—and that I would try to return as often as possible. The white-washed, rough stucco walls are hung with wood carvings, braids of garlic, dried herbs, old cooking pans, and pretty baskets. Each day a new menu is handwritten on pieces of graph paper, with a little drawing in the corner, and placed on the tables. This is the place for those who don't mind tackling a serious midday meal, one anchored by a filling bowl of gnocchi (Thursday only) or lasagna, followed by roast chicken or pork, lamb meatballs, or rolled beef stuffed and served with peas. Accompany your repast with a glass or two of the house Chianti. If

TELEPHONE
06 361 0305

OPEN
Mon–Sat: lunch 12:45–4 P.M.

CLOSED
Sun; Aug

RESERVATIONS
Not necessary

CREDIT CARDS
None

À LA CARTE
12.91–15.49€

MENÙ TURISTICO
None

COVER & SERVICE CHARGES
Cover 1.29€, service included

ENGLISH
Sometimes

this is not enough, there is always dessert—meringue cookies with lemon or a *crostata* with jam—and all for a final tab every Great Eater can appreciate.

TRATTORIA PIZZERIA LA CARAVELLA (3)
Via degli Scipioni, 32/32b at corner of Via Vespasiano

TELEPHONE
06 3972 6161

OPEN
Mon–Wed, Fri–Sun: lunch noon–3:30 P.M., dinner 6–11 P.M.

CLOSED
Thurs; Jan

RESERVATIONS
Not necessary

CREDIT CARDS
AE, DC, MC, V

À LA CARTE
18.08–25.82€

MENÙ TURISTICO
12.91€, 3 courses; cover and service included, beverage extra

COVER & SERVICE CHARGES
Cover 1.03€, service included

ENGLISH
Yes

Hearty cooking speaks to us all, and you can always find it at La Caravella, a busy, neighborhood, all-purpose trattoria with courteous service and a massive menu. The array of seasonal specialties, pizzas, and tried-and-true favorites will include something that appeals to everyone, from the diet-conscious to the diet-allergic. Also very appealing is the corner wraparound terrace that is filled to capacity during the warm weather. The *menù turistico* offers good value and plenty of first and second course choices, especially if you are seriously hungry and can polish off lasagna, veal scallops, or fried fish with a green salad, fried potatoes, and fruit salad for dessert. Cover and service are part of the package, but drinks are not.

Gelaterias

GIOVANNI FASSI (4)
Via Vespasiano, 56/ac

For details on this gelateria, please see page 148. All other information is the same.

TELEPHONE: None
OPEN: Tues–Sun: 12:30–8:30 P.M. (Sat till 1:15 A.M.)
CLOSED: Mon

Gourmet Dining in a Private Home

LA TORRE DEGLI ANNIBALDI–GRAZIELLA MELLO ($)

The Annibaldi Tower, located in the center of Rome, was built between 1200 and 1204 with stones from Emperor Nerone's Domus Aurea and from the Titus Baths. The purpose of the tower was to serve as a defensive fortification for Piero Annibaldi, the brother-in-law of Pope Innocent III. It is also said that St. Francis of Assisi stayed here while waiting to see the pontiff. Now the tower is the home of Graziella Mello, who restored it to its architectural and archaeological splendor, and opens it to guests for private cocktail parties, dinners, banquets, wedding receptions, and cooking lessons. The tower consists of two floors of rooms, a luxurious, partially covered garden, and a rooftop terrace with a view of St. Peter's, all of which she opens for entertaining.

Sra. Mello is a recognized Cordon Bleu chef who uses her love of fine food and cooking skills to create memorable dining experiences for her guests. She offers a choice of menus of either Italian or international cuisine, and she personally shops for all the ingredients, oversees the cooking, and acts as a gracious hostess. No detail is overlooked, from the fresh flowers and live musicians to the lovely place settings of china, crystal, and flatware. Her cooking classes, which include the recipes and a meal of what has been prepared, are held in her own kitchen for small groups; they last for eight weeks.

If you are traveling to Rome with a small group, need to entertain business clients, or wish to host a special event for friends or family, please contact Graziella Mello as far in advance as possible to make your arrangements.

TELEPHONE & FAX
06 481 8121

OPEN
By advance reservation *only*

CREDIT CARDS
None, cash only

PRICES
Prices on request; they depend on the type and style of event planned

ENGLISH
Yes

Food Shopping in Rome

Gourmet Food and Wine Shops

BUCCONE (17)
Via di Rippeta, 19 (Piazza del Popolo)

TELEPHONE & FAX
06 361 2154

OPEN
Mon–Sat: 9 A.M.–8:30 P.M.;
Sun: 10 A.M.–5 P.M.

CREDIT CARDS
AE, DC, MC, V

ENGLISH
Yes

Buccone has an amazing selection of wines, spirits, liqueurs, olive oils, and balsamic vinegars, and all of these can be shipped to any address on the planet. Please see page 110 for a description of their wine bar and restaurant.

CASTRONI (10)
Via Cola di Rienzo, 190, 196, 198 (The Vatican)

TELEPHONE
06 687 4383

INTERNET
www.castronigroup.it

Castroni, with two locations, is Rome's answer to Fauchon in Paris. The stores are a wonderland of regional specialties, plus they offer the largest selection of imported foods in Rome, which they will pack for you but not ship. The prices are on the high side, but if you are having Skippy extra-chunk peanut butter withdrawal pangs or want tacos and refried beans for dinner, here is the place to satisfy your fix.

The second store sells an array of American brands of cake mixes, soups, cereals, and even Pop Tarts. Also look for the small bottles of olive oil, truffle oil, and different types of dried pastas, which make great gifts to take home to lucky friends. The second location is at Via Ottaviano, 55, at the corner of Via Germanico; Tel: 06 3972 3279; Fax: 06 3972 3251.

CREDIT CARDS
MC, V
OPEN
Mon–Sat: 8 A.M.–8 P.M.
ENGLISH
Yes

ENOTECA COSTANTINI (13)
Piazza Cavour, 16 (The Vatican)

If you are a serious wine lover and connoisseur, Enoteca Costantini should be on your priority list of places to visit. The shop is on two levels, the first of which is devoted to an expensive restaurant and a wine bar, where, for a modest outlay, you can happily munch your way through a variety of cheeses and bar snacks while drinking a glass or two of wine. It also has shelf after shelf of distilled spirits, and bins of bargain—and not so bargain—wines. Downstairs is where the serious business of wine tasting and wine selling takes place. Every Wednesday the family holds wine-tasting seminars here amid the rows of magnificent wines they have been collecting for thirty years. These tastings, unfortunately, are not for the casual tourist, but for real aficionados who pay around 154.94€ for seven two-hour "wine-tasting lessons," where four wines are tasted and discussed. However, anyone can buy their wines, which range from 2.58 to more than 550€ a bottle, or stand at the bar upstairs and enjoy a glass or two of a fine vintage.

TELEPHONE
06 320 3575
FAX
06 321 3210
OPEN
Mon: 4:30–8 P.M.; Tues–Sat: 9 A.M.–1 P.M., 4:30–8 P.M.
CREDIT CARDS
AE, DC, MC, V
ENGLISH
Yes

FRANCHI (11)
Via Cola di Rienzo, 204 (The Vatican)

A rival to nearby Castroni, Franchi has a deli of your dreams, with wonderful antipasti and roast meats for creating gourmet picnics, fresh coffee ground to order at their coffee bar, and an enormous selection of ham, cheeses, and wines from all over Italy.

TELEPHONE
06 686 4576
INTERNET
www.franchigift.com
OPEN
Mon–Sat: 8:15 A.M.–9 P.M.
CREDIT CARDS
AE, DC, MC, V
ENGLISH
Yes

LA BOTTEGA DEL CIOCCOLATO (114)
Via Leonina, 82 (Colosseum)

TELEPHONE
06 482 1473
OPEN
Mon–Sat 9:30 A.M.–7:30 P.M.
CLOSED
July–Aug
CREDIT CARDS
AE, DC, MC, V
ENGLISH
Limited

Looking for a replica of the Colosseum, the Vatican, or Buddha in white or dark chocolate? Here is your source, an amazing little shop selling all sizes and shapes of chocolate replicas. A small Colloseum is 10.33€; a large one will set you back 30.99€. Everything can be gift wrapped, and you can design your own basket of chocolate goodies.

TRIMANI (97)
Via Goito, 20 (Train Station)

TELEPHONE
06 446 9661
FAX
06 446 9630
EMAIL
info@trimani.com
INTERNET
www.trimani.com
OPEN
Mon–Sat: 8:30 A.M.–1:30 P.M.,
3:30–8 P.M.; Sun: 10 A.M.–
1:30 P.M., 4–7:30 P.M.
CREDIT CARDS
AE, DC, MC, V
ENGLISH
Yes

Trimani has been considered one of Rome's premier wine and liquor shops since it opened in 1821. Naturally, you can buy a vintage cru that could cost more than your trip to Rome, but they also stock a good selection of wine at affordable prices, and they ship worldwide. They also have assorted dry pasta, jams, jellies, honey, dried fruits, and olive oils. To sample a few wines before you buy, go around the corner to their wine bar and restaurant (see page 147).

VOLPETTI (88)
Via Marmorata, 47 (Testaccio)

TELEPHONE
06 574 2352
INTERNET
www.fooditaly.com
OPEN
Mon–Sat: 8 A.M.–2 P.M.,
5–8:15 P.M.
CLOSED
Thur afternoon June–Oct
CREDIT CARDS
AE, MC, V
ENGLISH
Yes, ask for Claudio

Volpetti is recognized as not only one of the best food shops in Rome, but in all of Italy. At first glance, you may wonder why, but if you speak with Claudio, who is responsible for the care of their products, you will understand how it earned its deserved high reputation. Let's start with their cheeses, most of which come from Norica in Umbria and are stored in a climate-controlled cellar. Every day Claudio washes the rinds with whey and turns them, the way his mother did, to keep the cheeses clean and uniform. Claudio is passionate about his cheese and works twelve hours a day. He says, "Climate, terrain, and the hand of man make a cheese. The animal is the means to the cheese, but the land is the source." He can explain the cheeses, tell you what wine and foods to serve with them, offer samples, and put your choices in vacuum packs for the trip home. In addition to the fabulous cheeses, Volpetti sells a tremendous variety of meats, breads, aged vinegars, and interesting salsas. For a real taste of their foods and products, treat yourself to lunch at their cafeteria-style restaurant, Volpetti Piú, around the corner (see page 139). If you can't get to Rome to shop at Volpetti, shop online and have your order delivered to your door.

Grocery Stores and Supermarkets

CONAD AT TERMINI (103)
Forum Termini Mall, Termini Station

Located on the lower ground floor of the train station, this lifesaving mini-market is similar to a 7-Eleven, though the convenience comes at a high price.

OPEN
24 hours a day

CREDIT CARDS
MC, V

STANDA (83)
Viale Trastevere, 60 (Trastevere)

Standa is a supermarket in the basement of Oviesse, a dime store–quality department store. Both are good if you need a few things quickly, such as toothpaste, another cotton shirt, or a few snacks to take back to your hotel. Most of the produce is prepackaged, but the prices are fair and the grocery selections are outstanding.

NOTE: Two other branches of this supermarket are located near the Vatican (on Via Cola di Rienzo) and at Viale Regina Margherita, on the outskirts of Rome.

OPEN
Mon: 3:30–7:30 P.M.; Tues–Sat: 9 A.M.–7:30 P.M.

CREDIT CARDS
MC, V

ENGLISH
Limited

Indoor/Outdoor Markets

Rome has many food markets of all types and sizes. The most central and interesting are listed here. Most districts also have their own local morning food markets, which usually operate from 7 A.M. until 12:30 P.M. At all of these markets, do not count on much English being spoken and plan to pay in cash.

CAMPO DE' FIORI (66)
Piazza Campo de' Fiori

Campo de' Fiori has been a focus of Roman life since the sixteenth century, and it is still one of the most charming squares in the city. Today the colorful outdoor market attracts loads of camera-totting tourists. After the market is over, the square resembles a gigantic trash heap.

OPEN
Mon–Sat: 8 A.M.–1 P.M.

MERCATO DEI FIORI

OPEN
Tues: 10:30 A.M.–1 P.M.

Via Trionfale, 47/49 (northwestern edge of Rome)

This is an indoor wholesale flower market with bargain prices that is open to the public on Tuesday morning only.

PIAZZA DI S. COSIMATO (82)

OPEN
Mon–Sat: 7 A.M.–1 P.M.

West of Piazza Santa Maria in Trastevere

S. Cosimato is a smaller market, but with a good selection.

PIAZZA TESTACCIO (87)

OPEN
Mon–Sat: 8 A.M.–1 P.M.

Off Via Aldo Manuzio

This market is in a working-class neighborhood with prices to match. There are also a few clothing stalls and a lot of shoe stalls.

PIAZZA DELL' UNITA (9)

OPEN
Mon–Sat: 8 A.M.–7 P.M.

Off Via Cola di Rienzo (Vatican)

There are wonderful selections, good prices, and underground parking in this indoor market not far from the Vatican.

PIAZZA VITTORIO EMANUELE (113)

OPEN
Mon–Sat: 6:30 A.M.–1:30 P.M.

South of Santa Maria Maggiore (Train Station)

This big and busy market has everything from fish and produce to dairy products, meat, and dry goods. The wide selection appeals to people from different nationalities. Watch your money at all times, and especially watch out for gypsies who cruise through in packs about an hour before the market closes.

VIA DELL' ARANCIO (24)

OPEN
Mon–Sat: 8 A.M.–1 P.M.

Off Via Tomacelli at the end of Via di Ripetta (Spanish Steps)

This small market in a high-end neighborhood makes up in quality what it lacks in size. The few stalls sell *only* prime produce. If you keep going back to the same stall, after four or five visits you will be treated like a regular.

VIA MILAZZO (102)

OPEN
Tues–Sat: 8 A.M.–1 P.M.

Via Milazzo (near Termini Station)

This is a very typical neighborhood morning market with excellent produce. The lingerie stall is a throwback to the days when eighteen-hour bras, serious girdles, and garter belts were in vogue.

VENICE

Venetians know all too well that they are picturesque; in Venice one never loses the sense that life is being staged for the onlooker.

—*Jonathan Raban,* Arabia Through the
Looking Glass, *1979*

When I went to Venice, my dream became my address.
—*Marcel Proust, 1906*

Founded more than fifteen hundred years ago on a cluster of mudflats, Venice became Europe's trading post between the East and West, reaching the height of its power in the fifteenth century. Although it no longer enjoys such elite status, it remains a glorious reflection of its rich past, depending for its income now on the mass of visitors who arrive every year to marvel and experience enchantment.

In Venice, one always has the feeling of being suspended in time. Little has changed over the centuries to diminish the harmony of colors, lights, and sounds that float dreamlike over the canals and lagoons. Composed of more than 100 islets linked together by 354 bridges spanning 177 canals, it is little wonder how easy it is to get lost, even for a native. However, becoming hopelessly lost in the maze of *rio*s, *campo*s, and *campiello*s is one of the most pleasurable experiences of a visit to this romantic city on the Adriatic.

Since you cannot drive a car, hop on a bus, or hail a cab, what you will do in Venice is walk, walk, and walk. To save yourself supreme confusion, it is necessary to become familiar with the six districts, or *sestieri,* that make up the city, three per each side of the Grand Canal. They are Cannaregio, Castello, and San Marco to the east, and Dorsoduro, San Polo, and Santa Croce to the west. This is also how the listings in *Great Eats Italy* are organized, followed by restaurants on the outlying islands. Only three bridges cross the Grand Canal: Ponte degli Scalzi (at the train station), Rialto, and Accademia. Addresses are usually given only by the district and number (i.e., Dorsoduro 3437), often omitting the name of the street. All of the listings in the Venice section of *Great Eats Italy* include the name of the street and the number (i.e., Calle dell' Oro, 5678), with restaurants listed by district. This will help, but you will still get lost: street names may repeat in more than one district, some buildings have more than one set of numbers, and numbered addresses close to one another sequentially may indicate buildings at opposite ends of the district, since within *each* district there are some six thousand numbers with no clear-cut sequence. It is just as bizarre as it sounds, and often leads to hair-tearing and extreme frustration, especially when you mistakenly try to use logic—or a map.

Though you may be lost . . . *do not panic.* Look for the yellow signs posted throughout the city to find the direction you want. For example, look for the sign saying Rialto, the bridge that connects the San Marco district with San Polo, when you are going to shop at the Rialto Bridge. Accademia is your direction if you want to see the Galleria dell' Accademia, which has the most important collection of Venetian art in the world, or the Peggy Guggenheim Collection. If you are going back to get to your parked car, watch for signs saying Piazzale Roma. If your destination is St. Mark's Square, look for signs pointing to San Marco. If you are leaving Venice on the train, go in the direction marked *Ferrovia* (train station). For a definition of Venetian street terms, see page 180.

Venice celebrates a number of holidays (*feste*). The most important is Carnivale, held during the ten days before Lent and ending on Shrove Tuesday with a masked ball for the elite and dancing in St. Mark's Square for the rest of us. Crowds during this time defy description. Unless you enjoy elbow-to-elbow, pushing mob scenes and the-sky-is-the-limit prices in hotels and restaurants, it is best to avoid Venice at this time.

If you think food is pricey in Florence and Rome, you have not yet eaten in Venice, where even Italians used to runaway inflation consider dining out expensive. While Venice is a city of romantic enchantment, the high cost of living and the endless flow of tourists keep the prices in the stratosphere. Remember, nothing is produced or grown here—everything is brought in and hand carried to its destination, by foot or by boat. The best word-of-mouth recommendation for a Venetian restaurant is that the prices are not *too* high. My own feeling is that the short-term visitor should seriously consider casting aside thoughts of great economy and take the philosophical view that he or she may never pass this way again. This is not to say that good-value restaurants do not exist, because I have found many wonderful ones. This is just a warning that you will probably spend more for food in Venice than you want to.

One way to shave food costs is to lunch in a *baccari* (bar). Most Venetians do, and many order a plate of *cicchetti:* bite-size appetizers similar to Spanish tapas. To go with your plate, have an *ombra,* a glass of dry white wine. Another option is a plump *tramezzino,* a sandwich filled with almost anything you can think of. The cheapest eat will be a picnic you make up yourself from foods bought at a market or deli.

Venetian cuisine is known for its simplicity, and its best dishes often come from the sea, such as *granseole* (spider crabs), *molecche* (soft-shell crabs), *sarde in saor* (sardines marinated in vinegar, onions, and pine nuts), *bigoli in salsa* (thick, whole-wheat pasta with anchovies and onions), and *seppie in nero* (squid cooked in its own black ink and usually served with pasta or polenta). When ordering at a restaurant, remember that on Sunday and Monday the Rialto Market fish market is closed, so any fish served on these days will not be fresh that day. Risotto is the favored starch, sauced with delicate seafood or tender seasonal vegetables. Another popular rice dish is *risi e bisi*—a thick soupy dish of rice, peas, and pea pods. Polenta appears not only with fish but with the famous *fegato alla veneziana,* calves' liver with onions. Pastries and sweets abound. Try the ring-shaped cookies called *bussolai,* which are the specialty of Burano, or the thin, oval cookies called *baicoli.* Particular foods are traditional to eat on certain feast days. During Carnivale you will see small doughnuts known as *frittelle,* which come plain, with fruit (*con frutta*), or with cream (*con crema*). Buy a bagful and don't hesitate to eat them all right away, as they do not keep well. The most popular wines are from nearby Fruili and the neighboring Veneto, especially the white Soave or the red Valpolicella and Bardolino. Prosecco is a light, sparkling wine that is a delicious aperitif. Grappa, strong and fiery (so exercise caution), is made from plums, grapes, and juniper berries.

While most restaurants in other cities take their annual holidays in either July or August, the most popular months to close in Venice, in addition to July and August, are December, January, and February until the beginning of Carnivale, when the dampness and all-embracing cold of Venice subside. However, the period between Christmas and New Year's is becoming an increasingly popular time to visit Venice, so to meet the tourist demand, many restaurants will open during this time, then close again until Carnivale.

Because Venice exists primarily for tourists, many waiters and waitresses, and unfortunately restaurant owners as well, have become very jaded about the quality of service offered. If a place is very busy, often the Venetians get the service and the tourists are ignored, and you can only laugh when an old waiter slides the basket of bread down a long table, or reaches over your head to serve across the table. In an effort to improve its service image, especially in the better places, a group of independent restaurateurs called Ristoranti della Buona Accoglienza has been formed. This organization pledges a proper price-to-quality ratio, the use of fine products, and exceptional service in an agreeable atmosphere. Most of these restaurants are Big Splurges, but you are virtually guaranteed a wonderful meal. If you have any complaints about the food or service in any of the member restaurants, please call 041 528 5521, or write to them at Casella Postale No. 624, 30100 Venezia, Italy. The members listed in *Great Eats Italy* are:

Ai Gondolieri, page 212
Al Covo, page 191
Alla Madonna, page 222
Fiaschetteria Toscana, page 185
Ignazio, page 225
Osteria da Fiore, page 226

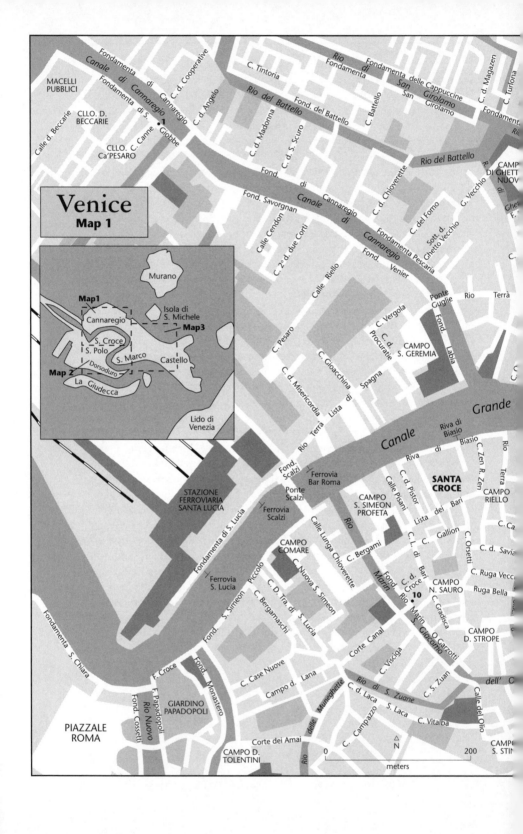

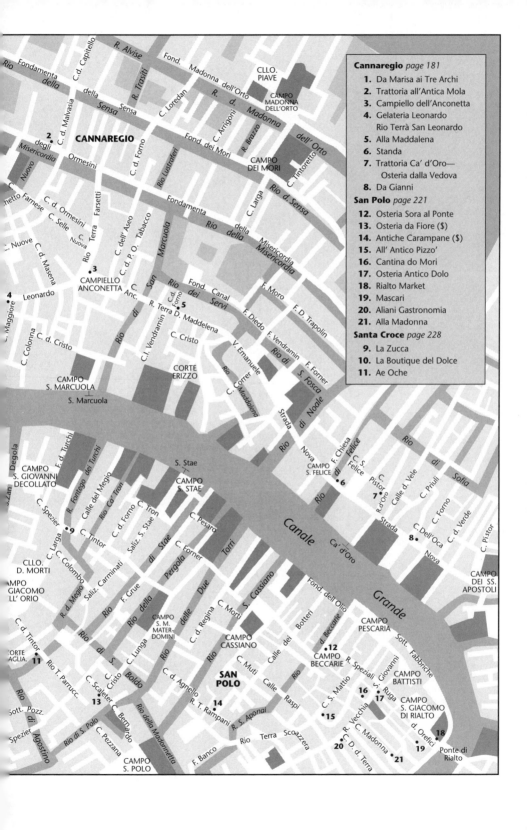

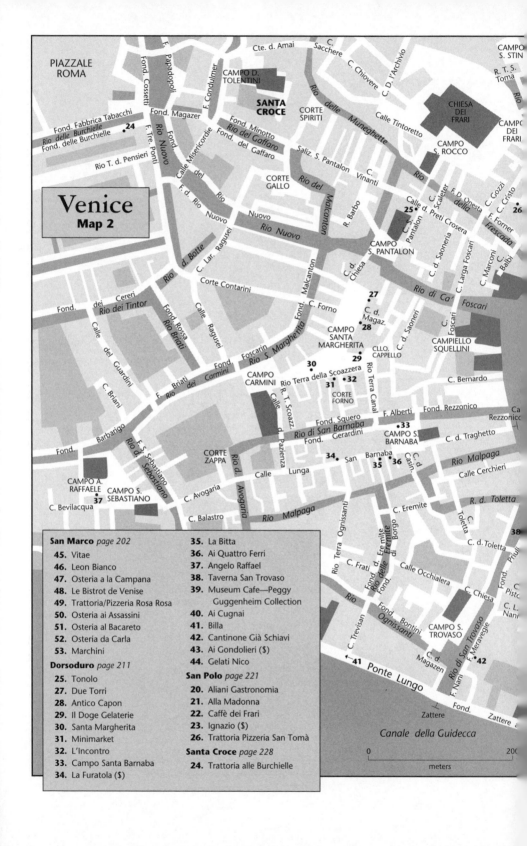

PIAZZALE
ROMA

Venice
Map 2

CAMPO
S. STIN

SANTA
CROCE

CHIESA
DEI
FRARI

CAMPO
DEI
FRARI

CAMPO D.
TOLENTINI

CORTE
SPIRITI

CAMPO
S. ROCCO

24

CORTE
GALLO

25

26

CAMPO
S. PANTALON

27

Corte Contarini

C. Forno

28

CAMPO
SANTA
MARGHERITA

CLLO.
CAPPELLO

CAMPIELLO
SQUELLINI

Rio dei Tintor

30

29

CAMPO
CARMINI

31 32

C. Bernardo

CORTE
FORNO

Ca
Rezzonico

Fond. Rezzonico

C. d. Traghetto

33

CAMPO S.
BARNABA

34

35 36

Rio Malpaga

Calle Cerchieri

CORTE
ZAPPA

CAMPO A.
RAFFAELE

37

CAMPO S.
SEBASTIANO

C. Bevilacqua

38

R. d. Toletta

C. d. Toletta

Rio Malpaga

C. Eremite

CAMPO S.
TROVASO

41 Ponte Lungo

42

Zattere

Zattere

Canale della Guidecca

0   200

meters

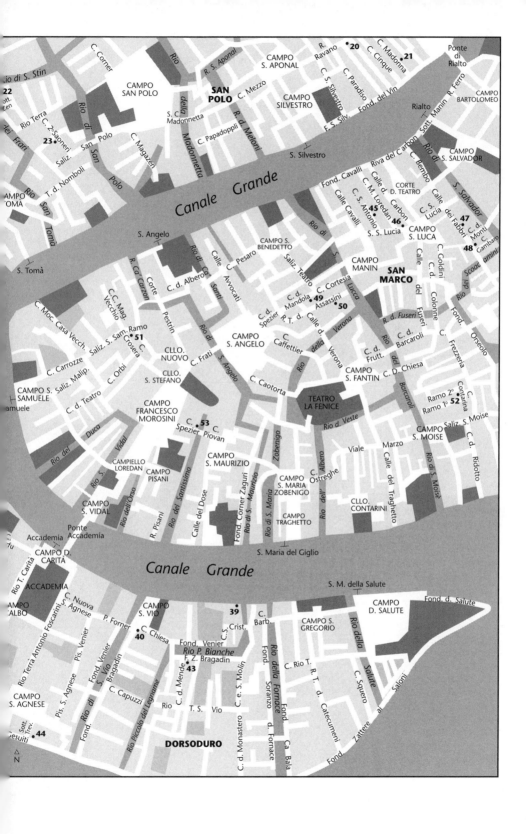

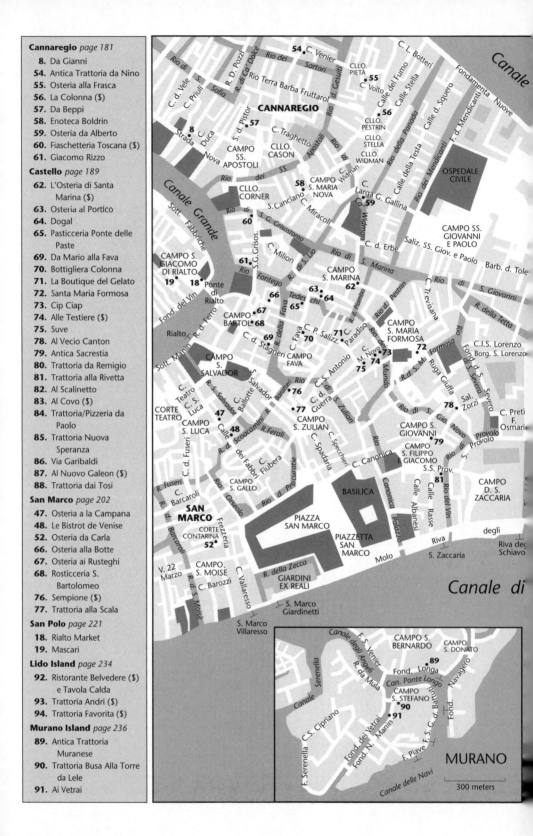

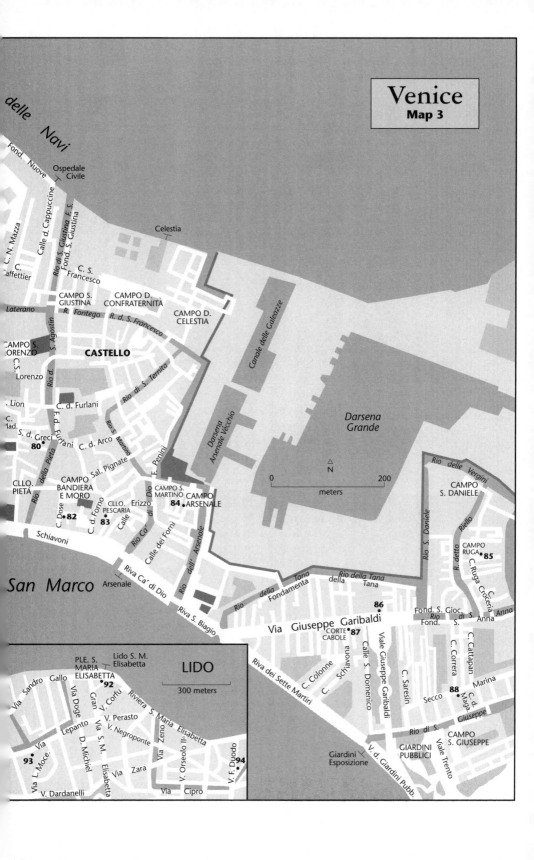

Venice
Map 3

delle Navi

Fond. Nuove

Ospedale Civile

C. N. Mazza

Calle d. Cappuccine

C. affettier

Rio di S. Giustina E. S.
Fond. S. Giustina

Celestia

C. S. Francesco

Laterano

CAMPO S. GIUSTINA

CAMPO D. CONFRATERNITÀ

R. Fontego

R. d. S. Francesco

CAMPO D. CELESTIA

S. Agostin

CAMPO S. LORENZO

C.S. Lorenzo

CASTELLO

Rio d.

Canale delle Galeazze

Lion

C. d. Furlani

C. lad.

F. d. Furlani

S. d. Greci

80

Rio S. Martino

C. d. Arco

Rio d. S. Ternita

Darsena Arsenale Vecchio

Darsena Grande

Rio della Pietà

Sal. Pignate

F. Penini

N

0   200

meters

Rio delle Vergini

CAMPO S. DANIELE

CLLO. PIETÀ

CAMPO BANDIERA E MORO

C. Dose

82

CLLO. Erizzo

PESCARIA

83

CAMPO S. MARTINO

84 ARSENALE

CAMPO

Rio S. Daniele

R. detto

Riello

CAMPO RUGA

85

C. Ruga Croceria

Schiavoni

C. d. Forno

Calle

Rio Ca di Dio

Calle dei Forni

Calle dell' Arsenale

Riva Ca' di Dio

Rio della Tana
della   Tana

Rio

della

Fondamenta

Tana

San Marco

Arsenale

Riva S. Biagio

86

Fond. S. Gioc,
Rio di S. Anna   Anna
Fond.   S.

C. Cattapan

C. Correra

Via Giuseppe Garibaldi

CORTE
CABOLE

87

Viale Giuseppe Garibaldi

Calle S. Domenico

C. Saresin

88

C. d. Maga

Marina

PLE. S. MARIA ELISABETTA

Lido S. M. Elisabetta

92

LIDO

300 meters

Via Sandro Gallo

Via Doge

Gran

V. Corfù

Riviera S. Maria Elisabetta

Riva dei Sette Martiri

C. Colonne

C.

Schiavona

Secco

Rio di S.

Giuseppe

GIARDINI PUBBLICI

Viale Trento

CAMPO S. GIUSEPPE

Via Lepanto

V. Perasto

Via S. M.

D. Michiel

V. Negroponte

Via Zeno

Via Orseolo II

Via S. Maria Elisabetta

93

Via

Via L. Moce.

Elisabetta

Zara

V. F. Duodo

94

V. Dardanelli

Via   Cipro

Giardini
Esposizione

V. d. Giardini Pubb.

Rolling Venice Card

If ever there was a discount-card deal for travelers between the ages of fourteen and twenty-nine, the Rolling Venice Card is it. Not only receiving discounts in participating restaurants, cardholders are entitled to at least a 10 percent discount on hotels, admissions to various museums (except the Accademia), and some store purchases. The participating establishments are listed on a map you receive when you get your card. The cost of the card and a map with all the discount locations on it is 2.58€. For 7.75€, in addition to the card and the map, you will get a Venice guidebook, an agenda, and a Rolling Venice T-shirt and tote bag. You can purchase the card at the train station from July through September, or any time of the year at major vaporetto ticket booths or at the address below. To get your card, you will need to show your passport and have a passport-size photo to affix to your card.

Comune di Venezia
Assessorato alla Gioventù
Calle Contarina, 1529, San Marco
Telephone: 041 274 7651
Open: Mon–Fri: 9 A.M.–1 P.M.; also Tues, Thur: 3–5 P.M.

Venetian Street Terms

Calle	main alleyway, often picturesque
Campiello	small square
Campo	square, usually with a church on it with the same name as the square
Corte	courtyard
Fondamenta	pavement along a section of water
Piscina	former pool that has been filled in
Ponte	bridge
Ramo	small side street linking two streets
Rio	small canal used by gondolas and cargo boats
Rio Terà	a canal filled in to make a street
Riva	major stretch of pavement along water
Ruga (and rughetta)	main shopping street
Salizzada	sometimes spelled *salizada,* the main street of a district
Sestiere	district
Sottoportico	small alley running beneath a building

Restaurants East of the Grand Canal

Cannaregio

This is the northern, most-populated *sestiere,* and the one most visitors first see if they arrive by train. It is also one of the most authentic districts because it does not have to rely solely on tourism. The area around the train station (Ferrovia) is the exception. It is very touristy, and if you don't know where to go, you can easily be overwhelmed by the assault of greasy spoons and questionable hotels. In the center of Cannaregio is the Jewish Quarter, sometimes referred to as the Jewish Ghetto; in fact, the Italian word *ghetto* became the universal term describing a restricted area for a poor, minority population. Part of the *sestiere* along the Grand Canal is lined with aging *palazzos,* the most famous of which is Ca' d'Oro, which holds an impressive art collection. In the northern part of the *sestiere* is the Madonna dell'Orto, a Gothic church with Tintoretto's *Presentation of Mary at the Temple.*

($) indicates a Big Splurge

Restaurants

ALLA MADDALENA (5)
Rio Terra della Maddalena, 2348

TELEPHONE
041 720 723

OPEN
Mon–Sat: bar 7:30 A.M.–9 P.M.;
hot lunch 12:30–2 P.M.

CLOSED
Sun; Aug

RESERVATIONS
Not accepted

CREDIT CARDS
None

À LA CARTE
Sandwiches from 1.55€, main
dishes from 4.13€, complete
lunch 9.81€

MENÙ TURISTICO
None

COVER & SERVICE CHARGES
No cover, service included

ENGLISH
Limited; as the barman said,
"We don't speak English, only
Venetian."

Where to go when you find yourself stranded in the dining desert around the train station and do not want to settle for the unappetizing tourist food that is the rule rather than the exception here? One answer is Alla Maddalena, a fine place for a sandwich, a plate of rigatoni, tagliatelle, or the daily hot special. All the food is made fresh daily and in some cases in limited supply, so when they run out of roast beef or the pasta of the day, you are out of luck. The desserts are brought in, so I recommend going to the *gelateria* across the street and having a scoop or two. At Alla Maddalena, you can enjoy your repast standing at the bar and kibitzing with the friendly bartenders or sitting on a tall stool by the window and watching the foot traffic hustle by.

ANTICA TRATTORIA DA NINO (54)
Salizada Seriman, 4858

TELEPHONE
041 528 5266

OPEN
Mon–Fri: bar 9 A.M.–9 P.M.,
lunch 11 A.M.–2:30 P.M., dinner
6:30–8:30 P.M.; Sat: bar 9 A.M.–
9 P.M., dinner 6:30–8:30 P.M.

CLOSED
Sat dinner, Sun; Jan, 2 weeks in
mid-Aug

RESERVATIONS
Not necessary

Every once in a while we need a port in a storm, and this little trattoria is just that. It is not worth a special trip, but if you are in the area—perhaps en route to the boat to Murano—and need a little sustenance, this is an answer. Leave your gourmet expectations at the door, order what can be prepared in the moment, and you will do fine. The interior used to be cluttered with collections of soccer scarves, plastic plants, and assorted posters, but the walls have been repainted white and now sport only Carnivale masks, framed sailor's knots, and pictures of Venice. The only piece of true kitsch left is the big wristwatch clock hanging over the bar.

The best meal deals are the seven *menù turistico*s. These range widely and include a bowl of spaghetti bolognese along with either a salad, grilled steak, or pork chop; spaghetti with fresh clams, followed by grilled sole or fried fish; a pizza served with a beer or soda; and a hamburger with fries. The house wine costs extra, but coffee is included. In the end, you will have had a filling meal and be soon on your way without having put a major hole in your budget.

NOTE: Please take a minute while you are in this area to visit Chiesa di S. Maria Assunta (Gesuiti), which contains works by Tintoretto. The church is located down the street from the restaurant and is open from 10 A.M. to noon and from 4 to 6 P.M. Mass is at 5:30 P.M.

CREDIT CARDS
AE, MC, V

À LA CARTE
23.22€

MENÙ TURISTICO
Seven menus from 6.20–18.08€, 2 or 3 courses with salad or vegetables, including cover and service charges, wine extra

COVER & SERVICE CHARGES
Cover 1.29€, 12% service added

ENGLISH
Yes, and menu in English

DA BEPPI (57)
Salizzada D. Pistor, 4550

One hundred years ago this was a rough-and-ready watering hole for the workers who cleaned the canals. Today, only the beamed ceiling remains as a reminder of those rowdy days. Inside this modest little trattoria near Ca' d'Oro are two wood-paneled rooms with the usual paintings of Venice. In front is a shaded patio that is perfect for warm-weather dining and people-watching. At Da Beppi, Delfina and her son Loris, who own it, create the type of Venetian homestyle cooking and atmosphere everyone hopes to find.

The daily specials depend on the season and whatever they find fresh at the market. No matter what time of year, you can expect to find *baccalà* (creamed salted cod) with polenta, marinated sardines, liver and onions, and a wonderful homemade chocolate almond cake with creamy chocolate frosting. The pastas are served in generous portions with a basket of crusty bread on the side to lap up the last drops of sauce.

TELEPHONE
041 528 5031

OPEN
Mon–Wed, Fri–Sun: lunch noon–3 P.M., dinner 7–10 P.M.

CLOSED
Thur; a week at Christmas, Jan–Feb (until Carnivale)

RESERVATIONS
Advised for weekends

CREDIT CARDS
MC, V

À LA CARTE
23.24–25.82€

MENÙ TURISTICO
None

COVER & SERVICE CHARGES
Cover 1.55€, service discretionary

ENGLISH
Yes

DA GIANNI (8)
Strada Nuova/SS. Appostoli, 4377

Most people rush right by Da Gianni, and that is too bad because it serves some of the best food along this tourist-trodden path. If tourists do stop, they make another mistake and that is consulting the multilingual, printed menu, which is best forgotten in favor of the imaginative, seasonal choices on the blackboard, most of which are fish based. The inside is properly set with

TELEPHONE
041 523 7268

OPEN
Mon–Tues, Thur–Sun: lunch noon–3 P.M., dinner 7–10 P.M.

CLOSED
Wed; Aug (dates vary)

RESERVATIONS
Advised

CREDIT CARDS
AE, DC, MC

À LA CARTE
20.66–25.82€

MENÙ TURISTICO
None

COVER & SERVICE CHARGES
Cover 1.55€, 10% service
added

ENGLISH
Yes

linens; outside offers prime tables overlooking the passing street parade. I thought the shrimp marinated in olive oil and lemon was wonderful, and my dining companion felt the same way about the typically Venetian liver, cooked to pink perfection and served with polenta. We each added a green salad and a glass of prosecco to start and soave wine to have with our meal. No, it wasn't Michelin-star material, but it was a simple, delicious Venetian lunch, one I would repeat often.

DA MARISA AI TRE ARCHI (1)
Fondamenta san Giobbe, 652

TELEPHONE
041 720 211

OPEN
Mon, Sun: lunch noon–2 P.M.;
Tues, Thur–Sat: lunch noon–
2 P.M., dinner 8–11 P.M.

CLOSED
Mon and Sun for dinner;
Wed; Aug

RESERVATIONS
Advised for Sun lunch

CREDIT CARDS
None

À LA CARTE
15.49–20.66€

MENÙ TURISTICO
None

COVER & SERVICE CHARGES
None

ENGLISH
Very limited

Unless you speak some Italian and can understand, even vaguely, a spoken menu, Marisa is probably not your Great Eat. On the other hand, if you want to rub elbows with a contingent of workers at lunch and lively locals at night and are willing eat whatever the cook bought at the market, you will be happy. I think the best time to go is for lunch on a warm, lazy Sunday, when time is not of the essence—you can sit at one of the canal-side tables, watch the boats float by in a corner of Venice seldom seen by the average visitor, and enjoy the moment. Another reason to aim for a Sunday is it is the only day the chef makes *zabaione,* and everyone agrees, it alone is worth the trip. Other dishes to look forward to are lusty stews, grilled fish, and risotto with bone marrow. This last is the house specialty, and it unfortunately makes infrequent appearances. To make your appearance, you can take the number 52 vaporetto and get off at Tre Archi.

ENOTECA BOLDRIN (58)
Salizzada San Canciano, 5550

TELEPHONE
041 523 7859

OPEN
Mon–Sat: 9 A.M.–9 P.M.,
lunch from noon–2:30 P.M.,
tramezzini any time

CLOSED
Sun; 10 days in July
(dates vary)

RESERVATIONS
Not necessary

CREDIT CARDS
None

À LA CARTE
Sandwiches from 1.55€, hot
foods 5.16–7.75€ per dish,
wines from 2.07€

In Venice you can spend the whole day getting lost inside the liquid maze of canals and narrow passageways that link one area to another. Adding to the fun are the mystifying maps, which do not necessarily spell the names of the streets the same way you will see them spelled on corner street signs or on business cards, if, in fact, they are even listed. A good case in point is Enoteca Boldrin, located on San Chianciano if you go by one map, or San Canciano if you go by the *enoteca*'s business card and another map. The restaurant is located in the same spot regardless, whichever way you spell the street, and that, ultimately, is all that matters.

What is the big news about another cafeteria-style lunch? First, this one is a hot ticket for locals, from overalled workmen to ladies draped in designer duds and gold jewelry. Why? Because the food is always fresh and plentiful, nicely prepared and displayed, and a quantum leap above the average deli-style dining that passes for lunch in Venice. There are at least a dozen first- and second-course choices, with an emphasis on fish, pastas (including risotto and lasagna), and colorful vegetables, but no desserts. Great Eating, even in a cafeteria, is always better with good wines, and there is no lack of them here—two walls are filled from ceiling to floor with more bottles than anyone cares to tally. At Boldrin, the M.O. is to get your food, pay, then hope you can snag a seat. Seating is along the walls next to the wine shelves, or at the wraparound bar where the dishes and *tramezzini* (sandwiches) are displayed.

MENÙ TURISTICO
None

COVER & SERVICE CHARGES
None

ENGLISH
Limited

FIASCHETTERIA TOSCANA ($, 60)
Salizzada San Giovanni Grisostomo, 5719

Fiaschetteria Toscana is the top choice of many Venetians for a celebration meal. In the two pleasant dining rooms, the Murano wall lights and candles cast a soft and romantic aura on the evening and the memorable food. On warm days, the prime seating is on the covered terrace across the street from the restaurant.

Fish plays a starring role in every course and is always excellent. The black *tagliolini* with lobster or white *tagliolini* with scampi and zucchini flowers are perfect pasta choices. For the second course, soft-shelled crab is a luxurious dish; the baked eel with bay leaves will please those who love something different, and the baked sea bass with potatoes will satisfy anyone. If you order their signature dish, *frittura della Serenissima*—a mixed, fried seafood platter—you will receive a complimentary plate to commemorate your meal. If fish isn't on your agenda, there are plenty of delightful alternatives, beginning with warm artichoke hearts or a plate of steamed white asparagus. Gnocchi with bacon and radicchio is an unusual treatment of this potato-based pasta, and it is much lighter than it sounds. The restaurant is also well-known for its *fiorentina* steaks (Chianina beef), either cooked with borolo wine, pepper sauce, or simply grilled. I think it is important to plan for dessert here, even if you only have room to share a bite or two. I am always torn between the *zabaione* served with crisp *baicoli* cookies, the caramel apple tart with a scoop of vanilla ice cream, and the smooth chocolate mousse with whipped cream.

TELEPHONE
041 528 5281

FAX
041 528 5521

OPEN
Mon, Wed–Sun: lunch 12:30–2:30 P.M., dinner 7:30–10:30 P.M.

CLOSED
Tues; 1 week after Carnivale, part of July and Aug (dates vary)

RESERVATIONS
Essential

CREDIT CARDS
AE, DC, MC, V

À LA CARTE
43.90–51.65€

MENÙ TURISTICO
None

COVER & SERVICE CHARGES
Cover and service charges included

ENGLISH
Yes, and menu in English

And usually, despite whatever I have promised my dining companion, I am reluctant to share in the end.

NOTE: Fiaschetteria Toscana is a member of Ristoranti della Buona Accoglienza; see page 173 for details.

LA COLONNA ($, 56)
Calle del Fumo, 5329 (at Campiello Pestrin)

TELEPHONE
041 522 9641

OPEN
Tues–Sat: lunch noon–2:30 P.M.,
dinner 7:30–10 P.M.

CLOSED
Mon, Sun; last 3 weeks of Jan

RESERVATIONS
Advised, especially at night

CREDIT CARDS
AE, DC, MC, V

À LA CARTE
30.99–36.15€

MENÙ TURISTICO
Menù regionale, 30.99€,
3 courses including dessert,
beverage extra; *menù degustazione,*
51.65€, 6 courses including
dessert and beverage; both must
be ordered by two

COVER & SERVICE CHARGES
No cover charge, 12% service
added

ENGLISH
Yes

"It's going to be good," I said to my dinner companion, "just look at the locals filling every table." Indeed, the neighborhood patrons know a good thing, and they like and respect what the talented chef can do with the Venetian bounty of succulent seafood. The small brick interior is correctly set with white linens, and the outdoor terrace is romantically lit at night. As you walk in, be sure to notice the beautiful window display of fresh fruits and produce that will be part of your meal. There are two set-price menus (which are not intended to be bargains), but unless you are amazingly hungry for fish, I would suggest ordering à la carte, which always reflects the chef's shopping safaris. You may sample crab with tiny asparagus tips, a special seafood risotto made to order for two, *tagliolini* with eggplant and calamari, fresh sardines prepared with onions and pine nuts and served with polenta, a beautiful grilled or baked fish, and for dessert, fat, juicy red strawberries. The satisfying food is cooked to order and served by one waiter, who manages to be gracious and accommodating despite the daunting table-to-server ratio. In the States, he would be unionized, and six people would need to be hired to do his job!

OSTERIA ALLA FRASCA (55)
Corte della Carità, 5176

TELEPHONE
041 528 5433

OPEN
Winter (Oct–May): Mon–Wed,
Fri–Sat, bar 8 A.M.–9 P.M.,
lunch noon–2:30 P.M., dinner
6:30–9:30 P.M.; Sun: bar 8 A.M.–
9 P.M., lunch noon–2:30 P.M.;
summer (June–Sept): Mon–
Wed, Fri–Sun, bar 8 A.M.–
11 P.M., dinner 6:30–9:30 P.M.

CLOSED
Thur; Sun dinner in winter;
lunch in summer; Jan, 2 weeks
in mid-Aug

RESERVATIONS
Advised

If you have yet to lose yourself in this sinking city's seductive byways, the hunt for this hidden gem is your golden opportunity. Actually, if you follow these directions, it may be disappointingly easy. From Fondamenta Nuove, walk down Calle del Fumo to Calle del Volto, turn right, and Corte della Carità is the second opening on your right; you will see the restaurant at the back of the little square. There is nothing touristy about this Venetian square; this is where everyday people live, hanging their weekly laundry to blow in the breeze and flap against the aging buildings. Bright flowers are lovingly tended in window boxes, dogs and children play after school, old ladies gossip, and the men talk politics and sports. For local color, it does not get much better.

The tiny *osteria* itself isn't much to look at, but it does have an interesting past as the storeroom where Tiziano kept his art supplies. All evidence of the artist is long gone, now replaced by four tables and a weekly menu taped to the refrigerator door—but no one, not even the cook, pays any attention to *that*. There are more tables outside, weather permitting. As you can imagine, the food here is comforting rather than trendy, and its mainstay is fish, served every day but Monday, when the special is *bollito* (boiled meat) and tripe. On Tuesday, it is fish and *pasta e fagoli;* Wednesday risotto of some sort; and the rest of the week, fish again. Dessert consists of hard cookies to dip in sweet wine; this may sound plain, but after a while, you will become addicted to this special Italian finale to your meal. While there are always one or two alternatives to fish, they are not recommended; stick to what they do best. *Cicchetti* are served at the bar, but if you sit down with yours, you will pay the cover charge.

CREDIT CARDS
None

À LA CARTE
Cicchetti from 1.03€, meals 18.08–20.06€

MENÙ TURISTICO
None

COVER & SERVICE CHARGES
Cover 1.55€, no service charge

ENGLISH
Yes

OSTERIA DA ALBERTO (59)
Calle Largo Giacinto Gallina, 5401

The rustic two-room *osteria* sits alongside a canal, with several tables overlooking the waterway. You might think tables on the canal would be the place to sit, and while this might be true late in the evening, at lunch you want to be up front near the bar where all the action is taking place. This is a place to come for fun, food, and Venetian-style camaraderie. The order of the day should be a plate with assorted *cicchetti,* or the daily hot dishes washed down with ample glasses of the *vino della casa.*

TELEPHONE
041 523 8153

OPEN
Mon–Sat: lunch 9:30 A.M.– 3 P.M., dinner 5:30–11 P.M.

CLOSED
Sun; Jan 15–22, last 2 weeks of July and first week of Aug

RESERVATIONS
Advised for dinner

CREDIT CARDS
None

À LA CARTE
From 1.29€ for *cicchetti;* 2 courses, 12.91€

MENÙ TURISTICO
None

COVER & SERVICE CHARGES
Cover and service included

ENGLISH
Yes

TRATTORIA ALL'ANTICA MOLA (2)
Fondamenta degli Ormesini, 2800

Venice exists today because of the huge influx of tourists who spend more than $150 million a year here. A visitor to Venice can easily become a sitting duck for dining rip-offs. With a little extra effort and some ingenuity, venturing off the beaten tourist track can yield not only better food but a great increase in value. Sitting along a canal on the edge of the Jewish Quarter is

TELEPHONE
041 717 492

OPEN
Daily: noon–midnight, continuous service

CLOSED
Aug

RESERVATIONS
Advised

CREDIT CARDS
AE, DC, MC, V
À LA CARTE
18.08–23.24€
MENÙ TURISTICO
None
COVER & SERVICE CHARGES
Cover 1.29€, service included
ENGLISH
Yes

Trattoria all'Antica Mola, where you will be assured a decent meal at a fair price, along with plenty of locals filling adjacent tables and enjoying the same. It is an unassuming place, but you will be able to spot it as you approach: it is the one with the flags flying beside the canal-side tables. The easiest way to find it is to cross the Campo di Quarter Nuovo to Fondamenta degli Ormesini and turn right, or walk along Rio Terrà Farsetti, cross the bridge, and turn left.

Time and tradition stand behind the food and the dowdy atmosphere. The two rooms are definitely in need of redecorating—hung as they are with old copper, postcards from regulars, and signed drawings on napkins—but Franco, the talkative owner, is certainly not thinking of doing anything like that any time soon. In warm weather, you won't care what the interior looks like because you will be sitting in the back garden or along the canal. For the most satisfying meal, focus on the simple pastas and second courses based on fish. If you want dessert, try the fruit-topped custard tarts or the orange cake. The house wines are good . . . and cheap. Another bonus: The food is served continuously from noon to midnight every day.

TRATTORIA CA' D'ORO—OSTERIA DALLA VEDOVA (7)
Calle del Pistor and Ramo Ca' d'Oro, 3912–3952 (off Strada Nova)

TELEPHONE
041 528 5324
OPEN
Mon–Wed, Fri–Sat: lunch
11:30 A.M.–2:30 P.M., dinner
6:30–10 P.M.; Sun:
dinner 6:30–10 P.M.
CLOSED
Thur; Sun lunch; 2 weeks after
Carnivale, Aug or Sept
RESERVATIONS
Advised
CREDIT CARDS
None
À LA CARTE
Cicchetti from 1.03€, 2 course
12.91–23.24€
MENÙ TURISTICO
None
COVER & SERVICE CHARGES
Cover 1.03€, service included
ENGLISH
Yes, and French

The name on the business card reads: Trattoria Ca' d'Oro—Osteria dalla Vedova. But on the window it's simply La Vedova, which is how it's known by all of its loyalists.

This spot has been in the same family for 135 years, and judging from the inside, little has changed in that time. The two rooms are filled with what looks like original furniture, a marvelous collection of copper pots hanging from the ceiling, and pretty antique lights. Any time you go you find the brother-and-sister owners, Lorenzo and Mirella, mixing and mingling with an interesting sampling of area regulars, who sit at the plain wooden tables sharing a bottle of *vino rosso* and arguing about Sunday's soccer scores or the latest Italian political scandal.

There is no proper menu, and they do not serve dessert, but this is a good place to keep in mind for a light lunch or dinner. Find out what the chef has prepared for that day, maybe a pasta with fresh clams, or a hearty soup, and add a plate of antipasti, a few chunks of bread, and a sturdy wine, and you will be all set. The service has been known to be cool, but after a few glasses of Tokai, or red wine from Padua, your Italian should improve, and you will feel more welcome.

Gelaterias

GELATERIA LEONARDO (4)
Rio Terra San Leonardo, 1525 (near Campo San Leonardo)

The strip of real estate leading from the *ferrovia* (train station) on Rio Terra di Spagna, across Campo S. Geremia and along Rio Terra San Leonardo, is full of tourist traps. You really need to be careful to avoid getting your budget soaked by poor-quality restaurants and greedy shopkeepers selling mostly garish junk. Clearly, this is not my favorite Venice neighborhood. However, most visitors travel this corridor at some point, and there are a few redeeming places worthy of a stop. Gelateria Leonardo is one to put on your snacking list if you are in the mood for a super *gelato produzione propria*—gelato made in house, and served in cones, cups, and fancy sundaes. This is the second shop owned by the gelato virtuosos who also run La Boutique del Gelato on Salizzada San Lio in Castello (see page 201).

TELEPHONE
041 710 000

OPEN
Daily: 10 A.M.–midnight (in winter till 8 P.M.)

CLOSED
Dec and Jan

CREDIT CARDS
None

PRICES
Cones from 0.77–2.32€, cups from 1.29–2.32€, sundaes from 2.58€

ENGLISH
Depends on server

Castello

Constituting the eastern portion of Venice, Castello is the largest of the *sestieri,* and the only one without real estate along the Grand Canal. The central building is the huge Gothic church of Santi Giovanni e Paolo, with the equestrian monument of Bartholomeo Colleoni by Andrea del Verrocchio. In back of the church is the Ospedale Civile, where the ambulance boats are tied up at the dock alongside the canal ready to respond to emergencies. Campo Santa Maria Formosa serves as a major crossing point between Piazza San Marco and the Rialto Bridge, and it's an interesting place to sip a cool drink in the afternoon and watch the neighborhood children gather to play while their mamas and nannies gossip or buy produce from one of the two stalls in the center of the square. Also in this district is the Arsenale—the shipyards of Venice—and the Riva degli Schiavoni, Venice's premier promenading ground, lined with grand hotels (such as the Danieli) and waves of tourists. Farther east is Rio Terà Garibaldi, the lusty workingman's quarter, and the only large green park in Venice, Giardini, which is where La Biennale, the famous international contemporary art exhibit, is held every two years.

($) indicates a Big Splurge

Restaurants

AL COVO ($, 83)
Campiello della Pescaria, 3968

People often ask me, "If you had only one meal to eat in a city, where would it be?" In Venice, the answer is simple: If I want fish, I would go to Al Covo for dinner. And I am not alone. The popularity of Al Covo is due both to the excellence of its cuisine, prepared by Cesare, and to the warm atmosphere created by his wife, Diane; this dynamic American/Italian couple opened the restaurant in 1987. At night, fresh flowers adorn the tables, which are formally set with floral-patterned china, heavy cutlery, and gleaming crystal.

While looking over the menu, a plate of bite-size appetizers are brought to your table, along with assorted breads served with iced butter curls, a treat found in few other Venetian restaurants. All of their dishes are prepared to order, using what the market offers each day and what products are in season. No frozen or canned foods are used, and neither are farmed fish. Cesare is justly well known for his imaginative and delicate preparations of fresh seafood, which are cooked without the use of butter or other animal fats. All the pastas are made daily in-house, and the tomato sauce is made from a recipe Cesare inherited from his grandmother. In winter, roasted wild local duck served with fresh mixed vegetables is an anticipated specialty of the house.

Their lunch offer has taken off like wildfire. In the tradition of trattorias, they have developed a midday menu consisting of a choice of appetizer or pasta dish of the day, main dish, and dessert. If you do not want this large of a meal, platters of mixed cheeses or vegetables, appetizers, soups, or just a bowl of pasta are available. The lunch atmosphere is casual, with bare tables, cloth napkins, and quick service geared to local workers who have only a limited time.

Whenever you eat at Al Covo—and some *Great Eats* readers have come here once and then eaten nowhere else for the rest of their Venetian stay—you absolutely must try at least one or two of Diane's homemade desserts. If the pear and prune cake with grappa sauce is available, have it for sure. It is so good it was featured in *Gourmet* magazine. The other choices are endless: zabaglione made at your table, bitter chocolate cake, walnut cake with caramel sauce and spiked with aged rum, *panna cotta*

TELEPHONE
041 522 3812

OPEN
Mon–Tues, Fri–Sun: lunch 12:45–2 P.M., dinner 7:30–10 P.M.

CLOSED
Wed–Thur; Jan, 2 weeks in Aug

RESERVATIONS
Essential

CREDIT CARDS
None, but they accept U.S. dollars and traveler's checks

À LA CARTE
Lunch 28.41–38.73€, dinner 41.32–49.06€

MENÙ TURISTICO
Menù osteria, lunch only: 30.77€, 3 courses, cover included; beverage and service extra

COVER & SERVICE CHARGES
Cover 3.62€, service not included

ENGLISH
Yes, and menu in English

with dark chocolate sauce. Whatever you order, your meal will be followed by a dish of nuts, chocolate, and mints as a complimentary grand finale.

Service by the English-speaking staff is attentive and helpful. While the lunch prices will fit into most budgets, the dinner prices are definitely not for budgeteers, so reserve this as a special occasion or final night in Venice with someone you love.

NOTE: Al Covo is a member of the Ristoranti della Buona Accoglienza; see page 173 for details.

ALLE TESTIERE ($, 74)
Calle del Mondo Novo, 5801 (off Salizzada San Lio)

TELEPHONE
041 522 7220

OPEN
Tues–Sat: lunch noon–2 P.M.,
dinner 7–10:30 P.M.

CLOSED
Mon, Sun; 3 weeks at Christmas, last 3 weeks in July

RESERVATIONS
Essential

CREDIT CARDS
None

À LA CARTE
38.73–43.90€

MENÙ TURISTICO
None

COVER & SERVICE CHARGES
Cover 1.29€, no service charge

ENGLISH
Yes

Where do the Venetians go for fish? When a place is "found," it is coveted, its name mentioned as guardedly as insider stock market tips. Such was the case when Alle Testiere opened. Everything about the spot is modest, except the quality of the fish and, potentially, the size of your check if you are not careful. Each of the bare tables has a Murano vase with fresh flowers. Seating is on hard bistro chairs, and service is quick . . . they have to turn those tables several times during a meal to keep out of the red. The server will recite the short menu, and fish plays a central role in every dish—it is always fresh, well prepared, and a delight to eat. From a very meager beginning, the restaurant is now the talk of the town; it has, you might say, achieved "blue chip" status as a solid dining investment. An added bonus for many is that the restaurant is completely nonsmoking.

AL NUOVO GALEON ($, 87)
Via Garibaldi, 1308

TELEPHONE & FAX
041 520 4656

OPEN
Wed–Sun: lunch 12:30–2:30 P.M., dinner 7:30–9:30 P.M.

CLOSED
Mon–Tues; Jan to Carnivale

RESERVATIONS
Advised

CREDIT CARDS
AE, DC, MC, V

À LA CARTE
33.57–38.73€

MENÙ TURISTICO
Lunch only Wed–Fri: 15.49€,
2 courses plus salad, beverage
extra

Via Garibaldi is a wide, bustling street that cuts through the eastern part of Castello. In the morning, it is filled with shoppers, and in the evening, with locals strolling down the middle and filling the bars. If you look along the side streets of this neighborhood, you will see bright red flower boxes at almost every window and laundry lines rustling in the breeze. The whole area is about as local as it gets. Just off Via Garibaldi are the public gardens where La Biennale, the international art exhibit, is held every two years.

So where does everyone eat? Besides bars, there are several choices, but for the best fresh fish, head for Al Nuovo Galeon. The restaurant's seafaring motif extends to the bar, which is an actual boat, and to the back rooms, which have wraparound murals of Venetian waterways. The set menu is a lunchtime Great Eat in that it offers four choices, including fish, for each course. You can start with *spaghetti alle vongole* (with clams), then have a mixed fried fish plate, potatoes, and a mixed salad all for less than just one of these courses could cost in the higher rent districts. Going à la carte can stretch your Venetian budget, especially if you order four courses. While there are plenty of choices other than fish, both on the set menu and à la carte, the restaurant is best known for fish.

COVER & SERVICE CHARGES
Cover 1.55€, 12% service added

ENGLISH
Yes, and menus in English

AL SCALINETTO (82)
Calle del Dose, 3803

The same family has been cooking here for forty-five years, and they show no sign of slowing down or changing their committment to serving high-quality food at sensible prices. The inside is small, as is the vine-covered back terrace as well as the tables, which are barely big enough to accommodate the plates of delicious, cooked-to-order food.

There are several set-menu options, including one with Venetian specialties and another featuring fish. These are good values in that they offer three or four choices for a filling three-course meal that includes vegetables and dessert. The food is seasonal, with daily specials, and as always, these reflect the best choices. Look for pastas sauced with clams, mussels, and shrimp, fish risottos for two, liver with polenta, mixed grilled platters, fried fish, and simple fruit desserts.

TELEPHONE
041 520 0776

OPEN
Mon–Thur, Sat–Sun: lunch noon–3 P.M., dinner 7–10:30 P.M.

CLOSED
Fri; 20 days in Nov, 20 days in Dec (dates vary)

RESERVATIONS
Advised

CREDIT CARDS
AE, MC, V

À LA CARTE
23.24–28.41€

MENÙ TURISTICO
Three 3-course menus: simple, 14.16€; fish, 16.53€, includes dessert; *Veneziano,* 21.69€, includes dessert or coffee

COVER & SERVICE CHARGES
None

ENGLISH
Yes, and menu in English

AL VECIO CANTON (78)
Corte Rotta, 4738/a (off Ruga Guiffa)

Yes, another shrine to pizza, but this one is hidden, the natives pack the place, and few tourists other than you and I know about it. Other points in its favor include its close proximity to St. Mark's Square, the swift and sure service, the staggering list of pizzas available for both lunch and dinner (forget all the other stuff on the second page of the menu), the fresh ingredients, and the high quality. The pizzas are, in a word, great, especially their specialty—starring tomatoes, *mozzarella di bufala,* and anchovies—which is deceptively rich and

TELEPHONE
041 528 5176

OPEN
Mon, Wed–Sun: lunch noon–2:30 P.M., dinner 7–10:30 P.M.

CLOSED
Tues; Aug

RESERVATIONS
Essential, especially for dinner and on the weekends

CREDIT CARDS
AE, DC, MC, V

À LA CARTE
Pizza 5.68–8.78€

MENÙ TURISTICO
12.91€, 2 courses and
vegetables; cover and service
included, beverage extra

COVER & SERVICE CHARGES
Cover 1.03€, service included

ENGLISH
Yes, and menu in English

delicious down to the last crumb of crispy crust. Finally, the prices will keep any Great Eater happy and in high spirits.

ANTICA SACRESTIA (79)
SS. Filippo e Giacomo, 4442, at corner of Calle de la Sacresta

TELEPHONE
041 523 0749

OPEN
Tues–Sun: lunch noon–
2:30 P.M., dinner 7–10:30 P.M.

CLOSED
Mon; a few days at Christmas

RESERVATIONS
Advised

CREDIT CARDS
MC, V

À LA CARTE
Pizza from 5.16€, full meals
20.66–23.24€

MENÙ TURISTICO
Menù turistico, 13.43€,
3 courses; *Vegetariano,* 20.66€,
3 courses and salad; *Veneziano,*
23.24€, 3 courses, all fish;
Pesce, 30.99€, 3 courses, all
fish; *Antica Sacrestia,* 51.65€,
house specialties from appetizer
to dessert; all menus include
cover and service, beverage
extra

COVER & SERVICE CHARGES
No cover charge, service
discretionary

ENGLISH
Yes

Your two teenagers are demanding pizza, your wife wants a vegetarian meal, your mother-in-law thinks pasta and a salad would hit the spot, and you are yearning for ham and eggs (and some relief from negotiating everybody's appetites). No problem: simply head for Antica Sacrestia, about a ten-minute meander from San Marco. As you've already guessed, this all-purpose Great Eat offers something for everyone . . . including some stiff cocktails and, best of all, prices that are easy on your travel budget. Thirty-eight pizzas are enhanced by a dozen specialties, four more feature white cheese and vegetable toppings, and for dessert, there is an orange liqueur–infused pizza and those topped with chocolate, banana, or kiwi. The five *menù turistico*s cover all the bases, from a basic three-course budget meal to two menus dominated by fish, one for vegetarians, and one described as having *porzioni enormi* (enormous portions) of all the house specialties. If this is not enough of a selection, there are two pages of à la carte menu items, which include pastas (including macaroni and cheese, crepes, and a vegetable torte), fifteen fish dishes, as many meat preparations, twenty-one desserts, and of course, the above-mentioned ham and eggs. If you can't find something to eat at Antica Sacrestia, I give up.

CIP CIAP (73)
Calle del Mondo Novo, 5799

TELEPHONE
041 523 6621

OPEN
Mon, Wed–Sun: 9 A.M.–9 P.M.,
continuous service

CLOSED
Tues; 3 weeks in Jan
(dates vary)

For some of the best *pizza al taglio di tutti tipi* (pizza slices of all types), a bulging calzone, or an assortment of minipizzas to munch on for a quick snack, do not miss this busy little corner establishment off the Campo Santa Maria Formosa. This is Italian fast food, and I love it. It was located close to my Venetian flat, and I will admit, I was a regular customer.

You can eat here if you want to stand along the Calle del Mondo Novo, or better, have your slices packaged to go. Everything is sold by weight from 0.93€ per 100 grams. Dole out a worthwhile 1.86€ or so per slice and a little more for the calzone, take your feast over to the Campo Santa Maria Formosa, and sit on a bench and watch the neighborhood at work and at play. It is a great way to feel Italian and have a satisfying Great Eat in the bargain.

RESERVATIONS
Not accepted

CREDIT CARDS
None

À LA CARTE
Pizza slices from 0.93€ per 100 grams; tortas and calzones from 1.29€ per 100 grams; whole pizzas from 3.87–6.20€

MENÙ TURISTICO
None

COVER & SERVICE CHARGES
No cover, service included

ENGLISH
Sometimes

DA MARIO ALLA FAVA (69)
Calle Stagneri, 5242

Da Mario alla Fava is attractively positioned between two narrow streets, just minutes from the tourist circus surrounding Rialto Bridge. As you can imagine, fine cuisine is not in great supply in this sector of Venice. However, the one exception is this delightful restaurant run by the same dedicated family since 1961. Inside, it is formally set with fresh flowers, crisp linens, and attractive lighting. One of the best features is the outdoor, shaded dining terrace that is mercifully secluded from the tawdry crowds just a half block away. The menu is seasonal, the pastas and desserts made here, and the quality and attention to detail apparent in every dish served. You might start with a light appetizer of scallops and fresh asparagus or prosciutto with kiwis. The *tagliolini* with clams and mushrooms is filling, but not so much so that you can't do justice to turbot with artichokes, grilled sea bass or a light veal scaloppine served with fresh vegetables. Even though the cakes and zabaglione are tempting, I have never had room for more than a refreshing bowl of mixed berries, splashed with grappa and topped with a little scoop of ice cream.

TELEPHONE
041 528 5147

OPEN
Daily: lunch noon–2:30 P.M., dinner 7–10:30 P.M.

CLOSED
20 days in Jan (dates vary)

RESERVATIONS
Essential for dinner, especially for the terrace

CREDIT CARDS
AE, DC, MC, V (only if ordering à la carte)

À LA CARTE
36.15–43.90€

MENÙ TURISTICO
18.08€, 3 courses (main course includes choice of fish or meat), including vegetable garnish and cover charge; service and beverage extra; no credit cards

COVER & SERVICE CHARGES
Cover 2.07€, 12% service added

ENGLISH
Yes, and menus in English

L'OSTERIA DI SANTA MARINA ($, 62)
Campo Santa Marina, 5911

A meal at Agostino Doria and Danilo Baldan's charming restaurant on the quiet Campo Santa Marina is a feast of extraordinary good cooking featuring superb fresh fish. In fact, I rate it as one of the best restaurants in Venice—one no Great Eater should miss. The intimate dining room has a bar to one side and an interesting

TELEPHONE & FAX
041 528 5239

INTERNET
www.osteriadisantamarina.it

OPEN
Mon: dinner 7:30–9:30 P.M.; Tues–Sat: lunch 12:30–2:30 P.M., dinner 7:30-9:30 P.M.

CLOSED
Mon lunch; Sun; Aug 15–31,
Jan 7–Feb 1

RESERVATIONS
Essential

CREDIT CARDS
MC, V

À LA CARTE
36.15–41.34€

MENÙ TURISTICO
Menù degustazione (must be
ordered by entire table):
51.65€ per person, includes
3 antipasti, 1 pasta, 1 main
course, 1 dessert, coffee and
water; wine extra

COVER & SERVICE CHARGES
Cover 2.58€, service
discretionary

ENGLISH
Yes, and menu in English

collection of French black-and-white sketches collected by Danilo's grandfather. The room seats only forty, and an additonal ten or twenty can be served on the covered summer terrace. There is only one seating for every mealtime, which encourages guests to relax and linger over their lunch or dinner. The gracious service is always very friendly and helpful, whether guiding you through the seasonal, fish-based menu or ordering just the right bottle of wine to complement your meal.

While you are trying to decide among the many delicious options, a complimentary appetizer is served; perhaps warm baby shrimp lightly tossed with shredded zucchini and resting on a bed of polenta. If you are ordering an antipasto, try the lukewarm spider crab delicately seasoned with a hint of lemon and olive oil, or the boiled octopus with red onion, grated orange peel, and balsamic vinegar, a bold combination of taste and texture that is unusual and very good . . . even if you don't like octopus. Pastas are simple, the way they should be when starring seafood. The sea bass and shrimp ravioli is a good example, and so is the *tagliolini* tossed with spider crab. For a second course, hope that the John Dory filet with summer vegetables is on the menu. It is an uncomplicated, simply prepared dish that allows the flavor of the fish to shine through. Tuna steak lightly seasoned with rosemary or the richly satisfying soft shell crabs with fresh artichokes are two more winning main courses. Portions are not overwhelming, so you can safely add a mixed green salad or a plate of lightly grilled vegetables, drizzled with extra-virgin olive oil. Desserts are, in a word, divine. If chocolate is your passion, don't miss the *tortino al cioccolato*—a rich chocolate pie that is worth every calorie. So is the lemon mousse, served with a light shower of chocolate sauce, a cluster of fresh currents, and a spun sugar cap. If you want a lighter but still sweet ending, the assortment of the chef's cookies (macaroons, dark chocolate brownie bites, and buttery nut wafers) goes perfectly with a glass of strawberry wine or an espresso.

OSTERIA AL PORTICO (63)
Calle della Malvasia, 6015, near Campo San Lio

This small picturesque place is crowded with copper pots, low beams, barflies, and wine barrels. Luigi, the affable owner, speaks English and welcomes everyone to his great Venetian hangout. Here you eat *cicchetti,* fish risotto when it comes out of the kitchen at 1 P.M., or any of the hot specials of the day, neatly written on a piece of olive-brown construction paper. Your wine will be from the Veneto and your check a Great Eat bargain.

TELEPHONE
041 522 9038

OPEN
Mon–Fri: bar 8 A.M.–10 P.M., continuous service for *cicchetti;* hot food noon–2 P.M., 7–9 P.M.; Sat: 8 A.M.–3 P.M.

CLOSED
Sat evening, Sun; 1 week in June, Aug and Nov

RESERVATIONS
Not necessary

CREDIT CARDS
None

À LA CARTE
Cicchetti from 1.29€, 2-course meal 15.49€

MENÙ TURISTICO
None

COVER & SERVICE CHARGES
No cover or service charges, but 2.07€ bread charge

ENGLISH
Yes

TRATTORIA ALLA RIVETTA (81)
Ponte San Provolo, 4625

Trattoria alla Rivetta, squeezed in on the right just before the Ponte San Provolo and off Campo S.S. Filipino e Giancomo, is a genuine and reasonable alternative to the many touristy alternatives that plague this area of Venice. A good sign, as always, is that the locals eat here in droves, filling every seat in the house almost as soon as it is open. You will see everyone from gondoliers on their breaks grabbing a snack at the bar and a glass of *vino della casa* to women out for a gossipy lunch with friends. True, it has been discovered, but that fact has not diminished its authenticity one bit. The menu is printed in English, and the restaurant serves full meals from 10 A.M. to 10 P.M., two distinct advantages for visitors.

Portions are not for the light eater. In fact, the bowl of mussels ordered as a first course will be plenty if you add a salad and the fresh bread that comes with every Italian meal. Hungry diners can start with the *tagliolini con granchio,* pasta with fresh crab, or a time-honored spaghetti with meat sauce. The squid cooked in its own ink served with polenta and the grilled jumbo shrimp are delicious entrées. There is also a full line of meats, including Venetian liver and onions, veal chops, and boiled beef with pesto sauce. Desserts are run-of-the-mill except for

TELEPHONE
041 528 7302

OPEN
Tues–Sun: 10 A.M.–10 P.M., continuous service

CLOSED
Mon; July 20–Aug 20

RESERVATIONS
Not accepted for over five

CREDIT CARDS
AE, MC, V

À LA CARTE
25.85€

MENÙ TURISTICO
None

COVER & SERVICE CHARGES
Cover 1.03€, 12% service added

ENGLISH
Some, and menu in English

the house tiramisù, that heavenly rum-spiked cake layered with triple-cream cheese and dusted with chocolate.

TRATTORIA DAI TOSI (88)
Secco Marina, 738

TELEPHONE
041 523 7102
OPEN
Mon–Tues, Thur–Sun: lunch noon–2:30 P.M., dinner 7–10 P.M.
CLOSED
Wed; 2 weeks in mid-Aug, few days at Christmas, last week of Jan or first week Feb (call to check, dates vary)
RESERVATIONS
Suggested for Sat and Sun
CREDIT CARDS
MC, V
À LA CARTE
20.66–23.24€, pizza from 5.16€
MENÙ TURISTICO
None
COVER & SERVICE CHARGES
Cover 1.55€, service included
ENGLISH
Yes, and menu in English

Trattoria dai Tosi occupies small but vibrant quarters that are further in spirit from tourist central than they are in kilometers. Located off Via Garibaldi (take Calle Correra until you get to Secco Marina, and it will be on your left), about a twenty-minute walk east of Piazza San Marco, this neighborhood gathering place is owned and run by two former waiters at Harry's Bar: Fabio, along with his wife, Lorena, and Paolo, with his English wife, Jackie. It is the wives who share cooking responsibilities. Jackie did not start out to be a chef. On a lark, she left her native Cornwall at age seventeen and came to the Lido, where she taught pony riding to children. She worked her way up, finally becoming well-known as a trainer for the top Italian show jumpers. Along the way she met Paolo, and the rest is history: they married, had two children, and became partners in this restaurant. Pictures of their children hang on the left wall in the room beyond the bar.

At noon, blue-collar workers troop in for Jackie's specials and her *pasta della casa,* an imaginative mix of vegetables, scampi, shrimp, calamari, pepperoni, zucchini, and carrots all tossed with spaghetti and a spoonful of cream. This makes a nice meal, accompanied by one or two crusty rolls, an *insalata mista,* and a glass of the house red wine. If you do go for lunch, be sure to take the time to see the oldest church in Venice, which is quite close by. The San Pietro di Castello is open daily from 8 A.M. to noon and 3 to 6 P.M., and on holidays from 8 A.M. to noon and 4:30 to 7:30 P.M.

The kitchen is closed for full dinner meals on Monday, Tuesday, and Thursday nights, but not the pizza ovens, which work overtime turning out almost fifty varieties of pizzas, ten of which are vegetarian. On these nights, you eat your pizza here or have it packed to go. On Friday, Saturday, and Sunday nights, the kitchen turns out its full menu, which includes pizza.

NOTE: Inexplicably, another place calling itself Trattoria dai Tosi has opened on the opposite corner. It won't take you long to figure out which is which . . . the Great Eat Tosi is the *small* one filled with locals, who spill onto the pavement in front on a summer evening or jam the bar in winter. The new Tosi is the big boring one with the chef standing in the doorway wondering when he will be busy.

TRATTORIA DA REMIGIO (80)
Salizzada dei Greci, 3416

At Trattoria da Remigio, all your choices are happy ones, whether for your appetizer, pasta, or fish or meat course. For a new twist on an old dish, try the *gnocchi alla pescatora,* potato-based pasta puffs with fish. For best results, always pay close attention to the handwritten daily specials, especially the seafood catch. The desserts will have you doing penance on a Thighmaster when you get home.

Arrive late and you will need a shoehorn to get in. The restaurant enjoys the fiercely devout patronage of Venetians, and they virtually pack it out day and night, so call ahead for a reservation and be on time.

TELEPHONE
041 523 0089

OPEN
Mon: lunch 12:30–2:30 P.M.;
Wed–Sun: lunch 12:30–
2:30 P.M., dinner 7:30–
10:30 P.M.

CLOSED
Mon dinner; Tues; Dec 20–Jan 20, last week of July and first week of Aug

RESERVATIONS
Essential

CREDIT CARDS
AE, DC, MC, V

À LA CARTE
25.82–30.99€

MENÙ TURISTICO
None

COVER & SERVICE CHARGES
Cover 1.55€, 12% service added

ENGLISH
Limited

TRATTORIA NUOVA SPERANZA (85)
Campo Ruga, 145

For an experience of local life in a hidden corner of Venice, it does not get any better than the simple lunch served at Trattoria Nuova Speranza, run by Lucciano and Massimo Salvagno. It all began in 1973 when Lucciano's mother opened a trattoria in Campo Ruga. For reasons only understood by Venetian bureaucrats—and their inordinant fondness for red tape and high taxes—she was forced to close. Then in 1984, Lucciano and his son Massimo bought the present Campo Ruga location. Technically Massimo only *helps* Lucciano, but in fact he is here every day.

It opens around 7:30 A.M. when the locals stop by for coffee. In the winter, workmen fill the old-fashioned knotty-pine dining room around noon, followed at 1 P.M. by the locals. In the summer, tables are placed on the campo, and everyone knows to arrive by noon to get an outdoor seat. Dinner is not served from June through September, and only by reservation the rest of the time. Specialties of the house include the Venetian favorites of

TELEPHONE
041 528 5225

OPEN
Daily: in summer, bar
7:30 A.M.–6 P.M., lunch
1–3:30 P.M.; in winter, bar
remains open till 8 P.M., lunch
is same hours, dinner by
reservation only

CLOSED
One week between Christmas
and New Year's, Aug 10–31
(dates vary)

RESERVATIONS
Not necessary for lunch;
required for dinner in winter

CREDIT CARDS
None

À LA CARTE
12.91–20.66€

MENÙ TURISTICO
12.91€, 2 courses, cover and
service included; beverage extra

COVER & SERVICE CHARGES
Cover 1.03€, 12% service
addded

ENGLISH
Yes, and *menù turistico* in
English

seppie in nero (cuttlefish cooked in its own ink) with polenta, and *bigoli in salsa* (spaghetti with sardines). Other crowd-pleasers, such as spaghetti carbonara, *sarde in saor,* and *baccalà,* are available. The two-course menu lists several options, including lasagna and *pasta al pomodoro* for the first course followed by roast chicken, pork, or the blue-plate special. Nothing is gourmet, but it's a taste of truly Venetian everyday cooking. Another Venetian characteristic is Lucciano and Massimo's "flexible" closing times. In the summer, they will often close after lunch, say around 4 P.M. And in the winter, they might close before 8 P.M. if there are no drinking customers or dinner reservations. The moral here? Arrive at lunchtime.

TRATTORIA/PIZZERIA DA PAOLO (84)
Campo Arsenale, 2389

TELEPHONE
041 521 0660

OPEN
Tues–Sun: lunch noon–3 P.M.,
dinner 7–10 P.M.

CLOSED
Mon; 2–3 weeks at Christmas
and New Year's, first or second
week in Sept

RESERVATIONS
Advised for dinner on weekends

CREDIT CARDS
None

À LA CARTE
15.49€, pizza 5.16–8.26€

MENÙ TURISTICO
None

COVER & SERVICE CHARGES
Cover 0.77€, 12% service
added

ENGLISH
Yes

You could not possibly ask for a better view of the commanding entrance to the Arsenale, the historic twelfth-century shipyard that hundreds of years ago employed 16,000 men who could assemble a galleon in twenty-four hours. The entire Arsenale covers 318 square meters and is still used by the Italian navy, but it is not open to the general public. Therefore, the stunning view of the lion-guarded entrance you have from a table on the terrace of Paolo's trattoria is about as close as you will get to this important Venetian landmark, unless you ride on the number 42 vaporetto, which cuts through the Arsenale.

Besides the location, what does Paolo's have going for it? If you order what they do best, it has alot going for it. If you stray too far from these items, not so much. In addition, the service can become distracted, and sometimes nonexistent, when it gets very busy. Warnings aside, I still recommend it and suggest you arrive early to get a good seat. And what do they do best? Order their *spaghetti della casa* with tomatoes, clams, muscles, and crayfish, or order a pizza, especially the house pizza loaded with vegetables, salami, and ham. Ask for a basket of warm pizza bread, drink the house Tokai white wine, take some pictures to show the family back home, and enjoy another lovely day in Venice.

Gelaterias

LA BOUTIQUE DEL GELATO (71)
Salizzada San Lio, 5727

Italians know good gelato, and nowhere is it better than here. This *gelateria* is easy to find: just look for the line that weaves down the narrow Salizzada San Lio. The line forms when they open around 10 A.M. and lasts until closing at 8:30 P.M. Run by an energetic duo—Sandra and Silvio Calvaldoro—this tiny operation does an amazing business. They are smart: they offer a few knockout flavors sold by the cone or cup, or packaged to go. There is no seating at all and no beverages available. I passed the shop coming and going to my flat each day, and every time it was all I could do not to stop in for a scoop of *nocciolosa* (a creamy chocolate gelato laced with nuts) or their specialty (and secret recipe) the *millefoglie*. Sandra and Silvio both speak English and have friends in San Francisco whom they often visit. If you are anywhere near either of their Venice *gelateria*, please have a scoop or two for me. For information on their second location, Gelateria Leonardo, see page 189.

TELEPHONE
041 522 3283

OPEN
Daily: 10 A.M.–8:30 P.M.

CLOSED
Jan

CREDIT CARDS
None

PRICES
Cones 1.03–2.58€, cups 1.29–2.58€, whipped cream 0.52€

ENGLISH
Yes

Pastry Shops and Bakeries

PASTICCERIA PONTE DELLE PASTE (65)
Ponte delle Paste, 5991, at end of Calle Carmine, off Salizzada San Lio

Aside from the mouthwatering display of pastries, I like this *pasticceria* because everyone is so friendly and nice. After a few visits in the morning you are treated as a regular. Monica and her staff know everyone, including the kind of coffee they prefer; often they have your pastry in hand before you have given your order. Around noon, trays of *tramezzini* (sandwiches), toast with ham and cheese, pizza slices, and salads are served in a tiny tea room. All the sugary delights can be packed to go.

TELEPHONE & FAX
041 522 2889

OPEN
Summer (June–Aug): Mon–Sat 7 A.M.–8:30 P.M., Sun 7 A.M.–2 P.M.; winter (Sept–May): Mon–Tues, Thur–Sun, same hours

CLOSED
Wed in winter; NAC

CREDIT CARDS
None

PRICES
Pastries from 1.03€, hot and cold sandwiches 1.55–3.10€

ENGLISH
Enough

San Marco

Piazza San Marco is the heart and soul of Venice, as it has been since the first rulers built the Doge Palace and St. Mark's Basilica. Often flooded, ringed with outrageously expensive shops and *caffès,* and populated by people and pigeons, it is the place every tourist visits and usually spends money. It is also the focus of the Carnivale season leading up to Lent, when crossing the square is virtually impossible due to the throngs of costumed posers and revelers. Many of Venice's essential sights are centered around San Marco, as well as posh hotels, shopping streets, and many overpriced restaurants. The don't-miss sights include the Correr Museum, a lovely untouched archaeological museum; the Bridge of Sighs; the Gothic San Stefano Church; the Palazzo Grassi, the city's most important venue for art shows; and La Fenice Opera, which tragically burned a few years ago but is being reconstructed amid great controversy.

RESTAURANTS

PASTRY SHOPS AND BAKERIES

($) indicates a Big Splurge

Restaurants

LE BISTROT DE VENISE (48)
Calle dei Fabbri, 4685

Le Bistrot de Venise tries to cover too much ground to give it a rousing two forks up. However, it does have its virtues, and if you are selective, you will like it. The kitchen promotes *la cucina classica Veneziana* and *cucina historica Veneziana*—classic and historical Venetian cuisine. You can mix and match the two types of food, starting with a classic serving of sardines stuffed with anchovies or pasta with scampi and fresh tomatoes. The traditional monkfish cooked with a hint of saffron and a dusting of almonds missed the mark, and so did the veal roll with artichokes and zucchini. Better to order a traditional plate of grilled fish or the historic sturgeon baked with wild fennel and garlic. The tried-and-true homemade desserts are not categorized and lean heavily on the can't-miss ingredients cream, chocolate, and sugar: try the rice pudding, cheesecake, or tiramisù.

From September through May, weekly poetry readings and live music performances are held. At these evening events, patrons are encouraged to hang around the bar and mix with the artists, which often turns out to be a pleasant way to feel part of Venice.

NOTE: Poetry and music performances start anywhere between 5 and 8 P.M. Call, email, or check their Website for the schedule.

TELEPHONE
041 523 6651

FAX
041 520 2224

EMAIL
bistrot@tin.it

INTERNET
www.bistrotdevenise.com

OPEN
Daily: noon–1 A.M., continuous service

CLOSED
Never

RESERVATIONS
Advised

CREDIT CARDS
MC, V

À LA CARTE
28.41–33.57€

MENÙ TURISTICO
None

COVER & SERVICE CHARGES
No cover, 15% service added

ENGLISH
Yes

LEON BIANCO (46)
Salizzada San Luca, 4153 (between Campo San Luca and Campo Manin)

When you want a snack or light meal and cannot face another slice of street pizza, try Leon Bianco, the type of place Venetians patronize day after day. Terrific *cicchetti* (finger-food snacks) and *tramezzini* (sandwiches) are served throughout the day, and hot food is offered only between noon and 3 P.M.

Rice or cheese croquettes, grilled shrimp, and roasted vegetables are only a few of the *cicchetti* you can pluck with a toothpick and pop into your mouth. There are always two or three hot dishes, and if you want to sample more than one, they will serve half portions. Every time I am in Venice, I always consider their *tramezzini* some of the best—toasted or plain bread filled with prosciutto, mushrooms, tomatoes, tuna, egg, shrimp, roast beef, or

TELEPHONE
041 522 1180

OPEN
Mon–Sat: snacks 8 A.M.–8 P.M., hot food noon–3 P.M.

CLOSED
Sun; NAC

RESERVATIONS
Not accepted

CREDIT CARDS
None

À LA CARTE
Cicchetti from 0.93€, sandwiches from 3.10€, hot dishes from 3.62€

MENÙ TURISTICO
None

COVER & SERVICE CHARGES
No cover, service included
ENGLISH
Limited

pork. You can rub shoulders standing at the marble counters and bar, or if you want to take a more relaxed approach to your meal, you can sit at a table in back and still not have any cover or service added to your bill. When you are finished eating, be local and take your dishes back up to the bar.

OSTERIA AI ASSASSINI (50)
Rio Terra dei Assassini, 3695

TELEPHONE & FAX
041 528 7986
INTERNET
www.osteriaaiassassini.it
OPEN
Mon–Sat: lunch 11:30 A.M.–3 P.M., dinner 6:30 P.M.–midnight
CLOSED
Sun; 2–3 weeks in Aug (dates vary)
RESERVATIONS
Advised
CREDIT CARDS
MC, V
À LA CARTE
Cicchetti from 1.81€; meals 18.08–23.24€
MENÙ TURISTICO
None
COVER & SERVICE CHARGES
Cover 1.03€, service included
ENGLISH
Yes

For years this was only a place to buy wine by the bottle or case. Then Giuseppe Galardi turned it into an *enoteca* (wine bar), and it has enjoyed popularity with the locals, probably because they are the only ones who can find it.

Actually, finding Rio Terra dei Assassini is not hard, but the fun of the hunt comes when trying to locate the *osteria* itself—there is no sign or name outside. You must look for the yellow light over the door, which is turned on when the place is open.

Every day the long wooden tables and benches are filled with people having lunch or *cicchetti* while sipping a glass or two of the eighty to ninety varieties of Italian wines available. *Cicchetti,* similar to Spanish tapas, range from a piece of bread with a slice of prosciutto to meatballs, deep-fried veggies, and whipped salt cod. For many, a few *cicchetti* with a glass of nice wine can easily substitute for lunch or be a light supper. The hot special changes daily, featuring a certain dish on each day of the week: on Monday it's a dish with white meat of some sort; Tuesday, stew or offal; Wednesday, *bollito,* boiled meat with four or five sauces; Thursday, *baccalà* with polenta; Friday, fish; and Saturday it's whatever the chef feels like cooking. Of course, pasta is served every day, and an impressive number of Italian wines are poured. The only dessert is a plate of homemade *biscotti* to dip in sweet wine.

OSTERIA AI RUSTEGHI (67)
Calletta della Bissa, 5529 (off Campo San Bartolomeo)

TELEPHONE
041 523 2205
OPEN
Mon–Sat: lunch 9:30 A.M.–3 P.M., dinner 5–8:30 P.M.
CLOSED
Sun; Aug (dates vary)
RESERVATIONS
Not accepted

Call it tiny. Call it local. Call it clean. But above all, call it good. Tucked away on a narrow alley only a heartbeat from the tourist madhouse on Campo San Bartolomeo, this wine bar is hard to find for the usual befuddled tourists—at least for those who see the McDonald's on the far, opposite corner of the campo and think they have found something. Roberto runs a tight ship, and hot meals are not part of his program. What you see in the *cicchetti* case is what you are going to eat . . . unless he decides to do a few sandwiches. No one speaks much English, but it is a good place to plunge in and practice your Italian, which will improve dramatically after your third *ombra* (glass of wine).

CREDIT CARDS
None

À LA CARTE
Cicchetti 1.03€, sandwiches 1.29€

MENÙ TURISTICO
None

COVER & SERVICE CHARGES
None

ENGLISH
Limited

OSTERIA A LA CAMPANA (47)
Calle dei Fabbri, 4720

"Where do you go for a good, cheap lunch in this neighborhood?" I asked Nellie, the friendly owner of Locanda Casa Petrarca, a nearby budget hotel (see *Great Sleeps Italy*). "I go to La Campana on Calle dei Fabbri," she said. Once you find it, you, too, will go back to this small, homey place with a dark wood interior that can charitably be called rustic. For the best selection at lunch, get there early, when the *cicchetti* are at their picture-perfect best. You can always find rice balls with a mozzarella cheese pocket inside, tuna or potato puffs, braised vegetables, frittatas, and chunks of cheese all displayed along a counter. For an even better deal, have your *cicchetti* standing at the bar, and you can deduct about 0.26€ per item.

If you want something more substantial, ask what the chef prepared that morning. There is a posted menu for lunch, but no one bothers looking at it. However, the English dinner menu is worth consulting in addition to the specials. Fish is the Friday special, and on other days look for bean soup, hearty stews, and assorted risottos and pastas.

TELEPHONE
041 588 5170

OPEN
Mon–Sat: lunch noon–3 P.M., dinner 7–10 P.M.

CLOSED
Sun; NAC

RESERVATIONS
Not necessary

CREDIT CARDS
AE, MC, V

À LA CARTE
Cicchetti from 1.29€, 2-course meal for 10.33–15.49€

MENÙ TURISTICO
None

COVER & SERVICE CHARGES
Cover 1.29€, service discretionary

ENGLISH
Yes

OSTERIA AL BACARETO (51)
Salizzada San Samuele, 3447 (at Calle delle Botteghe)

Emilio and his son Adriano told me, "You eat in this restaurant as a family." The house wine is good, the welcome always warm, the other diners interesting, and the prices fair. In short, this is a winner. Everyone seems to know one another at this comfortable family *osteria,* where you may see the neighborhood dogs sitting patiently by the door waiting for their masters to finish eating. At lunch, to feel part of the action, order a plate of *cicchetti* or a sandwich and a glass of the featured wine. Remember, if you stand at the bar to eat, you will save

TELEPHONE
041 528 9336

OPEN
Mon–Fri: lunch noon–3 P.M., dinner 7–10 P.M.; Sat: lunch noon–3 P.M.

CLOSED
Sat dinner; Sun; Christmas Day, Easter Day, Aug

RESERVATIONS
Advised

CREDIT CARDS
AE, MC, V

À LA CARTE
Cicchetti from 1.55€, full meals
23.24–30.99€
MENÙ TURISTICO
None
COVER & SERVICE CHARGES
Cover 1.55€, 12% service
added
ENGLISH
Yes, and menu in English

both the cover and the service charges. For dinner, reserve one or more of the sixteen places at any of the outside tables for a ringside seat on the evening *passeggiata*. If you stay with the chef's versions of Venetian dishes, the food will not disappoint. For example, *sarde in saor* (marinated sardines), the *risotti vari* (rice mixed with peas, squid, vegetables, or seafood), and the *bigoli in salsa* (wholemeal pasta with anchovy and onion sauce) are sure-fire first courses. Move on to the excellent seafood offerings, or liver and onions served with polenta, and close with your choice of the three house desserts: *Buranelli biscotti* (Venetian cookies from Burano dipped in dessert wine), tiramisù, or amaretto mousse.

OSTERIA ALLA BOTTE (66)
Calle della Bissa, 5482 (off Campo San Bartolomeo)

TELEPHONE
041 520 9775
OPEN
Mon–Wed, Fri–Sun: lunch
10 A.M.–3 P.M., dinner 6–11 P.M.
CLOSED
Thur; July, a few days at
Christmas
RESERVATIONS
Not necessary
CREDIT CARDS
None
À LA CARTE
Cicchetti from 1.03€, hot dishes
7.75–10.33€
MENÙ TURISTICO
None
COVER AND SERVICE CHARGE
No cover or service charge
ENGLISH
Yes

There must be ten or more *bacari* (wine bars) in a two-minute radius of Botte, each one interesting in its own way and worthy of a few visits until you find the one that suits you. At Botte, you can almost tell the time of day by the type of patrons jamming the bar. On a Sunday morning, it is the place where old men gather to jump-start the day with a grappa-laced coffee or a couple of straight shots of the potent elixir. During the week, businessfolk and shopkeepers dash in for a quick bite and a glass or two of their favorite *vino*. At lunch you can barely wedge your way in through the hungry throng, munching *cicchetti* at the bar or downing the daily hot dishes of *pasta e fagoli*, penne with *funghi porchini, bigoli in salsa,* or *baccalà* with polenta in the tiny dining area in back. When it reopens around 6 P.M., the crowd is a young mix, everyone smoozing, flirting, posing, and preening, whether inside or in the narrow alleyway in front. Later on, it is filled with couples drinking in the bar or having a simple Great Eat in back.

NOTE: There is no smoking allowed in the dining room, or from noon to 3 P.M. in the bar.

OSTERIA DA CARLA (52)
Corte Contarina, 1535 (off Frezzeria)

TELEPHONE
041 523 7855
OPEN
Mon–Sat: bar 7:30 A.M.–
10 P.M., lunch noon–3 P.M.,
dinner 6–10 P.M.
CLOSED
Sun; 15 days in Jan (dates vary)

Hidden? You bet. Discovered? Yes again, but by the cognoscenti in this part of Venice, who say, "Let's go to the Carla," and everyone knows exactly what they mean and where it is, even though the sign over the doorway reads Pietro Panizzolo. In short, if you didn't know about it, you would never find it, and that's the way the locals like it.

I was introduced to the Carla by a Great Eating pal from Florence who said he had been eating here for years and that I simply had to try it. We arrived late on a Saturday afternoon when the place was almost empty and the staff was preparing to close. It didn't matter—we were welcomed as if we were regulars. We settled in with a plate of assorted sandwiches and shared a bottle of beer. It was a perfect late lunch, and I knew I would come back when it was operating in full force. When I did, several times, I was always amazed. This place is super and the food is terrific. Every morning the menu is pinned to a barrel out front. There will be two or three pastas, including a risotto, a meat and a fish dish, fresh vegetables, and homemade tarts. Not ready for a big meal? Then order a sandwich from the bar and sit at one of the tables inside or, on a warm day, snag one of the tables placed in the walkway of the small courtyard on the side. The kitchen is closed from 3 to 6 P.M., but during this time the bar is open and you can always get a cold plate.

NOTE: Here's how to find Osteria da Carla coming from Piazza San Marco: Walk out the south exit from the piazza along Salizzada San Moisè and turn right on Frezzeria. The first archway on your left will be Sotoportego e Corte Contarina. This is it . . . you will see the barrel at the end of the court with a bouquet of fresh flowers on top and the menu of the day pinned on it. *Buon appetito,* and *tante grazie,* Frank.

RESERVATIONS
Not necessary

CREDIT CARDS
MC, V

À LA CARTE
Sandwiches from 3.10€, lunch or dinner 10.33€–12.91€

MENÙ TURISTICO
None

COVER & SERVICE CHARGES
None

ENGLISH
Yes

ROSTICCERIA S. BARTOLOMEO (68)
Calle de la Bissa, 5424/A (on Campo San Bartolomeo, near the Rialto Bridge)

If you are watching your food budget, do not go to the upstairs restaurant here. Instead stay downstairs, go through the self-service line, and take your food to one of the long bar tables by the window, thus avoiding the cover and service charges, as well as the higher prices, for almost the same food served in the restaurant.

The ground-floor cafeteria is a popular refueling stop for those who want a proper meal anytime between 9:30 A.M. and 9:30 P.M. Featured each day are salads, pastas, and hot dishes, which include the Venetian specialties of *baccalà alla Vicentina* (salt cod simmered in milk and herbs), deep-fried mozzarella, *seppie con polenta* (squid with polenta), and meat or vegetarian lasagne. There are all the usual desserts. The bottom line? For

TELEPHONE
041 522 3569

OPEN
Mon: 9:30 A.M.–4 P.M.; Tues–Sun: 9:30 A.M.–9:30 P.M., continuous service

CLOSED
Mon in winter; NAC

RESERVATIONS
Not accepted

CREDIT CARDS
AE, DC MC, V

À LA CARTE
From 1.03€ (for a sandwich) to 15.49€ for 3 courses, beverage extra

around 12.39€, you can get a two-course meal and a glass of house wine, and in Venice, that qualifies as cheap eats. Everything you see can be packaged to go.

NOTE: All prices quoted are for cafeteria dining.

SEMPIONE ($, 76)
Ponte Bareteri, 578

The beautiful canal-side setting, attentive service, and tempting Venetian cuisine draws me back to this family-run restaurant time after time. Its privileged location near St. Mark's Square and some of the city's most luxurious shops makes it an ideal stop for a leisurely lunch or dinner. The best tables, naturally, are by the leaded windows overlooking the canal and the gondolas quietly floating by. The food is simple, with unfussy preparations and a lavish use of olive oil. *Pennette* (small penne) tossed with a well-flavored *amatriciana* sauce of tomatoes and sweet red peppers is a hit. So is the pasta with spider crab and the *spaghetti Sempione* with prawns, mussels, and octopus. Finish every morsel, but save room for the heaping platter of scampi and squid, the calamari, or the fillet of *S. Pietro* cooked in butter. Meat lovers will be pleased to find liver and onions served with polenta, steaks, veal dishes, and roast chicken. For a pleasant ending, I like to have a bowl of fresh strawberries or a slice of pineapple.

TRATTORIA ALLA SCALA (77)
Corte Lucatello, 571

Given most of the slung-together food hapless visitors endure in this teeming tourist corner of San Marco, it is amazing to find someplace serving decent Venetian dishes at honest prices. Alla Scala is located on a tiny campiello near Mercerie, the busy main shopping street, which is literally clogged with people as long as the stores are open and people have money in their pockets. To escape this zoo-like atmosphere, take a break and have lunch or dinner at this family-owned trattoria, which has wooden bench banquettes and an assortment of varying art and Carnivale masks decorating its white walls. The old-fashioned cuisine is filling and covers all the usual Venetian dishes, including a selection of forty pastas. The *menù turistico,* available only at lunch, is a good deal if you can wade through all the courses;

otherwise, this is a place where you can feel comfortable ordering just one or two à la carte courses.

COVER & SERVICE CHARGES
Cover 1.81€, 12% service added

ENGLISH
Yes, and menu in English

TRATTORIA/PIZZERIA ROSA ROSA (49)
Calle della Mandola, 3709

While the trattoria menu lists a range of dishes—such as gnocchi with salmon; tagliatelle with onions, cherry tomatoes, and basil; grilled scamorza cheese with vegetables; and a rundown of meats—when you come to Rosa Rosa, think only of pizza. With the help of his wife and his mother, Cristiano has run Rosa Rosa since 1985. He specializes in thin-crust pies that are not too crisp, and offers enough toppings to please just about everyone. If you missed breakfast, order a pizza featuring bacon and eggs. For something a bit further out, there is one with horsemeat and another with goose. Less adventurous is the San Nicandro, with tomatoes, mozzarella, goat cheese, olives, onions, and capers. If, after consulting the three pages of options, you still don't see a pizza that pleases you . . . ask for what you want; they will customize.

TELEPHONE
041 523 4605

FAX
041 277 1045

OPEN
Mon–Tues, Thur–Sun: lunch noon–3 P.M., dinner 7–11 P.M.

CLOSED
Wed; NAC

RESERVATIONS
Not necessary

CREDIT CARDS
MC, V

À LA CARTE
20.66–25.82€, pizza from 6.71–10.33€

MENÙ TURISTICO
None

COVER AND SERVICE CHARGE
Cover 1.55€, 12% service added

ENGLISH
Yes, and menu in English

VITAE (45)
Calle Sant'Antonio, 4118

Vitae has a reputation as a happening place for lunch, which is the only time serious food is served. Later, the action shifts and it becomes the watering hole of the moment for a chic, black-clad crowd who keep the place jumping until the wee hours. During the peak lunch service, around 1 P.M., an air of organized chaos reigns, so be prepared to hang around the bar until a table clears. Use this time to watch the food being assembled by the hardworking owner and to decide what looks best: lasagne, eggplant Parmesan, gnocchi with four cheeses, risotto, dried beef on a bed of arugula, or perhaps a veal or pork dish. The only dessert decision is whether or not you want cream on your bowl of fresh fruit.

TELEPHONE
041 520 5205

OPEN
Mon–Fri: bar 9 A.M.–1 A.M., hot lunch 12:30–3 P.M.; Sat: bar 9 A.M.–1 A.M.

CLOSED
Sat lunch, Sun; NAC

RESERVATIONS
Not accepted

CREDIT CARDS
None

À LA CARTE
6.20–10.33€

MENÙ TURISTICO
None

COVER & SERVICE CHARGES
None

ENGLISH
Yes

Pastry Shops and Bakeries

MARCHINI (53)
Ponte San Maurizo, 2769,

TELEPHONE
041 522 9109, 041 528 7507

OPEN
Mon, Wed–Sun: 7 A.M.–8 P.M.

CLOSED
Tues

CREDIT CARDS
AE, MC, V

PRICES
Pastries from 0.77€, candies sold by weight

ENGLISH
Enough

Ask any Venetian where to buy some of the best cakes, chocolates, and pastries and the answer is always Marchini. One trip to this beautiful emporium of calories could satisfy your sweet tooth immediately and almost indefinitely, since they will pack as many bon bons, marzipan, and other candies as you can carry to take home with you.

NOTE: Ponte San Maurizo is not shown on most maps, but it is on Calle del Spezier, which is off Campo San Stefano.

Restaurants West of the Grand Canal

Dorsoduro

Dorsoduro, which lies between Santa Maria della Salute and the docks of San Nicolò in the southern part of Venice, is known for its beautiful churches, the magnificent art in the Accademia, and its contemporary counterpart, the Peggy Guggenheim Collection, which is beautifully housed in a *palazzo* along the Grand Canal. Dorsoduro is also the center of Venice's university population. Campo Santa Margherita, the heart of the *sestiere,* is one of the city's largest squares and a center of changing local activity. The small morning fish and produce stalls draw the housewives before lunch, in the afternoon the campo is filled with children playing, and at night it is a mecca for the under-thirty crowd.

GROCERY STORES AND SUPERMARKETS

Billa	**241**
Minimarket	**241**

OUTDOOR MARKETS

Santa Margherita	**242**
Campo Santa Barnaba	**242**

($) indicates a Big Splurge

Restaurants

AI CUGNAI (40)
Campo San Vio, 857

TELEPHONE
041 528 9238

OPEN
Tues–Sun: lunch noon–
2:30 P.M., dinner 7–9:30 P.M.

CLOSED
Mon; Aug 1–25

RESERVATIONS
Not necessary

CREDIT CARDS
None

À LA CARTE
20.66€

MENÙ TURISTICO
None

COVER & SERVICE CHARGES
Cover 1.03€, 10% service
added

ENGLISH
Limited, but menu in English

Those in search of a thrifty Great Eat near the Peggy Guggenheim Collection will do well to eat at Ai Cugnai. This cheapie, not too far from the Accademia vaporetto stop, has been run for fifty years by two sisters, their brother, and their combined families. Elegant it is not, but the down-home atmosphere makes for an authentic Venetian experience. At lunch, a cluster of neighbors stand at the bar, comparing notes on their day. Eventually, they will go on their way or sit at one of the tables in back to have a meal.

The food is far from fancy, but it is surprisingly good, especially the daily specials and their renditions of fresh crab, when it is in season. Be sure to ask which of the vegetables are fresh; you don't want canned spinach. For dessert, I would not miss a piece of their velvety chocolate cake for anything. But if it is all gone, the almond cake is special, too.

AI GONDOLIERI ($, 43)
Rio Terra San Vio, 366

TELEPHONE
041 528 6396

FAX
041 521 00 75

INTERNET
www.aigondolieri.com

OPEN
Mon, Wed–Sun: lunch noon–
2:30 P.M., dinner 7–10 P.M.

CLOSED
Tues; Christmas Day

When reserving your table at Ai Gondolieri, ask to be in the main dining room, where the linen-covered tables are set with smart china and crystal, fresh flowers, and glowing candles in the evening. The other narrow room, off the bar, has the same pretty place settings, but the wooden benches along the wall are uncomfortable, and the room serves as a corridor for restaurant patrons coming and going.

The food at Ai Gondolieri is more expensive than some, which is why it should be saved for a Big Splurge.

The detailed, creative menu is not translated, but this is not a concern because the waiters all speak English and willingly explain the dishes. The restaurant is well known for *not* serving fish—instead, arrive for its superb cheese list, for truffles from November to January, and for its homemade pastas, including two risottos served in a hollowed-out loaf of bread. The best buy is definitely the *menù degustazione*, since it includes all of chef Giovanni Trevisan's monthly changing, seasonally inspired dishes from appetizer to dessert. Wine is extra. You will start with three or four antipasti choices, including snails in Burgundy wine sauce, an unusual treatment of polenta cooked with smoky bacon, or a baby artichoke torte. Next will be homemade pasta, perhaps early spring asparagus tossed with buttery egg noodles or tiny ravioli with truffles. The main course might be a tender guinea hen garnished with seasonal vegetables, steak with mushrooms, perfectly cooked liver with polenta, or the chef's daily special. Wrapping it all up is a choice of such luscious homemade desserts as ricotta cheesecake with fresh strawberry sauce or a plate of specially selected cheese and an appropriate wine.

NOTE: Under the same management is the Museum Cafe at the Peggy Guggenheim Collection (see page 218).

RESERVATIONS
Advised, especially for dinner and Sun

CREDIT CARDS
AE, DC, MC, V

À LA CARTE
51.65–56.81€

MENÙ TURISTICO
Menù degustazione (minimum 2 persons), 51.65€, 6 courses; cover and service included; beverage extra

COVER & SERVICE CHARGES
Cover 4.65€, service included

ENGLISH
Yes

AI QUATTRO FERRI (36)
Calle Lunga San Barnaba, 2754/A

You can't beat a plate of *cicchetti,* an order of grilled vegetables, or that old Venetian standby, spaghetti with fresh clams, at this typical spot off of Campo Margherita run by Barbara and Bianca. No reservations are taken, so that means come early (when the best *cicchetti* and the *piatto del giorno* are usually still available) or be prepared to wait. Don't bother with the menu—no one can read it, and to compound things for a visitor, English is limited and becomes positively nonexistent when the owners are trying to keep up with the lunch trade. Still, these are not reasons to miss their daily specials, which always include fresh fish and a meat alternative. While probably not destination dining for dinner, it is a handy Great Eat for lunch with the locals . . . and at local prices.

TELEPHONE
041 520 6978

OPEN
Mon–Sat: lunch noon–2 P.M., dinner 6:30–10:30 P.M.

CLOSED
Sun; NAC

RESERVATIONS
Not accepted

CREDIT CARDS
None

À LA CARTE
12.91€

MENÙ TURISTICO
None

COVER & SERVICE CHARGES
1.03€ cover, no service charged

ENGLISH
Limited

ANGELO RAFFAEL (37)
Campo Angelo Raffaele, 1722

TELEPHONE
041 523 7456

OPEN
Wed–Sun: lunch 12:30–
2:30 P.M., dinner 7:30–
9:30 P.M.

CLOSED
Mon–Tues; 1 week in mid-Aug
(dates vary)

RESERVATIONS
Not necessary

CREDIT CARDS
None

À LA CARTE
18.08–23.24€

MENÙ TURISTICO
None

COVER & SERVICE CHARGES
Cover 1.29€, service included
inside, 10% service added
outside

ENGLISH
None

In tourist terms, Angelo Raffael (sometimes spelled Anzolo) is located a block beyond Mars, and the journey should be made mostly for anthropological reasons rather than culinary ones. Buried on a *campo* across from the Angelo Raffaele Church, it boasts true local color as the favored haunt for this blue-collar Venetian neighborhood. The cigar-smoking owner holds court behind the bar. The waitress serves an aging clientele, who show up every day sporting the same suits, telling the same stories—and probably also wondering about the "youth today" (i.e., the student crowd) occupying the outside tables. There is no proper menu; the waitress will tell you what's cooking, and it is nothing but fish. All the favorites are here, it just depends on what is in season at the Rialto Market and the mood of the chef. Veggies, salads, and desserts are afterthoughts. The house wine is not, and is enthusiastically consumed by all who eat here . . . including the owner.

NOTE: While you are here, take a minute to visit the fourteenth-century San Sebastiano Church on Fondamenta San Sebastiano. The interior of the church, designed and created by Paolo Veronese, is one of the most beautiful in Venice.

ANTICO CAPON (28)
Campo Santa Margherita, 3004

TELEPHONE & FAX
041 528 5252

OPEN
Daily: 11 A.M.–midnight,
continuous service

CLOSED
Never

RESERVATIONS
Not necessary

CREDIT CARDS
MC, V

À LA CARTE
Pizza from 5.16–12.91€

MENÙ TURISTICO
None

COVER & SERVICE CHARGES
Cover 1.55€, 12% service
added

ENGLISH
Yes

You must remember only one word when you come to Antico Capon: *pizza*. It is the only Great Eating option, but the varieties are endless . . . you name it, and they serve it atop one of their fifty crisp-crust, wood-fired pizzas. I think Antico Capon is best saved for warm-weather dining, when you can eat outside and have a ringside seat on the entertaining action taking place on this busy campo.

CANTINONE GIÀ SCHIAVI (42)
Fondamenta Nani, 992

Beginning with Giaccomo, three generations of the Schiavi family have kept up a 110-year-old tradition of selling fine wines from this canal-side location. Every family member has a specific role to play, right down to the black house mascot, Lupo, a dog who proudly rides with her master in the motorboat when he delivers wine orders, and snoozes on the bow in between. In addition to selling wines by the bottle and case, it has become a favorite local wine bar selling sandwiches and *cicchetti* at lunch. In fact, Alessandra, the wife of the present owner, Lino, makes over three hundred sandwiches *per day,* which sell out by 2 P.M. Multiply that by the week, month, and year, and not only is it amazingly prolific, it means they have a hit. If you are looking for something unusual to give as a gift, try a bottle of their *Fagolina Bianco* (strawberry wine), which you can sample by the glass and buy by the half-liter.

NOTE: When you arrive, don't be confused by the sign outside that reads "Vini: Al Bottegon"—you're at the right place.

TELEPHONE
041 523 0034

OPEN
Mon–Sat: bar 8 A.M.–2:30 P.M., 3:30–8:30 P.M., sandwiches noon–2:30 P.M.; Sun: bar 8 A.M.–2:30 P.M., sandwiches noon–2:30 P.M.

CLOSED
Sun afternoon; Aug 15–25

RESERVATIONS
Not accepted

CREDIT CARDS
None

À LA CARTE
Sandwiches from 2.58€, *cicchetti* from 1.03€

MENÙ TURISTICO
None

COVER & SERVICE CHARGES
No cover, service included

ENGLISH
Yes, usually

DUE TORRI (27)
Campo Santa Margherita, 3408

No one ever thumbed through a fat-free cookbook or called an interior decorator at this unchanging local pit stop, where the *cucina casalinga* (home cookin') is as hearty as the characters eating it. This no-frills lunch-time spot with plastic-covered tables is a gathering place for ruddy workers, who prefer to polish off a few glasses of red *before* digging into their pasta and fresh fish lunch. Those in a hurry stand at the bar and indulge in the selection of *cicchetti.* There is no printed menu, no dessert served, and no rules about smoking. Even the waiters may smoke on the job, but no one notices or minds, because they are busy puffing their brains out, too. In the afternoon, the older men return to play poker and toss down glasses of beer or grappa. Dinner is served on Friday and Saturday from July until mid-November, and from around May until October, tables are set outside on the campo.

TELEPHONE
041 523 8126

OPEN
Mon–Sat: bar 7 A.M.–9 P.M.; lunch noon–2:30 P.M.; dinner also Fri–Sat 7–10 P.M. from July 1–mid-Nov

CLOSED
Sun; between Christmas and New Year's, 3 weeks in Aug

RESERVATIONS
Not accepted

CREDIT CARDS
None

À LA CARTE
15.49–18.08€

MENÙ TURISTICO
None

COVER & SERVICE CHARGES
No cover, service included

ENGLISH
Limited

LA BITTA (35)
Calle Lunga San Barnaba, 2753

TELEPHONE
041 523 0531
OPEN
Tues–Sat: bar 9:30 A.M.–3 P.M.,
6:15 P.M.–midnight, lunch
12:30–3 P.M., dinner 7:30–
11:30 P.M.
CLOSED
Sun–Mon; NAC
RESERVATIONS
Advised for lunch, essential for
dinner
CREDIT CARDS
MC, V
À LA CARTE
18.08–25.82€
MENÙ TURISTICO
None
COVER & SERVICE CHARGES
No cover or service charge
(but tips are appreciated)
ENGLISH
Yes

Great Eats await you at La Bitta, a small trattoria with an even smaller walled back garden, which is where everyone wants to sit on a warm Venetian night. La Bitta is unusual in that it serves only meat. If you want fish, you need only walk down the street to La Furatola, a long-standing seafood favorite, which is under the same ownership (see below).

For lunch, the chalkboard menu changes daily, highlighting huge portions of Argentine beef, Canadian buffalo, and wonderful pastas. In the evening, if you are as lucky as I was, you can simply put yourself in your waiter's hands. I was all set to ask for a menu and order a pasta and a main course, but our waiter wasn't listening. He insisted my dining companion and I share a plate of air-dried beef with a grapefruit and olive oil dressing. When I asked what else there was for a starter, he just shrugged his shoulders and said *this* is what we would be eating. He was right . . . it was too big for one, just right for two, and absolutely delicious. Next, he brought us giant tortellini filled with spinach and ricotta in a butter and sage dressing. Good thing we also shared this, since the dish of the evening was roast kid. The kitchen only prepares this delicacy once a month, and we were fortunate enough to have arrived on that night, as this tender meat literally melted in our mouths. With it came fresh asparagus, zucchini spears, and roasted eggplant.

After this, I thought dessert was not just not an option but an impossibility. Again, the waiter turned a deaf ear and brought us two! One was a bowl of sweet strawberries with pepper and a few drops of balsamic vinegar, and the other was fresh pineapple laced with grappa. A plate of cookies finished the feast, which we both agreed was one of the more memorable meals we had had in Venice.

LA FURATOLA ($, 34)
Calle Lunga San Barnaba, 2869/A

TELEPHONE
041 520 8594
OPEN
Mon: dinner 7:30–10:30 P.M.;
Tues–Wed, Fri–Sun: lunch
12:30–2:30 P.M., dinner 7:30–
10:30 P.M.

La Furatola is a Venetian landmark famous for serving *only* seasonally fresh fish. The old-fashioned interior is appealing in its own way, especially the collection of black-and-white photographs of old Venice. Diners are seated at pink linen–covered tables that are decorated simply with a basket of bread sticks. Reservations are absolutely essential for dinner, and if you are thirty minutes late, your table will not be waiting for you.

I recommend starting with an antipasti mix of both warm and cold seafood. This is rich and filling, so if you need to pace yourself, perhaps skip the pasta if you are having a main course or consider the pasta as your entrée. If you do, the *spaghetti della casa,* topped with a seafood ragout, is wonderful. On Friday, the order of the day is always fish soup, followed by grilled sole, monkfish, sea beam, or whatever fish is best that day. Salads and vegetables make cameo appearances and are meant to garnish, not inspire. In the winter, zabaglione is the dessert to have; in summer, a glass of sweet wine with assorted dipping cookies is a refreshing finish. The house red or white wine is way above average, but if you are looking to upgrade, the featured Veneto and Friuli wines are also excellent.

If you don't want fish, reserve a table at La Furatola's sister restaurant, La Bitte (see above), which is down the street and serves only meat.

CLOSED
Mon lunch; Thur; last 3 weeks in July, Aug

RESERVATIONS
Advised for lunch, required for dinner (and held only 30 minutes)

CREDIT CARDS
AE, MC, V

À LA CARTE
36.15–41.32€

MENÙ TURISTICO
None

COVER & SERVICE CHARGES
Cover 2.58€, 10% service added

ENGLISH
Yes

L'INCONTRO (32)
Campo Santa Margherita, 3062A (near Ponte dei Pugni across Rio Terra Canal)

L'Incontro is the kind of place you always hope will be just around the corner, and it was for me. The first time I researched Venice for *Cheap Eats in Italy,* I lived on Campo Squellini, near the Campo Santa Margherita in Dorsoduro. Naturally, I tried every restaurant candidate in the vicinity, and L'Incontro topped my list of favorites. I liked it because it was local and extremely popular; it served dependable, well-priced food; and it was, until now, totally undiscovered. During my latest stay in Venice, while working on the fourth edition of this book, I ate here several times, and I am happy to say I still like the consistency of this restaurant.

The small establishment is composed of two rooms divided by a bar, plus a sidewalk terrace. The low-beamed ceilings, lacy window curtains, flowered tablecloths, baskets on the walls, and strawflower arrangements create a cozy, old-world atmosphere. If you go for dinner, arrive about 8:30 or 9 P.M. to give it a chance to fill up with other diners. When planning your meal, forget the long printed menu and stay strictly with the handwritten daily one, which changes for lunch and dinner. The owner, Luciano, is Sardinian, so the dishes reflect his love for the cooking of this region. The chef does not prepare any fish, concentrating instead on homemade

TELEPHONE
041 522 2404

OPEN
Tues–Sun: lunch 12:30–2:30 P.M., dinner 7:30–10:30 P.M.

CLOSED
Mon; July

RESERVATIONS
Advised

CREDIT CARDS
AE, DC, MC, V

À LA CARTE
25.82–30.99€

MENÙ TURISTICO
None

COVER & SERVICE CHARGES
Cover 1.55€, service discretionary

ENGLISH
Yes

pastas, fresh vegetables, wild game in season, Chianti beef, and grilled, roasted, or stewed veal and pork. The desserts are adequate but not thrilling, so I always pass on the sweet course and walk over to Il Doge Gelaterie (see page 220) for a scoop of my favorite gelato. The house wine is light and refreshing.

NOTE: When I first discovered L'Incontro, there was no sign. Now there is, but that does not mean the place is a snap to locate. It's toward the lower east end of Campo Santa Margherita as you head toward Campo Santa Barnaba and the floating vegetable market. At lunch and dinner, the daily menu is taped to a small window to the left of the door. The restaurant is next to a mask shop. When all else fails, ask a shopkeeper. Everyone knows it.

MUSEUM CAFE—PEGGY GUGGENHEIM COLLECTION (39)
Dorsoduro, 707 (follow signs after Ponte Accademia)

TELEPHONE
041 522 8688

FAX
041 521 0075

INTERNET
www.aigondolieri.com

OPEN
Mon, Wed–Sun: 10 A.M.–6 P.M., Sat until 10 P.M. in summer

CLOSED
Tues, and whenever the museum is closed

RESERVATIONS
Not necessary

CREDIT CARDS
AE, DC, MC, V

À LA CARTE
12.91–18.08€, sandwiches and desserts 5.16–10.33€

MENÙ TURISTICO
None

COVER & SERVICE CHARGES
None

ENGLISH
Yes, and menu in English

The Museum Cafe is as contemporary and inviting as its coolly elegant surroundings. Peggy Guggenheim was an extraordinary woman who amassed a brilliant collection of surreal and abstract art of the twentieth century. This museum, which was her home on the Grand Canal in Venice until her death in 1979, showcases her private collection of avant-garde paintings and sculpture.

The modern cafe wraps itself around a bar, an outside terrace, and several rooms displaying black-and-white photographs of the life of this remarkable and often controversial patron of the arts. The cafe is run by Giovanni Trevisan, the talented chef of Ai Gondolieri (see page 212), so you know it will be imaginative and delicious. The menu follows the seasons and offers large salads, pastas, main courses, sandwiches, and desserts. Many of the daily specials and first courses are the same as you would have at Ai Gondolieri, but for much less investment. You also have the option of ordering a full-scale meal or only a coffee. The cafe is open whenever the museum is, but to eat here you must buy a ticket for the museum, which in my opinion is certainly worth it.

TAVERNA SAN TROVASO (38)
Fondamenta Priuli, 1016

The small and very popular Taverna San Trovaso is a family-run effort of six brothers, their one sister, and assorted spouses and offspring. You *must* call ahead for reservations, and arrive on time if you expect to get a table. Readers of *Great Eats Italy* as well as smart Venetians know and recommend it as a restaurant where a delicious, uncomplicated meal can be had for a moderate price. In fact, I have never walked in without meeting someone walking out who didn't say to me, "This is *good!*" Restful and relaxing it is not, but instead it is full of happy locals eating well, having a good time, and sounding like it.

The *menù turistico* is a Great Eat value and offers enough choices to keep it interesting. The à la carte menu is varied and includes pizza noon and night, so it should appeal to everyone. The servings are tremendous and the wine very good, thus it is imperative to arrive hungry and thirsty in order to do justice to it all.

NOTE: There is a nonsmoking section.

TELEPHONE
041 520 3703

OPEN
Tues–Sun: lunch noon–2:50 P.M., dinner 7–9:50 P.M.

CLOSED
Mon; Dec 31–Jan 1, second week of July (dates vary)

RESERVATIONS
Essential (and don't be late)

CREDIT CARDS
AE, DC, MC, V

À LA CARTE
25.82€; pizzas from 5.16€

MENÙ TURISTICO
15.49€, 3 courses; beverage, cover, and service included

COVER & SERVICE CHARGES
Cover 1.55€, service discretionary

ENGLISH
Yes, and menu in English

Gelaterias

GELATI NICO (44)
Fondamenta Zattere ai Gesuiti, 922

The Zattere, the southernmost promenade in Venice, is popular with families, who like to spend Sunday afternoon strolling along the walkway that borders the Giudecca Canal. Along the way, there are several *gelaterie,* but Nico is far and away the best and most popular. I was first here on a freezing April afternoon during a driving rainstorm, and there were still ten people ahead of me in line waiting to dig into their specialty, a *gianduiotto:* a large slice of dense chocolate hazelnut ice cream buried in whipped cream and served in a cup. You can eat here, but Great Eaters will certainly order theirs to go, because then it will cost only 2.32€. To have it served at a tiny table inside, or on the deck overlooking the canal, sets you back about 4.13€. The same man has been dipping out *gianduiotti* for almost four decades; others have tried to imitate him, but none have ever equaled his version. There are other ice cream treats available, from sundaes to frappés, but almost everyone orders the famous *gianduiotto* no matter how many times they've had it before.

TELEPHONE
041 522 5293

OPEN
Feb–Sept: daily 6:45 A.M.–11:30 P.M.; Oct–Jan: Mon–Wed, Fri–Sun 7 A.M.–10:30 P.M., continuous service

CLOSED
Thur from Oct–Jan; Dec 15–Jan 12

CREDIT CARDS
None

PRICES
Gianduiotto to go, 2.32€; at a table, 4.13€; other ice cream from 3.62€

ENGLISH
Yes

IL DOGE GELATERIE (29)
Campo Santa Margherita, 3058A

TELEPHONE
041 523 4607

OPEN
Daily: 10:30 A.M.–midnight

CLOSED
Mon from Nov–Jan (can vary)

CREDIT CARDS
None

PRICES
Gelato cones and cups from
1.29–2.84€

ENGLISH
Limited

I must confess, I adore Italian gelato. Nowhere in Venice is it any better than at Il Doge Gelaterie, a shrine to this scrumptious treat. All the ice cream is made here, and there are more than forty superb flavors in the repertoire, including black-and-white coffee, rum, amaretto, *marron glace,* tiramisù, and zabaglione. There are also countless fruit *sorbettos* in summer and, to keep insistent dieters happy, soya gelato made with no sugar and several low-fat yogurts. The best of these is the coffee yogurt, which slips down like silk. However, please put your diet on hold, because there is one flavor you positively cannot miss, and that is their special *panna cotta del Doge,* a custard-based ice cream swirled with ribbons of caramel. Does it sound pedestrian? Let me assure you, after one taste you will agree that it is anything but. Just thinking about it makes me wish I was there right now eating another scoop or two of this celestial creation.

Pastry Shops and Bakeries

TONOLO (25)
Salizzada San Pantalon, 3764

TELEPHONE
041 533 7209

OPEN
Tues–Sun: 8 A.M.–9 P.M.,
continuous service

CLOSED
Mon; 2 days after Carnivale,
Aug

CREDIT CARDS
None

PRICES
Pastries from 0.83€

ENGLISH
Very limited

You will undoubtedly be the only tourist when you join the students, blue-haired dowagers, well-dressed businesspeople, and shopkeepers at Tonolo, the most popular spot to have a cappuccino and pastry in the San Pantalon area of Venice. Before arriving, sharpen your elbows and your determination, the better to edge your way to the counter where the young women somehow miraculously keep straight all the shouted early morning orders. Open from 8 A.M. until 9 P.M., this constantly crowded bakery makes some of the best high-calorie treats in Venice, and everyone knows it. There are no tables, so you must eat standing or have your order packaged to go. In the morning, indulge in a fresh cream-filled doughnut, a plain or almond-topped *cornetto* (croissant), raisin pound cake, or buttery brioche and a frothy cappuccino served in a pretty blue-and-white cup. At lunch, try two or three little pizzas. In the late afternoon, any one of their indulgent pastries or cakes will make you happy you came to Venice.

San Polo

San Polo occupies a middle section of the Grand Canal and is the smallest of the six *sestieri*. It is named after the ancient church of San Polo, which stands on Campo San Polo, the largest square in Venice after St. Mark's. The Rialto area, once the center of the city's bargaining, buying, and selling, is still famous for its colorful produce and fish markets and the countless tourist stalls that line the Ruga del Orefici. The Rialto Bridge is one of the three that crosses the Grand Canal, and it is one of the most photographed sites in Venice. No one should miss the enormous Gothic church of the Frari, with three of Venice's best altarpieces (one of these is Titian's *Assumption*), and the Scuola Grande di San Rocco, with its paintings by Tintoretto.

RESTAURANTS

GOURMET FOOD AND WINE SHOPS

OUTDOOR MARKETS

($) indicates a Big Splurge

Restaurants

ALIANI GASTRONOMIA (20)
Ruga Vecchia S. Giovanni, 654–655 (main street leading to Rialto Bridge)

TELEPHONE & FAX
041 522 4913

OPEN
Mon: 8 A.M.–1 P.M.; Tues–Sat: 8 A.M.–1 P.M., 5–7:30 P.M.

CLOSED
Mon afternoon, Sun; 2–3 weeks in Aug (dates vary)

RESERVATIONS
Not accepted

CREDIT CARDS
None

À LA CARTE
5.16–10.33€

MENÙ TURISTICO
None

COVER & SERVICE CHARGES
None

ENGLISH
Yes

For fast, flavorful, and fabulous deli-style takeout, one of the best and most central spots is Aliani Gastronomia near the Rialto Bridge. The shop, owned and operated by Bruno Aliani, his charming wife, Lucia, and their son, Davide, has been doing business in this location for over thirty years. Fresh daily pastas, roast meats, fish on Friday, Bruno's creamy *baccalà mantecata,* seasonal vegetables, a wide variety of Italian hams and cheeses, including *mozzarella di bufala* direct from the producer, and bottles of wine from the Veneto keep customers returning. There is also a good selection of top-quality extra-virgin olive oil and aged balsamic vinegar. There are no tables or bar areas for dining, and no beverages sold by the glass, so it is best to purchase drinks somewhere along this busy street and take your gourmet picnic elsewhere to enjoy.

Though the deli section is open for business on Monday, hot food is available only from Tuesday to Saturday. On Wednesday afternoon the meat and cheese section is closed.

ALLA MADONNA (21)
Calle della Madonna, 594

TELEPHONE
041 522 3824

FAX
041 521 0167

OPEN
Mon–Tues, Thur–Sun: lunch noon–3 P.M., dinner 7–10:30 P.M.

CLOSED
Wed; Aug 1–15, Dec 20–Jan 31

RESERVATIONS
Absolutely essential

CREDIT CARDS
AE, MC, V

À LA CARTE
28.41–33.57€

MENÙ TURISTICO
None

COVER & SERVICE CHARGES
Cover 1.55€, 12% service added

Alla Madonna is in a pivotal location on a narrow street on the San Polo side of the Rialto Bridge. Almost every guidebook to Venice lists it as one of the restaurants you *must* visit, and for good reason. The fresh fish is always delicious and reasonable, and the atmosphere is authentic and pleasing. The unadorned tables are filled every day with a mix of chattering Venetians and visitors. If you arrive without reservations—unless you are here the moment lunch or dinner service starts—you can expect to wait up to an hour for a table, so beware. Service by the white-coated waitstaff, some of whom have been on the job since time began, can be brusque, but given the number of tables they have to serve, it is easy to see why patience can run thin during the crunch.

From appetizer to pasta and main course, the star of the show is always fresh fish. At the entrance is an iced display of only some of the many delicacies awaiting you. The specialties are seafood risotto, spaghetti with black squid, squid with polenta, fried cuttlefish, a mixed fish fry, and grilled sole. Add a salad or fresh vegetable and a slice of Madonna cake (cream-filled sponge cake), and you will be in seventh heaven, or close to it.

NOTE: Alla Madonna is a member of Ristoranti della Buona Accoglienza; see page 173 for details.

ALL' ANTICO PIZZO' (15)
Calle San Mattio, 814

The Rialto Market is one of the top tourist attractions in Venice, and I recommend it highly. Today the old commercial meetingplace along the quay is a lively and colorful outdoor market crowded with countless stalls and shouting hawkers selling everything that is seasonally fresh. Housewives and chefs come early each morning for the best food available, and visitors wander through eager to soak up the local color and take advantage of the many interesting photo opportunities.

Whenever you are in this area, a good target for lunch is Antico Pizzo'. The two rooms with simply laid tables are filled every day with regulars, who come for the fine fish offered by Vittorio Marcolin and his two brothers, Mario and Fabio. As you enter, the fresh fish and antipasti display will tempt you. Fish is number one here, prepared without fanfare. Start with the fish risotto or the lasagna layered with fish. For the main course, I suggest the *fritto misto dell'Adriatico* (assorted fried Adriatic fish) or the *coda di rospo ai ferri* (grilled angler fish). Always ask what the daily specials are because they are bound to be winning choices. Other dishes are served—such as an omelette, liver with onions, and veal scaloppine—but stick to the fish. Desserts are not a high priority with the chef, and the kitchen definitely does not do pizza.

ANTICHE CARAMPANE ($, 14)
Rio Terra de le Carampane, 1911 (near Campiello Albrizzi)

Almost everything, from the formal atmosphere to the reliably tasty food, remains unchanged at Antiche Carampane, reported to be one of the oldest taverns in Venice. For a dress-up meal designed to impress your boss, difficult mother-in-law, or important date, this should do very well, provided everyone likes fish, since that is all they serve. To help casual guests not "in the know," a sign posted outside states that they do not serve pizza, lasagne, or pasta with *ragù* sauce, and there is no

ENGLISH
Yes, and menu in English

TELEPHONE
041 523 1575

OPEN
Tues–Sat: lunch 12:30–2:30 P.M., dinner 7:30–10 P.M.; Sun: lunch 12:30–2:30 P.M.

CLOSED
Mon; Sun dinner; 2 weeks in Jan, Aug (dates vary)

RESERVATIONS
Not necessary

CREDIT CARDS
MC, V

À LA CARTE
28.41–33.57€

MENÙ TURISTICO
None

COVER & SERVICE CHARGES
Cover 1.55€, service included

ENGLISH
Yes, and menu in English

TELEPHONE
041 524 0165

OPEN
Tues–Sat: lunch noon–3:30 P.M., dinner 7–11 P.M.

CLOSED
Mon, Sun; Aug

RESERVATIONS
Advised

CREDIT CARDS
AE, DC, MC, V

À LA CARTE
36.15–41.32€

MENÙ TURISTICO
None

COVER & SERVICE CHARGES
Cover 1.81€, service included

ENGLISH
Yes

fixed-price menu. They should add that there is no printed à la carte menu. The food you eat depends on what looked best that day at the Rialto Market. This is an old-school Big Splurge designed for those who prefer tradition over life in the fast lane.

CAFFÈ DEI FRARI (22)
Fondamenta dei Frari, 2564

TELEPHONE
041 524 1877

OPEN
Mon–Sat: 7:30–9 P.M.
(till 1 A.M. in summer),
continuous service

CLOSED
Sun; first or last week of Aug
(dates vary)

RESERVATIONS
Not accepted

CREDIT CARDS
None

À LA CARTE
Sandwiches from 1.81€

MENÙ TURISTICO
None

COVER & SERVICE CHARGES
Cover 0.77€ if occupying a
table, service discretionary

ENGLISH
Some

At this rambunctious *caffè* near the Campo dei Frari (at the foot of Ponte dei Frari), you will join Venetian students, men quaffing a third glass of Chianti far too early in the day, and elderly women fortifying their trip to the market with a *caffè macchiato* or cappuccino. There is always neighborly service and made-to-order savory sandwiches served from dawn to dusk by the casual crew. I like to go around noon and order a pocket-bread sandwich filled with slices of *prosciutto crudo* (air-dried salt-cured ham) and thin slices of provolone or *mozzarella di bufala* cheese. For the best people-watching, sit downstairs at one of the six round tables along the padded banquette, or in summer, at one of the tables outside facing the canal. As is the case in all cafés, if you sit at these tables, or one upstairs, you will pay an additional charge; here it is 0.77€ to have the waiter negotiate the narrow stairs with your order or bring it to you outside.

CANTINA DO MORI (16)
Calle do Mori, 429 (off Ruga Vecchia S. Giovanni)

TELEPHONE
041 522 5401

OPEN
Mon–Sat: 8:30 A.M.–9 P.M.,
continuous service

CLOSED
Sun; July 15–Aug 15

RESERVATIONS
Not accepted

CREDIT CARDS
None

À LA CARTE
Cicchetti from 1.03€, sandwiches
from 2.07€

MENÙ TURISTICO
None

COVER & SERVICE CHARGES
None

ENGLISH
Limited

For a glimpse of where the Rialto Market traders, delivery boys, and local officer workers go for wine and camaraderie, look no further than Cantina do Mori, which has a decidedly male-dominated atmosphere. Inside it is long, narrow, and dark, with hanging copper pots and a stand-up bar (there are no tables at all). You will eat great *cicchetti,* platters of local salami and prosciutto, enormous sandwiches, and drink wines sold by the glass. In existence since 1462, this time-worn *enoteca* is run by Rudi and Gianni, who will be happy to advise you on which wines you should drink with whatever you are eating. For instance, if it is salt cod, it should be a glass of prosecco. With winter sausage and beans, you will need a robust Cabernet.

NOTE: There are no toilets.

IGNAZIO ($, 23)
Calle Saoneri, 2749

Ignazio is named after Florenzo Scroccaro's father, who began this fine family-run restaurant in 1951. Then, as now, it served some of the best food in Venice. Just ask anyone who has ever eaten there and they will agree . . . I know I feel that way.

Everything is impressive, from the host's warm greeting to the last forkful of dessert. Great pains are taken to lay a handsome table using delicate china and attractive glass and silverware. Beautiful fresh flowers add color. In summer, a leafy green outdoor garden is open for alfresco dining. The English-speaking waitstaff carry out their duties with professionalism. For your meal, you will be in the hands of three talented, hardworking female chefs, including Ignazio's wife. It is clear that everyone is an important part of this extended family. When I was last there for lunch, one of the owner's daughters ran through the restaurant, heavy book bag in tow, and headed straight for the kitchen, where all work came to a halt and the girl was warmly greeted with kisses and hugs from everyone.

The meal begins with an assortment of antipasti, perhaps huge prawns bathed in a lemon and oil dressing or the mixed seafood plate. For the first course, I recommend their special *spaghetti alla trapanese con melanzane e zucchine* (egg pasta served with a mixture of eggplant, peppers, tomatoes, zucchini, and garlic in a light cream sauce). Although fish is king here, with grilled sole, lobster, or sea crab heading the list, also good are the Venetian-style sautéed liver and polenta and the veal escallope prepared "as you wish." Desserts, so often the least distinguished part of an Italian meal, are excellent, especially the homemade tiramisù, that rich favorite made with mascarpone cheese, and the their homemade chocolate cake. The wine list is varied and well priced.

NOTE: Ignazio is a member of Ristoranti della Buona Accoglienza; see page 173 for details.

TELEPHONE
041 523 4852

FAX
041 244 85 46

OPEN
Mon–Fri, Sun: lunch noon–3 P.M., dinner 7–10 P.M.

CLOSED
Sat; 1 week before Carnivale, last week of July–first 2 weeks of Aug

RESERVATIONS
Essential

CREDIT CARDS
AE, DC, MC, V

À LA CARTE
30.99–41.32€

MENÙ TURISTICO
None

COVER & SERVICE CHARGES
Cover 1.55€, 12% service added

ENGLISH
Yes, and menu in English

OSTERIA ANTICO DOLO (17)
Ruga Vecchia San Giovanni, 778 (often called Ruga Rialto)

For good wine and food near the Rialto Bridge, stop by Antico Dolo, a picture-postcard version of a typical *osteria* frequented by neighborhood residents. There are only twenty-five places in two little rooms, which are typically decorated with hanging pots and a lazy ceiling

TELEPHONE
041 522 6546

INTERNET
www.anticodolo.venezia.it

OPEN
Mon–Sat: lunch 10:30 A.M.–2:30 P.M., dinner 6:30–10:30 P.M.

CLOSED
Sun; July 1–15, Dec 23–Jan 6
(dates vary)

RESERVATIONS
Essential

CREDIT CARDS
AE, MC, V

À LA CARTE
20.66–25.82€

MENÙ TURISTICO
None

COVER & SERVICE CHARGES
Cover 1.55€, 12% service
added

ENGLISH
Yes

fan slowly moving the air. The size does not seem to deter the faithful, including gondoliers, who swear by the chef's dishes of country sausages, hearty seafood pastas, locally caught fish, and tripe with Parmesan cheese. The variety of wines is better than the one dessert option: *biscotti*.

OSTERIA DA FIORE ($, 13)
Calle del Scaleter, 2202

TELEPHONE
041 721 308

FAX
041 721 343

EMAIL
da_fiore@libero.it

INTERNET
www.dafiore.com

OPEN
Tues–Sat: lunch 12:30–
2:30 P.M., dinner 7:30–
10:30 P.M.

CLOSED
Mon, Sun; Dec 24–Jan 20, Aug

RESERVATIONS
Essential as far in advance as
possible

CREDIT CARDS
AE, DC, MC, V

À LA CARTE
77.47–90.38€

MENÙ TURISTICO
None

COVER & SERVICE CHARGES
No cover charge, 10% service
added

ENGLISH
Yes

Everyone has a favorite fish restaurant in Venice, and Da Fiore is at the top of many lists. Run by the charming Maurizio Martin, who works in front, and his wife, Mara, who is the capable chef, it has been in operation since 1978. Since that time they have built an enviable reputation for having the most sought-after tables for the best and freshest seasonal seafood available, and they have earned the only Michelin star awarded in Venice in the process. Because of the high demand, reservations are absolutely essential at least two weeks in advance. The well-designed interior is beautiful in its simple elegance. A vase of flowers graces each well-spaced table, set with soft yellow linen, large wineglasses, and shining cutlery. The formally dressed waitstaff are very helpful, explaining the menu and suggesting appropriate wines as needed. Please note that meat is not served.

The menu changes daily, but for delicious openers, you can always count on a seafood salad or a delicate fish soup. According to the time of year, you might see imaginative dishes featuring octopus, scallops, or razor clams. Also watch for delicate fried vegetables, which are light as feathers and not at all greasy. The first courses include a very light consommé with scampi and ravioli filled with a light whitefish. Be sure to save adequate room for the main courses, which also vary with the season. Look for grilled eel, fillet of striped bass splashed with balsamic vinegar, turbot baked in a potato crust, and soft-shell crab served with polenta. For dessert, the lemon *sorbetto* or the vanilla ice cream with a red wine–

soaked pear are light finishes to a lovely meal. Yes, this is definitely a Big Splurge, but one that is well worth it.

NOTE: Osteria da Fiore is a member of Ristorante della Buona Accoglienza; see page 173 for details.

OSTERIA SORA AL PONTE (12)
Ponte delle Becarie, 1588

The setting, just by the bridge leading to the Rialto fish market, should tell you what will be on your plate for lunch and dinner, as well as dominating the *cicchetti* at the bar. Four of the five set-price menus offer fish, and all incude the cover charge. You aren't reduced to eating just fried fish either: choices include *sarde in saor* (sardines marinated in vinegar with onions, pinenuts, and raisins), gnocchi with a salmon sauce, and *baccalà*. Some of the best à la carte dishes are those prepared for two: *sora al ponte* (an antipasti of barely cooked and marinated seafood), *tagliolini all'astice* (tagliolini with lobster), and a bountiful *grigliata mista*, a *secondo piatto* offering the best fish in the market. Add a salad and/or an order of grilled vegetables and you will understand why Sora al Ponte is such a success with everyone, from portly market workers to businesspeople and Venetian foodies—who hope this one stays a secret just a little longer.

TELEPHONE & FAX
041 718 208

OPEN
Tues–Sun: bar 8 A.M.–3 P.M., 7–10 P.M.; lunch noon–3 P.M.; dinner 7–10 P.M.

CLOSED
Mon; 2 weeks in Jan (dates vary)

RESERVATIONS
Advised

CREDIT CARDS
MC, V

À LA CARTE
25.82–36.15€

MENÙ TURISTICO
Sora al ponte: 18.08€, 2 fish courses, including vegetable, dessert, and service; *menu canova:* 15.49€, 2 fish courses, including salad, dessert, and service; *menu tiepolo:* 12.91€, 1 fish course, 1 meat course with potatoes, including dessert and service; *piatto combinato:* 10.33€, fish pasta, salad, including water or wine, cover, and service; unnamed menu: 7.75€, includes meat, potatoes, wine, cover, and service

COVER & SERVICE CHARGES
Cover 1.29€, 10% service added

ENGLISH
Yes

TRATTORIA PIZZERIA SAN TOMÀ (26)
Campo San Tomà, 2864A

Tasty pizza (with regular or whole-wheat crusts), delicious homemade pastas and bread, a friendly staff offering attentive service, a beautiful lighted garden, and an outside dining terrace perfect for people-watching—it all comes together to create a pleasing dining experience at Bernardo Di-Zio's trattoria. If you don't order a pizza or plate of pasta, consider his very special paella, which he makes only on Saturday and Sunday (otherwise you must order it ahead). When you order the paella,

TELEPHONE
041 523 8819

OPEN
Daily: lunch noon–3 P.M., dinner 7–10:30 P.M. (until 11 P.M. for pizza)

CLOSED
Closings can vary. Closed Tues from Jan–Mar 15 (except Carnivale), and closed some Tues in summer if the owner feels like it

RESERVATIONS
Advised for weekends and
holidays
CREDIT CARDS
AE, DC, MC, V
À LA CARTE
Pizza 5.16–10.33€, one-plate
meals from 12.91€, full meals
20.66–23.24€
MENÙ TURISTICO
13.94€, 3 courses; cover and
service included, beverage
extra; 24.27€ for Venetian
specialties, 3 courses, dessert,
wine, cover, and service
included
COVER & SERVICE CHARGES
Cover 1.03€, 12% service
added
ENGLISH
Yes, and menu in English

you get to keep the bib that protects your clothing from this juicy dish. Also on the menu are the usual Venetian standards of marinated sardines, fried fish, and liver with polenta.

An advantage for many Great Eaters is that a full three-course meal is *not* necessary. You can order one of the meal-size salads or a *piatto unico*—a one-plate dish of goulash with pasta, lasagna, and salad or chicken and fries—and still be treated as though you were ordering the works. Because all the servings are so big, dessert is kept to a minimum, with the emphasis on *sorbetto, tartufo,* or fruit.

Santa Croce

In the 1930s, the Fascists built the Piazzale Roma, the gigantic car park just over the bridge from Mestre. Toward the eastern part of the district are weaving walkways that are relatively tourist free. To the west, the area is mainly industrial and geared to dock and freight operations around the Stazione Marittima. Also here is the Manifattura Tabacci, the oldest industrial building in Venice still used for its original purpose: cigar and cigarette production. Flanking the Grand Canal are fading yet still imposing *palazzos.*

Restaurants

AE OCHE (11)
Calle del Tintor, 1552A-B

Ae Oche is young, fun, cheap, and good. This popular gathering ground for the Italian fast-food generation is *never* empty. I have yet to find a way to beat the Sunday crowd of families who arrive for one of the ninety varieties of crisp pizza and calzones. You can dine outside on a little deck, in a tented garden in the back, or at one of the inside booths with bench seats crafted from bed headboards.

Fire-eaters will love pizza No. 15, the *mangiafuoco* featuring spicy salami, pepperoni, paprika, and tabasco sauce. Tamer taste buds will appreciate No. 30, the *capricciosa* topped with prosciutto, mushrooms, and hearts of artichokes. The *disco volante* (flying saucer), two pizzas put together sandwich style, is not a stellar choice, and neither is the house wine. You are better off with something from their long international beer list, which offers brews from Australia, Mexico, the United States, and Spain, among others. There is also a regular trattoria menu with all the familiar antipasti, pastas, meats, and side dishes. However, this part of the menu is too long for all the food to be fresh . . . so order with extreme caution.

NOTE: There are two streets named Calle del Tintor, which is also spelled Tentor. You want the one that leads into Campo S. Giacomo dell' Orio.

TELEPHONE
041 524 1161

OPEN
Daily: winter, noon–3 P.M., 7 P.M.–midnight; summer, noon–midnight, continuous service

CLOSED
Never

RESERVATIONS
Advised, especially on weekends and holidays

CREDIT CARDS
MC, V

À LA CARTE
Pizza from 3.62–7.75€, full meal 15.49€

MENÙ TURISTICO
None

COVER & SERVICE CHARGES
Cover 1.29€, 12% service added

ENGLISH
Yes

LA ZUCCA (9)
Campo San Giacomo dell' Orio, 1762 (by the Ponte del Megio)

Collectors of unusual cuisine experiences take note: this may be your only chance to sample pumpkin pasta or pumpkin soup in Venice, two tasty treats from which this appealing little trattoria takes its name. Unfortunately, you will have to time your visit in the fall or winter, since these dishes are only available seasonally. The rest of the food on the daily changing menu shows a degree of originality as the young and enthusiastic owners strive to please a snappy group of youthful habitués, many of whom are vegetarians and appreciate the interesting ways the chef has with fresh vegetables for all courses.

TELEPHONE
041 524 1570

OPEN
Mon–Sat: lunch 12:30-2 P.M., dinner 7–10:30 P.M.

CLOSED
Sun; NAC

RESERVATIONS
Advised for dinner and holidays

CREDIT CARDS
AE, MC, V

À LA CARTE
18.08–20.66€

MENÙ TURISTICO
None

COVER & SERVICE CHARGES
Cover 1.29€, service included

ENGLISH
Yes

Aside from the pumpkin creations, pasta tossed several ways—including with tomato and fresh ricotta cheese—are the first-course front-runners. The chicken salad with nuts and a gorgonzola-spiked vinaigrette dressing and a Greek eggplant and potato tort are good lunch choices, while the roast pork or rabbit seem more appropriate for dinner. Vegetarians will want to try the carrots cooked with lemon and seasoned with curry, small onions simmered in prosecco wine, or the potato-provolone gratinée. For dessert, the *panna cotta* with chocolate on top and the chef's special lemon crostata display first-class simplicity.

I think the best seating is outside, overlooking the canal. On cool days, I like to sit toward the back at a window table on the Rio delle Megio canal rather than up front in the bar and kitchen area, where the shoulder-to-shoulder crowd can get a little loud. When you go, be sure to admire the modern paintings of pumpkins in every guise imaginable lining the oak-paneled walls.

TRATTORIA ALLE BURCHIELLE (24)
Fondamenta Burchielle, 393

TELEPHONE
041 710 342

OPEN
Tues–Sun: lunch noon–3 P.M., noon 7–10 P.M.

CLOSED
Mon; Jan

RESERVATIONS
Advised

CREDIT CARDS
AE, DC, MC, V

À LA CARTE
23.24–25.82€

MENÙ TURISTICO
None

COVER & SERVICE CHARGES
Cover 1.03€, 10% service added

ENGLISH
Yes, and menu in English

Trattoria alle Burchielle was founded on this site in 1503 and is considered one of the oldest trattorias in continuous operation in Venice. Ninety years ago, Bruno Pagin's uncle took charge, and now, under Bruno and his niece Serena's direction, it is still going strong as a local favorite best known for its treatment of fresh fish. The restaurant is along a pretty canal in a picturesque corner of Venice, not too far from Piazzale Roma. On a summer evening, it is wonderful to sit outside and watch the boats drifting by while enjoying textbook examples of traditional Venetian fish preparations.

Noteworthy among the first courses are the seafood lasagne and the spaghetti with whole clams. The most popular main courses are the *sogliola ai ferri* (grilled sole) and the giant prawns in a lemon, garlic, and olive oil marinade. There are a few meat dishes, but they are not the reason to eat here. And the sweets that adorn the pastry cart are not made in-house. A nice change of pace for dessert is a selection of Italian cheeses or sweet cookies dipped in *fragolino* (strawberry) wine. The regular menu is translated into English, but does not include the list of daily specials, so be sure to ask about them.

If you can't manage a full meal, try Grecia e Oriente, their new snack bar on the corner; it serves the usual sandwiches and *cicchetti* until the supply runs out, and around noon it offers a few hot pasta dishes.

Pastry Shops and Bakeries

LA BOUTIQUE DEL DOLCE (10)
Rio Marin, 890

On my long early-morning walks, I often passed by the large picture window of a bakery kitchen where a corps of hardworking women were busy pulling trays of pastries from the ovens, putting the finishing touches on decorated cakes, and filling individual tarts with fresh fruit. It was an impressive operation. After asking around, I found that this was the kitchen for a well-known Venetian pastry shop just across the canal. Of course, I rushed right over, and I liked what I found.

La Boutique del Dolce is owned by Gilda Vio, who makes all the divinely sinful pastries and is justifiably proud of the world acclaim her talents have brought her. If you have any guilt at all about indulging in these sinful treats, you may be somewhat assuaged to know that all of her products are made using only pure ingredients without coloring or additives. People in the know beat a daily path to her beautiful shop, which sells some of the best pastries in Venice—and let me assure you, the competition is stiff. Whenever you go, expect a crowd, especially on Sundays around noon, when handsome fathers with young children in tow walk here to purchase dessert for their midday meal. In the morning, order several fruit-filled croissants. Later on, vegetable-based puff pastries, individual pizzas, and sandwiches made on her own breads sell like hot cakes. In the afternoon, stop in for coffee and an airy rum meringue dusted with chocolate, or pick up a bag of their cookies or a box of hand-dipped chocolates for a special treat. Even if you don't buy a thing (a guaranteed impossibility), do go by to admire . . . and to smell.

TELEPHONE
041 718 523

OPEN
Mon–Tues, Thur–Sun: 6:30 A.M.–8 P.M., continuous service

CLOSED
Wed; Aug

CREDIT CARDS
None

PRICES
Pastries from 0.93€, individual pizzas from 1.29€, sandwiches from 1.81€

ENGLISH
None, but Gilda speaks French

Restaurants on the Islands

Burano Island

Burano is synonymous with lace. The best place to see the real thing is at the school in Piazza Galuppi and in its museum and shop. Shops selling more lace than you could ever wash and iron in three lifetimes line the main street that extends from the exit ramp from the boat dock clear across the island. Buyers along this stretch should beware, because most of the work comes straight from Hong Kong or the Philippines. Despite this, the island is a photographer's dream, with brightly colored houses nestled along narrow alleys and walkways. One purchase you can make without worry is a bagful of *bussolai,* the sweet local ring- or S-shaped biscuits that are perfect for dipping in sweet wine. Burano is still a fishing community, and as you walk around the island you will see the boats and nets lining the quays.

TRATTORIA AL GATTO NERO ($)
Via Giudecca, 88

TELEPHONE
041 730 120

FAX
041 735 570

EMAIL
maxpedro@libero.it

INTERNET
www.gattonero.com

OPEN
Tues–Sun: lunch noon–3 P.M., dinner 7:30–9 P.M.

CLOSED
Mon; 7–10 days in Jan, last 10 days of Nov

RESERVATIONS
Advised

CREDIT CARDS
AE, DC, MC, V

À LA CARTE
36.15–43.90€

MENÙ TURISTICO
None

COVER & SERVICE CHARGES
Cover 2.07€, service discretionary

ENGLISH
Yes, and menu in English

Most visitors come to Burano for two reasons: to buy the handmade lace and to eat fish. Tourists rarely stray from the Via Baldessare Galuppi, which is lined with shops selling linen and lace and a selection of overpriced eating places featuring greasy fried fish guaranteed to induce acute heartburn. Just beyond all of this is the most attractive part of Burano, one blissfully free of fellow travelers. It is here that you will find Al Gatto Nero. For the last four decades it has been owned by Ruggero, the chef; his son, Massimiliano; and the house cats: Tai, an independent red cat, and Ciccio, a contented, gray, fat cat who indicates his favoritism for certain customers by sleeping on an empty chair near their table.

Al Gatto Nero is widely recognized as the best trattoria on the island, thanks to its charm and character, not to mention outstanding food, which draws an international clientele. In addition to two large rooms inside, there is a covered canal-side terrace for warm-weather dining. One of the more impressive aspects of the service is the unique china, made especially for the restaurant. The large white dishes are ringed with an artist's conception of Burano buildings, and if you look very carefully, you will see Al Gatto Nero and Ciccio portrayed in the design. It is the most crowded at lunchtime, when local residents know to let the waiter guide their choices based on the daily specials of fresh fish. There is a menu, but as Massimiliano said, "We can't put everything we prepare on the menu, or it would be a bible!" You may want to skip the broiled eel, but not the fresh prawns, broiled sardines, turbot, or fresh sole. Desserts do not play a starring role, so you can concentrate fully on the rest of the meal. Of course, you will skip the meat dishes; they are real understudies.

Giudecca Island

Giudecca Island was where the wealthy Renaissance aristocrats built their summer palaces. Michelangelo stayed here when he left Florence in 1529. Today the wealthy hide out at the famed Cipriani Hotel and eat and drink in Harry's Dolce (a slightly less expensive spin-off of Harry's Bar in Venice). There is also a private garden, the Garden of Eden, named after the English gardener who began it, and Andrea Palladio's Church of La Zitelle. The panorama from the *fondamenta* along the water offers a magnificent view of Doge's Palace and the island of San Giorgio Maggiore.

ALTANELLA ($)
Calle delle Erbe, 268–270

Altanella has what Italians call a *buona forchetta* ("a good fork") and a *buon bicchiere* ("a good glass"). Buried halfway down a narrow street on Giudecca Island, at Rio de Ponte Lungo, the Stradella family restaurant has been in business since the turn of the century preparing *only* fish. It looks undiscovered because there is no sign, only a light outside, but it is firmly on the map. Hemingway was a customer in his day, as was François Mitterand. However, fame has not gone to anyone's head . . . the food is still marvelous.

During warm weather, reserve a table on the irresistibly romantic terrace overlooking the island's central canal. Otherwise, you can sit at one of the tables inside, where there are pictures of the restaurant in its early days and a photo of the founder over the kitchen door. Dishes I look forward to having again are the risotto with fish, the freshly made gnocchi with squid ink and sauced

TELEPHONE
041 522 7780

OPEN
Wed–Sun: lunch 12:30–2 P.M., dinner 7:30–9 P.M.

CLOSED
Mon–Tues; Jan–Carnivale, Aug 10–20

RESERVATIONS
Essential

CREDIT CARDS
None

À LA CARTE
30.99–36.15€

MENÙ TURISTICO
None

COVER & SERVICE CHARGES
Cover 1.55€, 10% service added

ENGLISH
Yes, and menu in English

with cuttlefish (a prized recipe of one of the grandmothers in the family), mussels and sweet peppers, the grilled sea bream, and the flavorful tuna. The desserts are made here, so be sure to plan on a piece of the lush chocolate cake, the unusual pumpkin cake, or if you are here at Easter, their special almond cake.

Lido Island

Early in the 1900s, Lido, which is Italian for "shore," was developed as a Belle Epoque resort. Today it is a playground with something for everyone's pocketbook and taste. It is known for its stretches of well-kept private beaches and dismal public ones, a gambling casino and film festival, and hotels—both dowager and flashy. One of the best ways to appreciate Lido is to rent a bike for the day and pedal. Lido is the only lagoon island with roads. It comes alive around Easter and closes down by the end of the year.

RESTAURANTS

($) indicates a Big Splurge

Restaurants

RISTORANTE BELVEDERE ($) E TAVOLA CALDA (92)

Piazzale la Santa Maria Elisabetta, 4

TELEPHONE
041 526 0115, 041 526 0164

OPEN
Tues–Sun: lunch noon–2:30 P.M., dinner 7–9:30 P.M.

CLOSED
Mon; Ristorante Belvedere: Nov–April; Tavola Calda: 2 weeks in Nov

RESERVATIONS
Advised for Ristorante, not accepted at Tavola Calda

CREDIT CARDS
DC, MC, V

If you are visiting Lido for the day, chances are you will want to eat. Unless you know where to go, most of the food is overpriced tourist pizza or deadly dull and ludicrously expensive hotel dining; there is not much middle ground. Enter the Ristorante Belvedere and its Tavola Calda snack bar next door, which are part of the Hotel Belvedere (see *Great Sleeps Italy*).

Everyone agrees that some of the best food to be had in this tourist mecca is at the Belvedere, right across the street from the Venice vaporetto stop. At the restaurant, famished Great Eaters will order the *menù turistico*, a

18.08€ value that includes three courses, cover and service charges, but not beverages. The food, which features fresh fish, is served on a pretty streetside terrace or in the formal hotel dining room with big picture windows.

Confirmed card-carrying bargaineers will skip the *ristorante* side completely and head straight for the Tavola Calda, which adjoins it. This is just the answer for the visitor with lots on the agenda and no time, desire, or money for a fancy meal. The same kitchen is used for both places, but the prices here are much lower. Every day there are pastas, roast chicken, fish, and an excellent selection of vegetables, salads, and made-to-order sandwiches. Another benefit is that it is open year-round Tuesday through Sunday, while the hotel restaurant is closed from November to Easter.

À LA CARTE
Ristorante, 41.32€; Tavola Calda, sandwiches from 1.29€, hot meals 7.75–10.33€, beverage included

MENÙ TURISTICO
Ristorante:18.08€, 3 courses; cover and service included, beverage extra

COVER & SERVICE CHARGES
Ristorante, cover 2.07€, service included; Tavola Calda, none

ENGLISH
Yes, and menu in English at Ristorante

TRATTORIA ANDRI ($, 93)
Via Lepanto, 21

Trattoria Andri is in a pretty neighborhood only a ten-minute stroll from the usual tourist track on the island of Lido. There are ninety places outside on a covered terrace and maybe fifty more inside this lovely old villa. The interior is open and airy, featuring white walls hung with modern abstract paintings and brass platters. Silk flowers adorn each table, and a fresh bouquet brightens up the bar. The same family has been serving Lido residents for more than thirty years.

The best first course is the house specialty: *spaghetti Andri,* featuring fat shrimp. Grilled turbot or filet of sole sautéed in butter make winning main-course selections, as do all the daily specials of seasonal seafood. The seriously hungry will consider the *menù Andri,* a multi-course fish feast featuring numerous selections for each course plus dessert, wine, and grappa. Dessert calls for something light, and the best choice, in my opinion, and in the opinion of a hundred other diners *per day,* is not listed on the menu and does not have a name. Ask for the *limone digestif*—a frothy, refreshing mix of lemon, ice, sparkling wine, and vodka blended together like a milkshake and served in a champagne flute.

TELEPHONE
041 526 5482

OPEN
Wed–Sun: lunch noon–3 P.M., dinner 7:30 P.M.–midnight

CLOSED
Mon–Tues; Jan, Feb

RESERVATIONS
Advised

CREDIT CARDS
MC, V (but not when they are busy, and Andri decides that)

À LA CARTE
30.99–36.15€

MENÙ TURISTICO
Menù Andri: 46.48€, 4 courses, including dessert, wine, and grappa

COVER & SERVICE CHARGES
Cover 2.07€, service discretionary

ENGLISH
Yes, and menu in English

TRATTORIA FAVORITA ($, 94)
Via Francesco Duodo, 33

TELEPHONE
041 526 1626

EMAIL
lucapradel1@tin.it

OPEN
Tues: dinner 7:30–10:30 P.M.;
Wed–Sun: lunch 12:30–
2:30 P.M., dinner 7:30–
10:30 P.M.

CLOSED
Mon; Tues lunch; Jan

RESERVATIONS
Essential, at least 2–3 days in
advance

CREDIT CARDS
AE, DC, MC, V

À LA CARTE
36.15–43.90€

MENÙ TURISTICO
None

COVER & SERVICE CHARGES
Cover 2.58€, service included

ENGLISH
Yes, and menu in English

The regulars at Trattoria Favorita come for the wine and the dependable fish preparations turned out by a hardworking squad of chefs. I like it because of its location: hidden in a pretty residential district about a twenty-minute walk from the Santa Maria Elisabetta vaporetto stop.

Summer seating on the vine-covered terrace is always in demand, but the seats are hard plastic with thin cushions, and thus not many deals are made or romances begun while sitting here. The inside is more comfortable, and it is air-conditioned, a real bonus during the sizzling Venetian summers. The two large rooms have great atmosphere, with heavy beams, a nice collection of country furniture, liberal use of green plants and fresh flowers, and soft pink table linens.

The kitchen does not feature daily specials; instead, it concentrates on doing a superb job with everything listed on the sensible menu. The emphasis is on fish. In fact, besides fish, there are just two entrée choices: steak, either plain or with peppers. The gnocchi with crab is perfect, and so is the spaghetti with fresh clams. Grilled filet of sole, bass, a mixed grilled fish platter, and turbot make up the bulk of the main courses. Their specialty is San Pietro, and when you order this dish, you will be given a collector's plate to commemorate your meal. The wine list is exceptional, listing only regional wines in all price categories. If something sweet is called for at the end of your meal, sip the vodka-lemon-prosecco smoothie.

Murano Island

Visitors to Venice make the trip to Murano either to buy glass or to eat fish—or both. Most of the restaurants are closed for dinner, so plan accordingly.

RESTAURANTS

Restaurants

AI VETRAI (91)
Fondamenta Manin, 29

The best time to experience Ai Vetrai is on a warm Sunday, when you want to arrive early for lunch and nab one of the canalside tables. The inside goes on forever, and is perfectly acceptable, but why not be reminded every minute that you are fortunate enough to be dining in this picturesque part of Venice? The menu reads well, but only if you are ordering fish—everything else is beside the point, especially the restaurant's nod toward meat . . . horse salami with polenta. Salmon carpaccio and *sarde in saor* are two promising starters. Best pastas are the spaghetti with lobster, *tagliolini* with spider crab, or the seafood risotto for two. The mixed grilled or fried fish arrives on an oversized platter . . . so be ready for it. Don't worry about dessert; they are reruns you see everywhere: tiramisù, *panna cotta* with berries, and gelato.

TELEPHONE
041 739 293

OPEN
Mon–Wed, Fri–Sun: lunch noon–3 P.M.

CLOSED
Thur; NAC

RESERVATIONS
Advised in the summer

CREDIT CARDS
AE, MC, V

À LA CARTE
28.41–36.15€

MENÙ TURISTICO
None

COVER & SERVICE CHARGES
Cover 1.03€, 12% service added

ENGLISH
Yes

ANTICA TRATTORIA MURANESE (89)
Fondamenta Cavour, 20

Situated on the canal about halfway down from the Venice vaporetto stop is the Antica Trattoria Muranese, a reliable bet for an unassuming seafood lunch in Murano. Thanks to the tourists who arrive by the boatload from Venice, Murano stays in business selling its famous glass. There are few real "local" spots, but at least here the food is honest and cheap . . . for Murano. There is a summer garden in back with tables and umbrellas. In the cooler months, seating is inside two steamy rooms with little in the way of interior decoration.

Budgeteers are going to want the *menù turistico*. Haute cuisine is not one of the kitchen's strengths, so for maximum results, think simple. Rely on what has to be prepared to order, such as grilled fish or whatever they are pushing as the special. The *menù turistico* offers three non-fish pastas or a fish risotto as a first course, and for the second, four fish choices or veal scaloppine, all served with mixed vegetables or a salad. The uninteresting bakery desserts make it easy to bypass this course, and besides, you have to pay extra for it if you are doing the *menù turistico*. The house wine is okay, but a beer is probably better.

TELEPHONE
041 739 610

OPEN
Daily: lunch noon–3 P.M.

CLOSED
Never

RESERVATIONS
Not necessary

CREDIT CARDS
AE, MC, V

À LA CARTE
20.66–25.82€

MENÙ TURISTICO
18.08€, 3 courses; cover and service included, beverage extra

COVER & SERVICE CHARGES
Cover 1.03€, 12% service added

ENGLISH
Some

TRATTORIA BUSA ALLA TORRE DA LELE (90)
Campo S. Stefano, 3

TELEPHONE
041 739 662

OPEN
Daily: lunch 11:30 A.M.–
3:30 P.M.

CLOSED
Jan 10–30

RESERVATIONS
Advised

CREDIT CARDS
AE, DC, MC, V

À LA CARTE
28.41–33.57€

MENÙ TURISTICO
None

COVER & SERVICE CHARGES
Cover 1.55€, 12% service
added

ENGLISH
Yes, and menu in English

Welcome to Lele and Christina's trattoria, where knowledgeable Venetians eat when they visit the island of Murano. Lele, a big man with red hair and a twinkle in his eye, is a Murano fixture who meets and greets his guests with gusto. His wife, Christina, keeps things moving from behind the bar. The waiters offer casual service, and time should not be a top priority on your visit here. There are two rooms inside the thirteenth-century building, but if weather permits, sit outside. Settle in at one of the terrace tables on the *campo* by the clock tower and enjoy a romantic, leisurely lunch, accompanied by a nice bottle of Venetian wine and someone very special . . . and be glad you are not home mowing the lawn or paying bills.

The food probably will not sweep you off your feet, but the kitchen does know how to turn out classic fish dishes with finesse and just the right amount of dash. You will have the best success if you stick to any of the fresh fish offerings, and, as usual, pay close heed to whatever the chef offers for the daily special. The pasta with fresh clams, a brimming fish soup, and *tagliolini* with crab are only a few of the regular first courses, and sixteen main courses feature local fish.

Sant' Erasmo Island

Sant' Erasmo Island is known as the garden island because it provides many of the best vegetables, particularly artichokes and asparagus, sold at the Rialto Market. Although the island is larger than Venice, its population is sparse. There is one church, one bar, one restaurant, no doctor, no policeman, no school, and no tourism. You can, however, rent a bicycle and ride around the island, admiring the fields and the peace and quiet of it all. The only boat servicing the island is the number 13, leaving from Fondamente Nuove. The trip takes about forty-five minutes. If you do make a day of it and bike around the island, make sure you know what time the last boat goes back to Venice, since there are no hotels either.

CA' VIGNOTTO
Via Forti, 71

Tired of the tourist mob scene in Venice? Yearning for something different, a look at a Venice that the rank-and-file visitor never sees? Are you hungry enough for a meal that never seems to stop? If the answer is yes, then hop on the vaporetto number 13 from Fondamente Nuove and take the forty-five minute trip to Sant' Erasmo Island, which is light years away from Venice in sophistication and pretense. Whether or not you rent a bicycle to tour the rural island, you can dine at Ca'Vignotto, a pretty farmhouse restaurant that serves only multicourse set meals; Sunday lunch and weekday dinners are the best and most lively times to be here.

The restaurant is about a fifteen-minute walk from the vaporetto stop, and finding it is part of the adventure, since of course there are no signs. Here is what to do. Get off the vaporetto at Chiesa, the third stop on Sant' Erasmo. Face the church and take Via dei' Spironi, a dusty road to the left. Be careful not to take the narrow road alongside the church, or you will wind up in someone's backyard, as I did. Stay on Via dei' Spironi until you come to the end, then turn left on Via Forti. The restaurant is on the lefthand side at Via Forti, 71, but the number is nowhere to be seen. Still, at this point you can't miss it: just look for the fountain in the front and the masses of red geraniums in glorious bloom.

Is the food worth this safari? Indeed it is. But be prepared for a huge fish, meat, or vegetarian meal. The waitstaff troops out course after course in a rustic, barnlike dining room paneled in knotty pine. In April and May you can count on artichokes everywhere: in risotto and pasta and served boiled or fried as side dishes. In June, the fried zucchini flowers are crispy bites of heaven. The meal begins with two appetizers, then two pasta servings, a main course with at least two vegetables, all the red or white wine you can drink, and ends with dessert. If you haven't done the bike trip around the island, maybe now is the time.

TELEPHONE
041 528 5329

OPEN
Mon, Wed–Sun: lunch and dinner by appointment only

CLOSED
Tues; last 3 weeks in Jan

RESERVATIONS
Required

CREDIT CARDS
None

À LA CARTE
None

MENÙ TURISTICO
18.08€ for meat or vegetable meal, 25.82€ for fish; all include multiple courses, wine, cover, and service charges

COVER & SERVICE CHARGES
None

ENGLISH
Yes, ask for Rodrigo

Food Shopping in Venice

Gourmet Food and Wine Shops

BOTTIGLIERA COLONNA (70)
Calle della Fava, 5595 (Castello)

TELEPHONE & FAX
041 528 5137

EMAIL
botcol@libero.it

OPEN
Mon–Sat: 9 A.M.–1 P.M.,
4–8 P.M.

CLOSED
Sun; Jan 15–31

CREDIT CARDS
None

This small shop has a good selection of Italian wines from small producers. They also have a good supply of grappa and speak English, but they do not ship or take credit cards.

GIACOMO RIZZO (61)
San Giovanni Grisostomo, 5778 (Cannaregio)

One of the best gourmet food shops in Venice is Giacomo Rizzo, which has been dispensing its hand-made pastas, balsamic vinegars, truffles, extra-virgin first-pressed olive oils, honeys, and dried mushrooms since 1905. The dried pastas are made without preservatives or colors, and range from a simple spinach tagliatelle to others flavored with radicchio, smoked salmon, cuttlefish, and beetroot.

TELEPHONE & FAX
041 522 2824

OPEN
Mon–Sat: 8:30 A.M.–1 P.M.;
Mon–Tues, Thur–Sat: 3:30–
7:30 P.M.

CLOSED
Wed afternoon, Sun; a few days
in Aug

CREDIT CARDS
None

MASCARI (19)
Rugha Orefici, 381 (San Polo)

In the front, it looks like a gourmet grocery store with bags of *funghi porcini,* bottles of specialty olive oils, aged balsamic vinegar, spices, jams, jellies, hard candies galore, and even jars of dijon mustard. The best part about Mascari is its large Italian wine selection, which are in the back rooms. Ask for Gabriele, one of the sons; he speaks English well and can help you select just what you want. They do not ship.

TELEPHONE
041 522 9762

EMAIL
iginioma@tin.it

INTERNET
www.imascari.com

OPEN
Mon–Sat: 8 A.M.–1 P.M.,
4–7:30 P.M. (also Sun at
Christmas)

CLOSED
Sun; Aug 1–17, 2 days at
Christmas and New Year's

CREDIT CARDS
None

Grocery Stores and Supermarkets

Big supermarkets do not exist in Venice, and most of the so-called supermarkets are well hidden. Hours are usually from 8:30 A.M. to 12:30 or 1 P.M. and 3:30 to 7:30 P.M. from Monday through Saturday, except Wednesdays, when they are closed in the afternoon. Sunday, of course, is a full day of rest.

The largest market is Standa (6), Strada Nova, 3660 (Cannaregio), which has a second location on Lido at Via Corfù. Smaller markets include: Billa (41), Zattere al Ponte Lungo, 1491 (Dorsoduro); Dogal (64), Calle del Pistor, 3989 (Castello); Minimarket (31), Campo Santa Margherita 3019/3112 (Dorsoduro); and Suve (75), corner of Salizzada San Lio and Calle Mondo Nuovo, 5812 (Castello). Suve is the most central market, and it has a good meat and cheese selection; it is open nonstop Monday to Saturday from 8:30 A.M. to 7:30 P.M.

Outdoor Markets

Open-air markets selling fruits, vegetables, and flowers are set up in various squares every day but Sunday. They are all open in the mornings and sometimes in the afternoon. You will find them at Santa Maria Formosa (Castello), Via Garibaldi (Castello), Santa Margherita (Dorsoduro), Campiello dell'Anconetta (Cannaregio), Rio Terrà San Leonardo (Cannaregio), and on a barge off Campo Santa Barnaba (Dorsoduro). Generally speaking, the hours are from Monday to Saturday 8:30 A.M. to 12:30 P.M., and afternoons, except Wednesday, from 3:30 to 7:30 P.M.

The market to end all markets, however, is the famous Rialto Market (San Polo), next to the Rialto Bridge. The hawker stalls lining the bridge sell everything from T-shirts, masks, jewelry, and glassware to fake and real lace. These sellers are open from around 9 A.M. until 6 P.M. in winter and later in summer. The vegetable market (*erberia*) is the best, least expensive, and most colorful in Venice. It is open *only* in the morning from Monday to Saturday, 7:30 or 8 A.M. to 1 P.M. One of the best stalls is run by a friendly young man named Simone, who speaks English and is eager to serve foreigners as well as his regular Venetian customers. How do you find Simone? He is the stall right in front of the fresh pasta shop on the corner of Campo de la Cordaria, 219, and Calle Cesare Battista. The Rialto fish market (*pescheria*) is one of the finest in Europe. Here you will see every known variety of fish and seafood, and some you never knew existed. This is worth a trip, and don't forget your camera. It is open Tuesday to Saturday from 8 A.M. to 1 P.M.

Glossary of Italian Words and Phrases

Everyone should try to be Italian, at least once a year.
—Judy Witts, an adopted Florentine who runs
Divine Cucina, a cooking school in Florence

This glossary is broken down into two sections: the first half gives Italian equivalents for some general words and phrases you might need to use while ordering in a restaurant. The second half gives English translations of Italian words you might find as you read a menu. Many restaurants have menus in English, but invariably they do not include the daily specials, which most often are the best items to order. This glossary is designed to help you make sure there will not be a difference between what you order and what you actually eat.

General Phrases

Hello (telephone)	*pronto*
Hello/good-bye (familiar)	*ciao*
Good morning	*buon giorno*
Good afternoon	*buon pomeriggio*
Good evening	*buona sera*
Goodnight	*buona notte*
Good-bye	*arrivederci*
Please	*per favore*
Thank you	*grazie*
You are welcome	*prego*
Yes/No	*si/no*
Excuse me	*Mi scusi*
I am sorry	*Mi dispiace*
I want/I would like . . .	*Desidero, vorrei . . .*
Do you speak English?	*Parla inglese?*
I don't speak Italian	*Non parlo italiano*
I understand	*Capisco*
I don't understand	*Non capisco*
Where are the restrooms?	*Dov'è la toilette (per signore* [women], *per signori* [men])?
How much is it?	*Quanto costa?*
A little/A lot	*poco/tanto*
More/Less	*più/meno*
Enough/Too much	*abbastanza/troppo*
Open/Closed	*aperto/chiuso*
Please telephone for a taxi	*Per favore, telefoni per un tassi*
No smoking	*vietato fumare*
I am hungry	*Ho fame*

I am diabetic	*Ho il diabete*
I am on a diet	*Sono a dieta*
I am vegetarian	*Sono vegetariano (a)*
I cannot eat	*Non posso mangiare*
It is hot/cold	*È caldo/freddo*
Please give me . . .	*Per favore, mi dia . . .*

Days of the week

today	*oggi*
tonight	*stastera*
tomorrow	*domani*
yesterday	*ieri*
Monday	*lunedì*
Tuesday	*martedì*
Wednesday	*mercoledì*
Thursday	*giovedì*
Friday	*venerdì*
Saturday	*sabato*
Sunday	*domenica*

Numbers

1	*uno*
2	*due*
3	*tre*
4	*quattro*
5	*cinque*
6	*sei*
7	*sette*
8	*otto*
9	*nove*
10	*dieci*
11	*undici*
12	*dodici*
13	*tredici*
14	*quattordici*
15	*quindici*
16	*sedici*
17	*diciasette*
18	*diciotto*
19	*diciannove*
20	*venti*
21	*ventuno*
30	*trenta*
40	*quaranta*
50	*cinquanta*
60	*sessanta*
70	*settanta*
80	*ottanta*
90	*novanta*
100	*cento*

Restaurant Basics

A table for ___, please	*Un tavolo per___persone, per favore*
waiter/waitress	*cameriere/cameriera*
breakfast	*prima colazione*
lunch	*pranzo*
dinner	*cena*
snack	*un spuntino*
takeaway	*da portare via*
The menu, please	*La lista, per favore*
The wine list, please	*La lista dei vini, per favore*
I would like this	*Vorrei questo*
The bill, please	*Il conto, per favore*
The bill divided by two	*Uno diviso due*
The bill is not correct	*Il conto non è giusto*
cover charge	*pane e coperto*
service charge	*servizio*
Is the service included?	*Il servizio è incluso?*
Service is included	*Il servizio è compreso/incluso*
appetizers	*antipasti*
first courses	*primi piatti*
second courses	*secondi piatti*
side dishes	*contorni*
dessert	*dolce*
fixed-price menu	*menù turistico/prezzo fisso*
dish of the day	*piatto del giorno*
specialty of the house/ homemade	*specialità della casa/fatto in casa*
half portion	*una mezza porzione*
in season	*di stagione*
I need a . . .	*Ho bisogno di . . .*
knife	*un cotello*
fork	*una forchetta*
spoon	*un cucchiaio*
cup	*tazza*
plate	*piatto*
side dishes	*contorni*
dessert	*dolce*
ashtray	*portacenere*
chair	*sedia*
highchair	*seggiolino*
table	*tavola*
napkin	*il tovagliolo*
I would like . . .	*Vorrei . . .*
a cup of	*una tazza di*
a glass of	*un bicchiere di*
a bottle of	*una bottiglia di*
a half bottle of	*una mezza bottiglia di*
a carafe of	*una caraffa di*
a liter of	*uno litro di*

Places

alimentari	grocery store
baccaro	Venetian wine bar
caffè	café
drogheria	dried and packaged foods
enoteca	wine shop/bar
gastronomica	grocery store
gelateria	ice cream shop
il forno	bread shop, bakery
latteria	cheese and dairy store
osteria	wine bar
paninoteca	sandwich bar
pasticceria	pastry shop
salumeria	shop for dried, cured meats and cheese
tabaccheria	tobaccanist, a place to get newspapers, bus tickets, lottery tickets, pens, stamps, and so on
tavola calda	cafeteria-style food

Reading the Menu

Cooking Methods

affumicato	smoked
al dente	firm, not overcooked (as in pasta)
al ferro	grilled without olive oil
al forno	baked
alla brace	barbecued, charcoal grilled
alla griglia/ferri	grilled
allo spiedo	on the spit
al sangue/poco cotto	rare
al vapore/in úmido	steamed/stewed
arrosto	roast
ben cotto	well-done
bollito/lesso	boiled
brasato	braised, cooked in wine
carpaccio	thinly sliced raw meat or fish
cotto	cooked (not raw)
crudo	raw
fritto	fried
in camicia	poached
involtini	wrapped or rolled
milanese	fried in egg and breadcrumbs
pizzaiola	cooked in tomato sauce
ripieno/ farcito/stufato	stuffed
spiedo	spit roasted
surgelato	frozen

Types of Pasta

agnolotti	similar to ravioli, usually filled with meat
bavette	long, narrow pasta
bigoli	large, whole-wheat pasta (Venice)
bombolotti	short, tube shaped
bucatini	hollow spaghetti
cannelloni	stuffed pasta tubes
capelli d'angelo	angel hair pasta

conchiglie	pasta shells
crespelle	crepes
farfalle	butterfly-shaped pasta
fettuccine	long, thin flat pasta
fusilli	spiral-shaped pasta
gnocchi (con granseola)	small potato dumplings (spider crab sauce, Venetian specialty)
lasagne	large, flat noodles layered with ingredients and baked
maccheroni, maccheroncini	macaroni
orecchiette	ear-shaped pasta
paglia e fieno	green and yellow tagliatelle
pappardelle	wide noodles
pasta verde	spinach noodles
pasticcio	baked pasta pie with cheese, vegetables, and meat
penne	narrow, diagonally cut macaroni
ravioli	filled pasta squares
rigatoni	large macaroni
risotto (ai funghi, al zafferano)	rice (with mushrooms, saffron)
rotelle	spiral-shaped pasta
tagliatelle	thin, flat egg pasta ribbons
taglierini	thin pasta ribbons
tagliolini	thin, flat noodles
tonnarelli	square-shaped spaghetti
tortelli	ravioli with a filling of potato or spinach and ricotta cheese
tortellini	small meat or cheese-filled pasta dumplings
tortelloni	large tortellini
vermicelli	thin spaghetti
ziti	short, wide, tube-shaped pasta

Pasta Sauces

aglio e olio (e peperoncino)	tossed in garlic and olive oil (and hot peppers)
al burro (e salvia)	with butter (and sage)
al sugo	with puréed tomatoes
amatriciana	bacon or sausage, tomatoes, onion, and hot pepper
arrabbiata	spicy tomato sauce with chilies
bolognese	meat sauce, usually with tomato
bucaniera	seafood, tomato, garlic, parsley, and oil
cacciatore	tomato, onion, peppers, mushrooms, garlic, herbs, and wine sauce
cacio e pepe	cheese and ground pepper
carbonara	cream, ham or bacon, egg, and Parmesan cheese
frutta di mare	seafood
funghi	mushroom
gricia	chili, onion, and sausage
matriciana	pork and tomato sauce
norma	tomato, eggplant, and salted ricotta cheese
panna	cream
parmigiano	Parmesan cheese
pesto	ground pine nuts, basil, garlic, and pecorino cheese
pomodoro/pomodoro fresco	tomato sauce/raw tomatoes

puttanesca	tomatoes, capers, red peppers, anchovies, garlic, and oil
quattro formaggi	with four cheeses
ragù	tomato-based meat sauce
sugo (di pomodoro)	puréed tomato sauce
vóngole	clams, tomatoes, and garlic

Pizza

Most pizzerias have dozens of variations on the following basics.

calzone	stuffed pizza
capricciosa	ham, hard-boiled or fried egg, artichokes, and olives
frutti di mare	seafood, usually mussels, prawns, squid, and clams
funghi	mushrooms (from a can unless specifies *funghi freschi*)
margherita	tomato, mozzarella, and basil
marinara	plain tomato sauce, oregano and sometimes anchovies, never cheese
pizza bianca	without tomato
pizza napoletana	thick-crust pizza
pizza romana	thin-crust pizza
pizza al taglio	slice of pizza
pizzelle	small fried pizza with tomato and Parmesan cheese
quattro formaggi	four cheeses
quattro stagioni	literally means "four seasons": mozzarella (winter), artichoke or arugula (spring), fried egg (summer), and mushrooms (fall)
salsiccia	sausage, tomato, and mozzarella

Drinks

acqua	water
acqua minerale senza gas/gassata	mineral water, still or gas
acqua di selz	soda water
aranciata, il succo d'arancia	orange drink, orange juice
aperitivo	before-dinner drink
bicchiere	glass
birra	beer
caffè	coffee
cioccolata calda	hot chocolate
dolce	sweet
ghiaccio (con ghiaccio)	ice (on the rocks)
granita	iced drink
grappa	potent liquor made from grape mash
Hag	brand name of the most popular decaf coffee; used to mean decaffeinated in general
latte	milk
latte intero/parzialmente scremato/scremato	whole milk, low fat milk, nonfat milk
limonata	lemonade
limoncello	sweet lemon liqueur, best served ice cold
liquore	liqueur
litro	liter
mezzo litro	half liter
ombra (Venice)	glass of white wine in a bar

prosecco	dry, sparkling white wine
quarto litro	quarter liter
spremuta	fresh fruit juice
spritz al bitter (Venice)	Venetian aperitif: white wine, selzer, dash of bitters (such as Campari), lemon twist
secco	dry
succo (di frutta)	juice (fruit)
tè	tea
tisana	herbal tea
vino (locale, bianco, rosso)	wine (local, white, red)
vin santo	sweet dessert wine
whiskey scozzese, lo scotch	scotch

Other Menu and Food Terms

A

abbacchio	milk-fed spring lamb
aborio	best rice to make risotto
acciughe	anchovies
aceto	vinegar
acqua cotta	thick vegetable soup poured over bread
affettai misti	assorted cold cuts
affettato	sliced
aglio	garlic
agnello	lamb
agrume	citrus fruit
albicocca	apricot
alici/marinati	fresh anchovies/ marinated
all'alla/alle/allo	in the style of/with
alloro	bay leaf
ananas	pineapple
anatra	duck
aneto	dill
anguilla (Veneziana)	eel (cooked with lemon and tuna)
antipasti misti	assorted appetizers
antipasto	appetizer
aperitivo	apéritif
a piacere	as you like it
aragosta	lobster, crayfish
arancia	orange
aringa	herring
arista	roast pork
arrosto	roast
asciutto	dry
asparagi	asparagus
assaggio	a taste
assaggi	a series of small portions
astice	crayfish

B

baccalà	dried salt cod, sometimes simmered in milk or fried in batter
baccalà mantecata	creamy cod
bacelli	fava beans (Tuscan)

baicoli	famous Venetian dessert cookie
banane	bananas
barbabietola	beet
basilico	basil
Bel Paese	soft, mild cheese
bieta, bietola	Swiss chard
bigoli in salsa	fat, often whole-wheat spaghetti with anchovies and onion sauce (Venetian specialty)
biscotti	cookies
bistecca	beef steak
bistecca alla fiorentina	T-bone steak, grilled over coals, served very rare
bollito misto (con salsa verde)	mixed boiled meats (with vinegar and parsley sauce)
braciola	steak, chop, slice of meat
branzino	sea bass
bresaola	air-cured beef, thinly sliced
briosca	croissant (also called *cornetto)*
broccoli siciliani	broccoli
broccolo	green cauliflower
brodetto	fish stew
brodo (pastina in brodo)	broth (with pasta pieces)
bruschetta	toasted bread rubbed with raw garlic topped with tomatoes, olive oil, or olive paste
budino di cioccolato	chocolate pudding
bue	beef, ox
burro	butter
bussolài buranèli	"s" or doughnut-shaped cookies made on Burano

C

cacciagione	game
calamari (calamaretti)	squid (baby squid)
caldo	hot/warm
camomilla	chamomile tea
cannellini	white beans
cannoli (Siciliana)	custard-filled pastry with pieces of candied fruit (pastry shells filled with ricotta cheese and dusted with sugar)
cantuccini	hard almond biscuits to dip in *vin santo*
caparosoli	clams
caponata	eggplant salad
cappe sante	scallops
capperi	capers
capra (capretto)	goat (baby goat)
caprese	fresh tomato, mozzarella, and basil salad
capriolo	venison
carbonade	beef stewed with red wine
carciofo (alla giudia) (alla romana)	artichoke (deep-fried) (cooked with garlic, parsley and mint)
carne	meat
carotte	carrots
carpaccio	thinly sliced raw beef
casalinga	homestyle
cassata	ice cream with candied fruit
castagne	chestnuts

cavolfiore	cauliflower
cavolo (nero)	cabbage (dark)
ceci	chickpeas
cerfoglio	chervil
cernia	grouper
cervello	brains
cervo	venison
cetriolo	cucumber
chianina	Tuscan beef
cicchetti	snacks (Venice)
cicoria	green, leafy vegetable similar to dandelion greens
ciliegia	cherry
cinghiale	wild boar
cioccolato	chocolate
cipolla	onion
coccómero	watermelon
coda di bue alla vaccinara	oxtail stew
coda di rospo	monkfish
congelato	frozen
coniglio	rabbit
contorni	side dishes (vegetables, salads, potatoes)
coperto	cover charge added per person to bill
cornetto	croissant (also called *briosca*)
costoletta	chop or cutlet
cozze	mussels
crema	custard
crespelle	crepes
crostata	open-faced fruit tart
crostini	toasted bread, topped with grilled cheese spread with pâté
crudo	raw (as in *prosciutto crudo,* raw ham)
cucina	kitchen, cooking
cuore	heart

D

da portare via	to take out
datteri	dates
degustazione	tasting
di stagione	of the season
dolce	dessert

E

erbe	herbs

F

fagiano	pheasant
fagioli	Tuscan whitebeans
fagiolini	green string beans
fave	fava (broad) beans
fegatelli	pork livers
fegatini	chicken livers
fégato (alla Veneziana)	calves' liver (with onions and olive oil)
fettunta	garlic bread with fresh olive oil (Florence)
fichi	figs
filetto	filet

finocchio	fennel
fior di latte	mozzarella made from cow's milk
fior di zucca/fiori di zucchino	zucchini flowers stuffed with mozzarella and anchovies, dipped in bread batter and quickly fried
fiorentina	thick, rare Tuscan steak
focaccia	flat bread made with olive oil
Fontina	delicate, buttery cheese
formaggio	cheese
fragole	strawberries
fragoline	tiny wild strawberries
freddo	cold
fritelle	Venetian fritters made only at Carnivale, filled with raisins or cream
frittata	unfolded omelette
fritto	fried
fritto misto	assorted deep-fried foods (fish, vegetables)
frutta	fruit
frutti di bosco	woodland berries
frutti di mare	shellfish
funghi	mushrooms
funghi porcini	wild boletus mushrooms

G

gamberetti	shrimp, prawns
gelato	ice cream
ghiaccio	ice
gianduiotto	chocolate hazelnut ice cream treat
gnocchi/gnocchetti	small potato dumplings
Gorgonzola	blue-veined cheese
granchio/granseola	crab/spider crab
grissini	bread sticks

I

imbottito	stuffed
insalata (di mare)	salad (seafood)
integrale	whole wheat
involtini	stuffed meat or fish rolls

L

lampone	raspberries
lattuga	lettuce
legumi	vegetables
lenticchie	lentils
lepre	wild hare
lesso	boiled
limone (limonata)	lemon (lemonade)
lingua	tongue
lombatine	veal chops
lumache	snails

M

macedonia di frutta	dessert of chopped fresh fruit
maiale, maialino	pork, piglet
mandarino	tangerine
mándorla	almond

manzo	beef
mela	apple
melanzane	eggplant
melone	melon
menta	mint
merluzzo	cod
miele	honey
millefoglie	layers of puff pastry filled with custard cream
minestra	soup
minestrone	vegetable soup
more	blackberries
mozzarella di bufala	delicate fresh cheese made from the milk of a water buffalo

N

nazionale	domestic, meaning made in Italy
noce	walnut
nocciola	hazelnut

O

oca	goose
olio di oliva extravergine	first press, extra-virgin olive oil
orata	sea bream
ossobuco	veal shanks
ostriche	oysters

P

pajata	baby veal intestines
pancetta	spicy, salted bacon
pane (tostato)	bread (toast)
pane e coperto	bread and cover charge
panettone	light yeast cake with candied fruit peel
panna	cream
panna cotta	vanilla cream pudding
panna (montata)	cream (whipped)
panino	sandwich or roll
panzanella	Tuscan specialty salad made with stale bread, olive oil, tomatoes, and onions
parmigiano	Parmesan cheese
pasta e ceci	pasta and chickpea soup
pasta e fagioli	pasta and barlotti bean soup
patata	potato
pecorino	sheep's cheese
pepe	black pepper
peperonata	grilled peppers served in olive oil
peperoncini	hot red peppers
peperoni	peppers
pera	pear
pesca/pesche	peach/peaches
pesce	fish
pescespada	swordfish
piccione	pigeon
pignoli	pine nuts
pinzimonio	appetizer of raw vegetables to be dipped in olive oil
piselli	peas

polenta	cornmeal
pólipo/polpo	octopus
pollo	chicken
polpette/polpettini	meatballs
pomodori (ripieni)	tomatoes (stuffed)
pompelmo	grapefruit
porchetta	roast piglet
porri	leeks
prezzemolo	parsley
primavera	with spring vegetables
primi piatti	first courses
produzione artiginale, propria	homemade, usually ice cream
prosciutto/con melone	air-dried, salt-cured ham/ with melon
prosciutto cotto	cooked prosciutto
prosciutto crudo	raw prosciutto
provolone	smooth, cow's-milk cheese
prunga	plum
prunga secca	prune
puntarelle	wild chicory greens dressed with oil, vinegar, mashed anchovies (Roman specialty)
purè di patate	mashed potatoes

R

radicchio	red chicory
radice	radish
rosmarino	rosemary
rape	turnip greens
ravanello	radish
ribollita	bean, bread, cabbage, and vegetable soup (means "reboiled")
ricci di mare	sea urchins
ricotta	soft, mild white cheese
ripieno	stuffed
risi e bisi	rice and pea soup, sometimes with ham and Parmesan cheese
rombo	turbot
rognoni	kidneys
rucola, rughetta	arugula

S

sale	salt
salmone	salmon
salsiccia	sausage
saltimbocca	veal rolls with ham, flavored with sage
salvia	sage
San Pietro	John Dory fish
sarda/sardella/sardina	sardine
sarde (in saor)	sardines (marinated in vinegar, onions, pine nuts, and raisins)
scaloppa	thinly sliced meat
scampi	prawns
secondi piatti	main courses
sedano	celery
semifreddo	soft frozen, ice cream mousse

senape	mustard
seppie in nero	squid (cuttlefish) cooked in its own ink
servizio	service charge
sformato	soufflé-like vegetable pudding
sogliola	sole
sorbetto	sherbet
spezzatino	stew
spiedini	spit-roasted kebabs, skewers
spigola	type of sea bass
spinaci	spinach
straccetti	stir-fried strips of veal or beef
stracciatella	broth with egg and Parmesan cheese stirred in at the last minute
straccino	soft cream cheese

T

tacchino	turkey
tartufo	ice cream coated in hard chocolate
tiramisù	rich, creamy dessert made with mascarpone cheese, liqueur, espresso, chocolate, and ladyfingers (means "pick-me-up")
toast	toasted ham and cheese sandwich
tonno	tuna
torta	cake/tarte/pie
torta della nonna	cake with custard and nuts
torta di mele	apple custart tarte
tostato	toasted
tramezzino	sandwich (also called *panino*)
trancia	slice
trippa (alla romana)	tripe (in tomato sauce)
trota	trout

U

un etto	100 grams, about 4 ounces
uova	egg
uva	grape
uva secca	raisin

V

verdure (cotte)	green vegetables (cooked)
verza	cabbage (also called *cavolo*)
vitello, vitella, vitellone	veal
vongole	clams

Z

zabaione, zabaglione	custard dessert made in a copper pot to order with beaten egg yolks, sugar, and white or marsala wine, and served warm
zucca	pumpkin
zucchero	sugar
zuppa de pesce	fish soup
zuppa inglese	trifle

Index by City

FLORENCE

BIG SPLURGES IN FLORENCE

ROME

BIG SPLURGES IN ROME

GELATERIAS

PASTRY SHOPS AND BAKERIES

VENICE

BIG SPLURGES IN VENICE

GELATERIAS

PASTRY SHOPS AND BAKERIES

Readers' Comments

In *Great Eats Italy,* I recommend places as they were when I visited them and as this book went to press. I hope they will stay that way, but as all travelers know, there are no guarantees. This is especially true when it comes to prices; in fact, there is usually a 10 to 20 percent price increase between editions of this guide. While every effort has been made to ensure the accuracy of the information presented, the reader must understand that menu selections, staff and management, opening and closing times, vacation schedules, and ownership can change overnight. Therefore, the author and publisher cannot accept responsibility for any changes that occur that result in loss or inconvenience to anyone.

Great Eats Italy is updated and revised on a regular basis. If you find that someplace has changed, or make a discovery you want to pass along, please send me a note stating the name and address of the restaurant, the date of your visit, a description of your findings, and any other information you think is necessary. Your comments are extremely important to me, and I read and follow through on every letter I receive. Because of this, I do not provide an email address, since the volume of mail it would generate would make it impossible to personally reply to each message. I hope you will understand and please take a few minutes to send me an old-fashioned letter with your comments, tips, new finds, or suggestions for *Great Eats Italy.*

Please send your letters to Sandra A. Gustafson, *Great Eats Italy,* c/o Chronicle Books, 85 Second Street, Sixth Floor, San Francisco, CA 94105.

For more information about all of the books in the Great Eats/Great Sleeps series, and for updates as I travel, please visit my Website at www.greateatsandsleeps.com.